JOY &
STRENGTH

"The joy of the Lord is your strength"

JOY &
STRENGTH

Selected by

MARY WILDER
TILESTON

WORLD WIDE
PUBLICATIONS

1303 Hennepin Ave., Minneapolis, MN 55403

ISBN: 0-89066-084-0
1986 PRINTING

PRINTED IN THE UNITED STATES OF AMERICA

preface

THIS little book, like its predecessor, "Daily Strength for Daily Needs," is a selection from writers of many countries and centuries, of thoughts of courage, faith, hope, and love, to cheer and inspirit the pilgrim in his daily journey, whether it be in clouds or sunshine; and to remind him of what he can do to help his fellow-travellers. And may his evening and morning be serene as in the old story — "The Pilgrim they laid in a large upper chamber, whose window opened towards the sun-rising: the name of the chamber was Peace; where he slept till break of day, and then he awoke and sang."

MARY WILDER TILESTON

Boston, October, 1901.

foreword

SINCE receiving my first copy of *Joy and Strength* many years ago, it has been a constant source of exactly that—joy and strength.

What I like about the book is that it is a compilation of writings from God's choice servants down through the ages including St. Augustine, George MacDonald, Samuel Rutherford, Hannah Whitall Smith and many others.

Indexes in the back provide the dates when these people lived and page numbers where additional material by them may be found. In this way one becomes acquainted with otherwise unknown saints and life is enriched not only by what they said but who they were and, even occasionally, what they did.

To me it is a classic.

Ruth Bell Graham

Montreat, November 1986

Joy and Strength

Be strong and of good courage . . . fear not, nor be dismayed; for the Lord God, even my God, will be with thee; He will not fail thee, nor forsake thee.
1 CHRONICLES xxviii. 20

That we should serve in newness of spirit.
ROMANS vii. 6

HELP us, O Lord! behold we enter
Upon another year to-day;
In Thee our hopes and thoughts now centre,
Renew our courage for the way;
New life, new strength, new happiness,
We ask of Thee; oh, hear, and bless!
JOHANN RIST

THE year begins; and all its pages are as blank as the silent years of the life of Jesus Christ. Let us begin it with high resolution; then let us take all its limitations, all its hindrances, its disappointments, its narrow and common-place conditions, and meet them as the Master did in Nazareth, with patience, with obedience, putting ourselves in cheerful subjection, serving our apprenticeship. Who knows what opportunity may come to us this year? Let us live in a great spirit, then we shall be ready for a great occasion.
GEORGE HODGES

Walk cheerfully and freely in God's service.
ST. TERESA

JANUARY 2

As the mountains are round about Jerusalem, so the Lord is round about His people from henceforth even forever.

PSALMS CXXV. 2

I HOPE it may be the happiest year of your life, as I think each succeeding year of everybody's life should be, if only everybody were wise enough to see things as they are; for it is certain that there really exists, laid up and ready to hand, for those who will just lay hands upon it, enough for every one and enough forever. I am quite sure that the central mistake of all lives that *are* mistaken is the not taking this simple unchangeable fact for granted, not seeing that it is so, and cannot but be so, and will remain so "though we believe not." I think I can trace every scrap of sorrow in my own life to this simple unbelief. How could I be anything but quite happy if I believed always that all the past is forgiven, and all the present furnished with power, and all the future bright with hope, because of the same abiding facts, which don't change with my mood, do not crumble, because I totter and stagger at the promise through unbelief, but stand firm and clear with their peaks of pearl cleaving the air of Eternity, and the bases of their hills rooted unfathomably in the Rock of God?

JAMES SMETHAM

2

Let all those that seek Thee rejoice and be glad in Thee; let such as love Thy salvation say continually, The Lord be magnified.

PSALMS xl. 16

Then will I go unto the altar of God; unto God, my exceeding joy.

PSALMS xliii. 4

WE doubt the word that tells us: Ask,
  And ye shall have your prayer;
We turn our thoughts as to a task,
  With will constrained and rare.

And yet we have; these scanty prayers
  Yield gold without alloy;
O God, but he who trusts and dares
  Must have a boundless joy!

GEORGE MACDONALD

TELL them that, until religion cease to be a burden, it is nothing,—until prayer cease to be a weariness, it is nothing. However difficult and however imperfect, the spirit must still rejoice in it.

EDWARD IRVING

From a weary laborer, worn with slavish and ineffectual toil, I had become as a little child receiving from God the free gift of eternal life and of daily sustenance; and prayer, from a weary spiritual exercise, had become the simple asking from the Heavenly Father of daily bread, and thanking Him.

ELIZABETH RUNDLE CHARLES

JANUARY 4

*He will be very gracious unto thee at the voice of
thy cry; when He shall hear it, He will answer
thee.*

ISAIAH XXX. 19

THAT was the Shepherd of the flock; He knew
   The distant voice of one poor sheep astray;
It had forsaken Him, but He was true,
   And listened for its bleating night and day.

    •   •   •   •   •

And *thou*, fallen soul, afraid to live or die
   In the deep pit that will not set thee free,
Lift up to Him the helpless homeward cry,
   For all that tender love is seeking thee.

ANNA L. WARING

OUR Divine Shepherd followed after His lost
sheep for three and thirty years, in a way so painful
and so thorny that He spilt His heart's blood and left
His life there. The poor sheep now follows Him
through obedience to His commands, or through a
desire (though at times but faint) to obey Him,
calling upon Him and beseeching Him earnestly for
help; is it possible that He should now refuse to turn
upon it His life-giving look? Will He not give ear to
it, and lay it upon His divine shoulders, rejoicing over
it with all His friends and with the angels of Heaven?
For if our Lord ceased not to search most diligently
and lovingly for the blind and deaf sinner, the lost
drachma of the Gospel, till He found it, how is it possible that He should abandon him who, as a lost
sheep, cries and calls upon his Shepherd?

LORENZO SCUPOLI

*Be ye therefore followers of God as dear children;
and walk in love, as Christ also hath loved us, and
hath given Himself for us an offering and a sacrifice to God.*

EPHESIANS v. 1, 2

O JOY supreme! I know the Voice,
　　Like none beside on earth or sea;
Yea, more, O soul of mine, rejoice,
　　By all that He requires of me,
　　I know what God Himself must be.
JOHN G. WHITTIER

EITHER there is a God supremely good, One
whom His children may love and trust to the very
uttermost point without the slightest fear of the
reality falling short of the heart's desire, or else there
is no God, no love, no forgiveness, no redress. God is
wholly good, if good at all, and those who hope in
Him will be wiser if they hope with all their hearts
than if they hope with only half their hearts.

WILLIAM R. HUNTINGTON

As mighty and as wise as God is to save man, as
willing He is. For Christ Himself is the ground of all
the laws of Christian men; and He taught us to do
good against evil. Here we may see that He is Himself
this charity, and doth to us as He teacheth us to do:
for He willeth that we be like Him in fulness of endless love.

MOTHER JULIANA

We know what God is like because we know the
character of Jesus Christ.

GEORGE HODGES

5

And when they had opened their treasures, they presented unto Him gifts; gold, and frankincense, and myrrh.

MATTHEW ii. 11

GIVE yourselves anew to God and to God's service, and He will give you the desire and the power to open your treasures; to give to Him, it may be wealth, it may be time, it may be personal service, it may be life itself. In His store there is a place for all, for the tears of the penitent, the barley loaves of the child, the two mites of the widow, the savings of the Philippians' "deep poverty," as well as for Mary's ointment, for the land of Barnabas, for the gold and incense and myrrh of these Eastern sages. And if the vision of Christ be before his eyes, and the love of Christ be in his heart, the man of wealth will give his large offering, the man of learning his dear-bought knowledge, the man of business his hard-earned leisure, for the glory of God, for the benefit of his fellow-men, for the Church or for the poor; to feed the hungry, or to teach the ignorant, to help the struggling, or to guide the erring; and each gift will be welcomed by Him who gave Himself for us all, and who asks in return for ourselves as a living sacrifice to Him.

JOHN ELLERTON

Let every one of us please his neighbor for his good.

ROMANS xv. 2

Let us consider one another.

HEBREWS x. 24

LOOK around you, first in your own family, then among your friends and neighbors, and see whether there be not some one whose little burden you can lighten, whose little cares you may lessen, whose little pleasures you can promote, whose little wants and wishes you can gratify. Giving up cheerfully our own occupations to attend to others, is one of the little kindnesses and self-denials. Doing little things that nobody likes to do, but which must be done by some one, is another. It may seem to many, that if they avoid little unkindnesses, they must necessarily be doing all that is right to their family and friends; but it is not enough to abstain from sharp words, sneering tones, petty contradiction, or daily little selfish cares; we must be active and earnest in kindness, not merely passive and inoffensive.

LITTLE THINGS, 1852

The labor of the baking was the hardest part of the sacrifice of her hospitality. To many it is easy to give what they have, but the offering of weariness and pain is never easy. They are indeed a true salt to salt sacrifices withal.

GEORGE MACDONALD

He maketh the storm a calm, so that the waves thereof are still. Then are they glad because they be quiet; so He bringeth them unto their desired haven.

PSALMS cvii. 29, 30

As thou learnest this lesson, to carry all thy sorrows to God, and lie at thy Saviour's feet, and spread thy grief before Him, thou wilt find a calm come over thee, thou knowest not whence; thou wilt see through the clouds a bright opening, small perhaps and quickly closed, but telling of eternal rest, and everlasting day, and of the depth of the Love of God. Thy heart will still rise and sink, but it will rise and sink, not restlessly, nor waywardly, not in violent gusts of passion; but resting in stillness on the bosom of the ocean of the Love of God. Then shalt thou learn, not to endure only patiently, but, in everything against thy will, humbly and quickly to see and to love the loving Will of God. Thy faith and thy love and thy hope will grow, the more thou seest the work of God with thee; thou wilt joy in thy sorrow, and thy sorrow will be turned into joy.

EDWARD B. PUSEY

In nothing be anxious; but in everything by prayer and supplication with thanksgiving let your requests be made known unto God. And the peace of God, which passeth all understanding, shall guard your hearts and your thoughts in Christ Jesus.

PHILIPPIANS iv. 6, 7 (R. V.)

JUST think of having His wonderful peace guarding one's heart and one's thoughts all day long. But it is only on condition that we fulfil the sixth verse, "In nothing be anxious,"—this is a distinct command, and, if we fail to fulfil it, we shall not get the blessing. Sorrow even is anxiety, and should be laid upon our blessed Lord. Then in prayer and supplication we must not forget that thanksgiving is also distinctly commanded; we must praise God for His dealings with us, even though we cannot make them out at times. Pray God to make you cease from anxiety about yourself and your plans; just be willing to do the work our dear Father gives you at the time.

JOHN KENNETH MACKENZIE

Oh, how great peace and quietness would he possess who should cut off all vain anxiety and place all his confidence in God.

THOMAS À. KEMPIS

9

JANUARY 10

I girded thee, though thou hast not known me.

ISAIAH xlv. 5

For I know the thoughts that I think toward you, saith the Lord; thoughts of peace and not of evil, to give you an expected end.

JEREMIAH xxix. 11

> THOU knowest,—oh, the precious truth
> That bids my soul be strong!
> The care, the never-weary care
> That cannot lead me wrong!
> There is a blessed end for me,
> Whereon thine eyes are set;
> Thou hast a comfort in Thy love,
> Too great to show me yet.
>
> ANNA L. WARING

NO room for a discouraged or depressed feeling is left you. If your sphere is outwardly humble, if it even appears to be quite insignificant, God understands it better than you do, and it is a part of His wisdom to bring out great sentiments in humble conditions, great principles in works that are outwardly trivial, great characters under great adversities and heavy loads of encumbrance. Let it fill you with cheerfulness and exalted feeling, however deep in obscurity your lot may be, that God is leading you on, girding you for a work, preparing you for a good that is worthy of His divine magnificence. If God is really preparing us all to become that which is the very highest and best thing possible, there ought never to be a discouraged or uncheerful being in the world.

HORACE BUSHNELL

*The secret of the Lord is with them that fear Him;
and He will show them His covenant.*

PSALMS XXV. 14

THEN shall my days be Thine,
    And all my heart be love;
And joy and peace be mine,
    Such as are known above.
Come, Holy Spirit, quickly come,
    And make my heart Thy lasting home.

ANDREW REED

IT is a sign that the soul is living in God, if it maintain calmness within through the consciousness of His Presence, while working for Him in active ministrations. Such restfulness will show itself in the commonest ways, in doing common duties at the right time, in preserving a sweetness and evenness of temper in the midst of ordinary interruptions and disturbances, in walking to and fro quietly on the day's varied errands, in speaking gentle words, in sweetly meeting unexpected calls. A calm, restful temper grows as self is learning to lose itself in God. Such grace tells gradually on the daily life; even the minutest detail may be brought under the power of God, and carried out in union with Him.

T. T. CARTER

See that ye hasten the matter.

2 CHRONICLES xxiv. 5

AND grant me, Lord, to do,
With ready heart and willing,
Whate'er Thou shalt command,
My calling here fulfilling;
And do it when I ought,
With all my strength, and bless
The work I thus have wrought,
For Thou must give success.

JOHANN HEERMANN

No unwelcome tasks become any the less unwelcome by putting them off till to-morrow. It is only when they are behind us and done, that we begin to find that there is a sweetness to be tasted afterwards, and that the remembrance of unwelcome duties unhesitatingly done is welcome and pleasant. Accomplished, they are full of blessing, and there is a smile on their faces as they leave us. Undone, they stand threatening and disturbing our tranquillity, and hindering our communion with God. If there be lying before you any bit of work from which you shrink, go straight up to it, and do it at once. The only way to get rid of it is to do it.

ALEXANDER MACLAREN

She constantly yielded to that kind of selfishness which makes the writing, or not writing, a letter depend upon the inclination of the moment.

SARAH W. STEPHEN

Let us not therefore judge one another any more.
ROMANS xiv. 13

"TELL not abroad another's faults
  Till thou hast cured thine own;
Nor whisper of thy neighbor's sin
  Till thou art perfect grown:
Then, when thy soul is pure enough
  To bear My searching eye
Unshrinking, then may come the time
  Thy brother to decry."
  "Jesu, Saviour, pitying be;
Parce mihi, Domine!"
LYRA MYSTICA

THE habit of judging is so nearly incurable, and its cure is such an almost interminable process, that we must concentrate ourselves for a long while on keeping it in check, and this check is to be found in kind interpretations. We must come to esteem very lightly our sharp eye for evil, on which perhaps we once prided ourselves as cleverness. We must look at our talent for analysis of character as a dreadful possibility of huge uncharitableness. We are sure to continue to say clever things, so long as we continue to indulge in this analysis; and clever things are equally sure to be sharp and acid. We must grow to something higher, and something truer, than a quickness in detecting evil.

FREDERICK WM. FABER

I will hear what God the Lord will speak; for He will speak peace unto His people.

PSALMS lxxxv. 8

Now, O my God,
My comfort, portion, rest!
Thou, none but Thou, shalt reign within my breast.
Call me to Thee! call me Thyself—oh, speak,
And bind my heart to Thee, whom most I seek!

GERHARD TERSTEEGEN

JUST as in prayer it is not we who momentarily catch His attention, but He ours, so when we fail to hear His voice, it is not because He is not speaking so much as that we are not listening. We must recognize that all things are in God and that God is in all things, and we must learn to be very attentive, in order to hear God speaking in His ordinary tone without any special accent. A man must not stop listening any more than praying when he rises from his knees. No one questions the need of times of formal address to God, but few admit in any practical way the need of quiet waiting upon God, gazing into His face, feeling for His hand, listening for His voice. "I will hearken what the Lord God will say concerning me." God has special confidences for each soul. Indeed, it would seem as though the deepest truths came only in moments of profound devotional silence and contemplation.

CHARLES H. BRENT

Wait on the Lord: be of good courage, and He shall strengthen thine heart; wait, I say, on the Lord.
PSALMS xxvii. 14

WITH smile of trust and folded hands,
The passive soul in waiting stands
To feel, as flowers in the sun and dew,
The One true Life its own renew.
JOHN G. WHITTIER

THE whole duty and blessedness of waiting on God has its root in this, that He is such a blessed Being, full, to overflowing, of goodness and power and life and joy, that we, however wretched, cannot for any time come into contact with Him, without that life and power secretly, silently, beginning to enter into us and blessing us. God is Love! God's love is just *His delight to impart Himself and His blessedness* to His children. Come, and however feeble you feel, just wait in His presence. As a feeble invalid is brought out into the sunshine to let its warmth go through him, come with all that is dark and cold in you *into the sunshine of God's holy, omnipotent love,* and sit and wait there, with the one thought: Here I am, in the sunshine of His love. As the sun does its work in the weak one who seeks its rays, *God will do His work in you.*

ANDREW MURRAY

JANUARY 16

The very hairs of your head are all numbered.

I will go in the strength of the Lord God.

No trouble is too small wherein to see the will of God for thee. Great troubles come but seldom. Daily fretting trials, that is, what of thyself would fret thee, may often, in God's hands, conform thee more to His gracious will. They are the daily touches, whereby He traces on thee the likeness of His divine will. There is nothing too slight wherein to practise oneness with the will of God. By daily practice in slight crosses of our own will, do we learn the lesson our Lord taught, "Not as I will, but as Thou." All the things whereof men daily complain may perfect thee in the will of God. The changes of the seasons, bodily discomforts or ailments, rude words, petty slights, little jealousies, unevenness of temper in those with whom thou livest, misunderstandings, censures of thy faith or practice, severe judgments, thanklessness of those thou wouldest benefit, interruptions in what thou wouldest do, oppressiveness or distraction of thy labors,—whatever thou canst think of, wherein others fret themselves, and, still more, thyself; therein thou seest how to be of one will with God.

EDWARD B. PUSEY

*Ye shall know that I have not done without cause
all that I have done, saith the Lord God.*

EZEKIEL xiv. 23

> Joy is the lesson set for some,
> For others pain best teacher is;
> We know not which for us shall come,
> But both are Heaven's high ministries.
>
> SUSAN COOLIDGE

THE outward features of our life may not be all that we should choose them to be; there may be things we wish for that never come to us; there may be much we wish away that we cannot part from. The persons with whom we live, the circumstances by which we are surrounded, the duties we have to perform, the burdens we have to bear, may not only be other than what we should have selected for ourselves, but may even seem inconsistent with that formation and discipline of character which we honestly wish to promote. Knowing us better than we know ourselves, fully understanding how greatly we are affected by the outward events and conditions of life, He has ordered them with a view to our entire and final, not only our immediate, happiness; and whenever we can be safely trusted with pastures that are green, and waters that are still, in the way of earthly blessing, the Good Shepherd leads us there.

ANTHONY W. THOROLD

I delight to do Thy will, O my God; yea, Thy law is within my heart.

PSALMS xl. 8

CROWN us with love, and so with peace;
  Transfigure duty to delight;
Our lips inspire, our faith increase,
  Brighten with hope our darkest night.
Bring us from earthly bondage free
To find our heaven in serving Thee.

HENRY WILDER FOOTE

WE often make our duties harder by thinking them hard. We dwell on the things we do not like till they grow before our eyes, and, at last, perhaps shut out heaven itself. But this is not following our Master, and He, we may be sure, will value little the obedience of a discontented heart. The moment we see that anything to be done is a plain duty, we must resolutely trample out every rising impulse of discontent. We must not merely prevent our discontent from interfering with the duty itself; we must not merely prevent it from breaking out into murmuring; we must get rid of the discontent itself. Cheerfulness in the service of Christ is one of the first requisites to make that service Christian.

FREDERICK TEMPLE

Therefore all things whatsoever ye would that men should do to you, do ye even so to them; for this is the Law and the Prophets.

MATTHEW vii. 12

TAKE the trouble to spend only one single day according to God's commandments, and you will see yourself, you will feel by your own heart, how good it is to fulfil God's will (and God's will in relation to us is our life, our eternal blessedness). Love God with all your heart; value with all your strength His love and His benefits to you, enumerate His mercies, which are endlessly great and manifold. Furthermore, love every man as yourself,—that is, do not wish him anything that you would not wish for yourself; do not let your memory keep in it any evil caused to you by others, even as you would wish that the evil done by yourself should be forgotten by others; do unto them as you would do unto yourself, or even do not do unto them as you would not do unto yourself; and then you will see what you will obtain in your heart,—what peace, what blessedness! You will be in paradise before reaching it,—that is, before the paradise in heaven, you will be in the paradise on earth.

FATHER JOHN

*Though I walk in the midst of trouble, Thou wilt
revive me; Thou shalt stretch forth Thine hand
against the wrath of mine enemies, and Thy right
hand shall save me.*

PSALMS cxxxviii. 7

HOLY Spirit, Joy divine,
Cheer this saddened heart of mine;
Bid my troubled thoughts be still;
With Thy peace my spirit fill.

ANDREW REED

THEREFORE, in the evil hour, lie still, feel thy
stay, till His light which "makes manifest" arise in
thee, and clear up things to thee. And think not the
time of darkness long; but watch, that thy heart be
kept empty, and thy mind clear of thoughts and belief
of things, till He bring in somewhat which thou
mayest safely receive. Therefore, say to thy thoughts
and to thy belief of things (according to the represen-
tation of the dark power, in the time of thy darkness),
"Get thee hence!" And if that will not do, look up to
the Lord to speak to them; and to keep them out if
they be not already entered, or to thrust them out if
they be already got in. And if He do not so presently,
or for a long time, yet do not murmur or think much,
but wait till He do. Yea, though they violently thrust
themselves upon thee, and seem to have entered thy
mind, yet let them be as strangers to thee; receive
them not, believe them not, know them not, own
them not.

ISAAC PENINGTON

Be of good courage, and He shall strengthen your heart, all ye that hope in the Lord.

PSALMS xxxi. 24

Lord, all my desire is before Thee.

PSALMS xxxviii. 9

THINK not again the wells of Life to fill,
By any conscious act of your own will;
Retire within the silence of your soul,
And let God's Spirit enter, and control.
The springs of feeling which you thought were stilled,
Shall so be deepened, sweetened, and refilled.

ANNA J. GRANNISS

WHEN you find that weariness depresses or amusement distracts you, you will calmly turn with an untroubled spirit to your Heavenly Father, who is always holding out His arms to you. You will look to Him for gladness and refreshment when depressed, for moderation and recollection when in good spirits, and you will find that He will never leave you to want. A trustful glance, a silent movement of the heart towards Him will renew your strength; and though you may often feel as if your soul were downcast and numb, whatever God calls you to do, He will give you power and courage to perform. Our Heavenly Father, so far from ever overlooking us, is only waiting to find our hearts open, to pour into them the torrents of His grace.

FRANÇOIS DE LA MOTHE FÉNELON

Then said I, Lo, I came ... to do Thy will, O God.

HEBREWS x. 7

Commit thy works unto the Lord.

PROVERBS xvi. 3

OH, let Thy wisdom be my guide,
Nor take Thy light from me away;
Thy grace be over at my side,
That from Thy path I may not stray;
But, feeling that Thy hand is o'er me,
In steadfast faith my course fulfil,
And keep Thy word, and do Thy will,
They love within, Thy heaven before me!

WOLFGANG C. DESSLER

"I COME to do Thy will, O God."

That is what we are here for,—to do God's will. That is the object of your life and mine,—to do God's will. Any of us can tell in a moment whether our lives are right or not. Are we doing God's will? We do not mean, Are we doing God's work?—preaching, or teaching, or collecting money,—but God's *will*. A man may think he is doing God's work when he is not even doing God's will. And a man may be doing God's work and God's will quite as much by hewing stones, or sweeping streets, as by preaching or praying. So the question means just this, Are we working out our common every-day life on the great lines of God's will?

HENRY DRUMMOND

So shall we ever be with the Lord.

1 THESSALONIANS iv. 17

They shall walk with me in white; for they are worthy.

REVELATION iii. 4

WE are taught to believe of the Blessed, that they "serve Him day and night in His temple," that "His servants shall serve Him." And this must be with powers and endowments developed in harmony with higher worlds, so that all the tastes, the desires, the affections, the artistic powers, the intellectual gifts, which belong to each individual, each with his own special capacities, trained and developed and exercised in spiritual modes of life, will be suited to that higher world, where they dwell in the presence of the Almighty God, and the "Lamb who is in the midst of them." The activities of a condition of life such as we cannot yet conceive, we shall enter upon, if fitted for it, trained for it, by the exercise of our gifts during our life in this world; we shall be like weapons in the Hand of God, ready for what Service He may will.

THOMAS THELLUSON CARTER

For those who live, as she did, with their whole talents dedicated to God's service, death is only the gate of life,—the path from joyous work in this world to greater capacities and opportunities for it in the other.

HORATIA K. EDEN

The throne of God and of the Lamb shall be in it; and His servants shall serve Him; and they shall see His face; and His name shall be in their foreheads.

REVELATION xxii. 3, 4

> AND doubtless unto thee is given
> A life that bears immortal fruit
> In such great offices as suit
> The full-grown energies of heaven.
> ALFRED TENNYSON

IF we are to be thus disciplined and trained, as workmen in various orders of work, instruments thus formed for God's service, what may we look to become hereafter? May not instruments thus formed, when this passing scene is over, and we appear in God's presence, cleansed and disciplined, with the true workman's hand, may we not be set to work in higher spheres, in grander ministries, in a world of nobler service? We speak of heaven as a sort of rest, of sweet consolation, of communion with God, such as we cannot know on earth; but consistently with this perfect sweetness, heaven is full of activity, of ministrations infinite. For God is active, and out of His activity He formed all creatures. As in the deep seas in their endless movements there is calm beneath, so in God are depths of peace as infinite as the activity of His creation. So, too, His creatures partake of infinite peace and intensely active service.

T. T. CARTER

I can do all things through Christ which strengtheneth me.

PHILIPIANS iv. 13

Let him take hold of my strength.

ISAIAH xxvii. 5

THOU canst o'ercome this heart of mine,
　Thou wilt victorious prove;
For everlasting strength is Thine,
　And everlasting love.

CHARLES WESLEY

WE are conscious of our own weakness and of the strength of evil; but not of the third force, stronger than either ourselves or the power of evil, which is at our disposal if we will draw upon it. What is needed is a deliberate and whole-hearted realization that we are *in Christ*, and Christ is *in us* by His Spirit; an unconditional surrender of faith to Him; a practice, which grows more natural by exercise, of remembering and deliberately drawing by faith upon His strength in the moments of temptation and not merely upon our own resources. "In the name of Jesus Christ of Nazareth I will do thus and thus." So we too may form, like St. Paul, the habit of victory.

CHARLES GORE

JANUARY 26

That ye might be filled with the knowledge of His will in all wisdom and spiritual understanding, that ye might walk worthy of the Lord unto all pleasing.

COLOSSIANS i. 9, 10

SOMETHING for Thee! Lord, let this be
Thy choice for me from day to day;
The life I live it is not mine,
Thy will, my will, have made it Thine!
Oh, let me do in Thine own way
Something for Thee!

ELIZABETH PRENTISS

ACT faithfully according to thy degree of light, and what God giveth thee to see; and thou shalt see more clearly. Hearken to the low whispers of His voice within thee, and thou shalt hear more distinctly. Above all, do not stifle any motions of conscience. Meditate daily on the things of Eternity; and, by the grace of God, do something daily which thou wouldest wish to have done when that day cometh. Above all things, in all things, "look unto Jesus, the Author and Finisher of thy faith." If thou failest, look to Him to uphold thee; if thou stumblest, hold swift His hand to help thee; if thou fallest, lie not hopelessly there, but look to Him to raise thee; if, by His grace, thou doest well, look to Him in thanksgiving, that He has helped thee, and pray that thou mayest do better.

EDWARD B. PUSEY

As the hart panteth after the waterbrooks, so panteth my soul after Thee, O God.

PSALMS xlii. 1

Singing and making melody in your heart to the Lord.

EPHESIANS v. 19

LORD, make my heart a place where angels sing!
   For surely thoughts low-breathed by Thee
Are angels gliding near on noiseless wings;
   And where a home they see

Swept clean, and garnished with adoring joy,
   They enter in and dwell,
   And teach that heart to swell
With heavenly melody, their own untired employ.

JOHN KEBLE

LET your heart and desires continually hold converse with God, in heartfelt simplicity. Reflect on Him with feelings of love and reverence, and often offer up your heart, with all that you have and are, to Him, in spirit and in truth, as cordially and sincerely as possible. If through weakness or unfaithfulness you forsake this exercise, which is so incredibly helpful and beautiful, all you have to do is, meekly and heartily to begin again; and do not be weary of it, although in the beginning you may not find any great advantage from it, or make any rapid progress in it. It is not true that such a mode of life is hard; it is easy and pleasant to the spirit, and becomes in due time like a heaven upon earth. A little patience and courage alone are needed.

GERHARD TERSTEEGEN

JANUARY 28

In Thine hand is power and might; and in Thine hand it is to make great, and to give strength unto all.

CHRONICLES xxix. 12

WHEN I have nothing in my hand
　　Wherewith to serve my King,
When Thy commandment finds me weak
　　And wanting everything,
My soul, upon Thy greatness cast,
　　Shall rise divinely free;
Then will I serve with what Thou hast,
　　And gird myself with Thee.

ANNA L. WARING

HOW are we to approach such blessed strength? First of all, through a steadfast will to refuse nothing that God requires of us, and to do nothing deliberately which can displease Him. Next, we must learn to take our faults humbly, as proofs of our weakness, and use them to increase our trust in God, and our mistrust of self. Neither must we be discouraged at our own wretchedness, or give way to the thought that we cannot do or bear any special thing; our duty is, while confessing that of ourselves it is impossible, to remember that God is all-powerful, and that through Him we can do whatever He may require of us. We must learn to say with St. Augustine, "Give me what Thou commandest, and command what Thou wilt."

JEAN NICOLAS GROU

The Lord is good unto them that wait for Him, to the soul that seeketh Him.

LAMENTATIONS iii. 25

B E patient till your wings are grown. I fear very much that you are too vehement and headlong in your wishes and attempts to fly. You see the beauty of spiritual light and good resolutions; you fancy that you have almost attained, and your ardor is redoubled; you rush forward, but in vain, for your Master has chained you to your perch, or else it is that your wings are not grown; and this constant excitement exhausts your strength. You must indeed strive to fly, but gently, without growing eager or restless. You resign yourself, but it is always with a BUT; you want this and that, and you struggle to get it. A simple wish is no hindrance to resignation; but a palpitating heart, a flapping of wings, an agitated will, and endless, quick, restless movements are unquestionably caused by deficient resignation. Do you know what you must do? You must be willing not to fly, since your wings are not yet grown. Do not be so eager with your vain desires, do not even be eager in avoiding eagerness; go on quietly in your path—it is a good path.

ST. FRANCIS DE SALES

And the Lord said, I have surely seen the affliction of my people which are in Egypt, and have heard their cry by reason of their taskmasters; for I know their sorrows.

EXODUS iii. 7

THOU knowest, Lord, the weariness and sorrow
  Of the sad heart that comes to Thee for rest;
Cares of to-day, and burdens for to-morrow,
  Blessings implored, and sins to be confessed:
I come before Thee at Thy gracious word,
And lay them at Thy feet,—Thou knowest, Lord.

JANE BORTHWICK

THAT sorrow which can be *seen* is the lightest form really, however apparently heavy; then there is that which is *not* seen, secret sorrows which yet can be put into words, and can be told to near friends as well as be poured out to God; but there are sorrows beyond these, such as are *never* told, and cannot be put into words, and may only be wordlessly laid before God: these are the deepest. Now comes the supply for each: "I have *seen*" that which is patent and external; "I have heard their *cry*," which is the expression of this, and of as much of the external as is expressible; but this would not go deep enough, so God adds, "I *know* their sorrows," down to very depths of all, those which no eye sees or ear ever heard.

F. R. HAVERGAL

His heart fretteth against the Lord.

PROVERBS xix. 3

I know, O Lord, that Thy judgments are right and that Thou in faithfulness hast afflicted me.

PSALMS cxix. 75

AND my soul complaineth not,
For no pain or fears dismay her;
Still she clings to God in faith,
Trusts Him though He seem to slay her.
'Tis when flesh and blood repine,
Sun of joy, Thou canst not shine,

JOHANN J. WINCKLER

IMPATIENCE and fretting under trial does not increase our suffering, whereas meek submission sanctifies all suffering, and fills the tortured heart with peace amid its anguish. Worship Him in every sorrow; worship Him in deed and word, but still more in humble and loving acceptance of each pang and heart-ache. Be sure that your mere silent willing endurance is a true act of adoration; and thus, come what may, weariness, pain, desolation, destitution, loneliness, all will carry on His gracious work in you, and, amid the sharpest pressure of suffering, you will be sending up to His eternal throne the precious incense of submission and trust.

ABBÉ GUILLORÉ

FEBRUARY 1

And now, brethren, I commend you to God, and to the word of His grace, which is able to build you up, and to give you an inheritance among all them that are sanctified.

ACTS XX. 32

ONLY the rays of God can cure the heart,
Purge it of evil; there's no other way
Except to turn with the whole heart to God.

In heavenly sunlight live no shades of fear;
The soul there, busy or at rest, hath peace;
And music floweth from the various world.

WILLIAM ALLINGHAM

BREAK off things which displease God, and, whatever ye do, do it to please Him. Dedicate, morning by morning, the actions of the day to God; live in His Presence; offer to Him your acts beforehand; recall yourself, if the case admits, into His Presence, in the midst of them; give Him the glory with thy whole heart, if they be well done, since nothing good is our own; if they be amiss, grieve to Him. If we make God our end, He who gave us the grace thus to seek Him, will give us His love; He will increase our longing desire for Him; and whom in all we seek, whom in all we would please, whom in all we would love, Him shall we find, Him possess, here in grace and veiled, hereafter, in glory.

EDWARD B. PUSEY

I will refine them as silver is refined, and will try them as gold is tried.

ZECHARIAH xiii. 9

As the purifying process is carried on, "the refiner watches the operation, with the greatest earnestness, until the metal has the appearance of a highly polished mirror, reflecting every object around it: even the refiner, as he looks upon the mass of metal, may see himself as in a looking-glass, and thus he can form a very correct judgment respecting the purity of the metal. When he is satisfied, the fire is withdrawn, and the metal removed from the furnace." See Jesus, as the Refiner, watching "with the greatest earnestness" the purifying of thy soul in the furnace of earth. His hand has lighted the fire which is now separating the pure metal of holiness from the dross of sin in thee. His loving eye is ever eagerly watching for the moment when the purifying work is done. Then, without a moment's delay, He withdraws the fire, and the purified soul is removed from the furnace. See, again, when it is that the purification is completed; it is when the Image of Christ is reflected in us, so that He can see Himslef in us as in a mirror. Raise your eyes, then, amidst the flames, and see the Face of Jesus watching you with the tender pity and intense interest of His love.

GEORGE BODY

FEBRUARY 3

I will not fail thee, nor forsake thee. Be strong, and of a good courage.

JOSHUA i. 5, 6

And all the people answered with one voice, and said, All the words which the Lord hath said will we do.

EXODUS xxiv. 3

OUR Lord teaches us not to shrink from the consequences which we may see to be involved in any course of duty which we have undertaken. He leads us to accept the results of any high choice as they open to our mind,—to regard trustfully, in every act of self-dedication, in every resolve we are led to make, whatever possibilities there may be of coming trial, foreseen or unforeseen,—to realize in calmness the future, whatever that future may be. If the calling of God is clear, if the sense of duty become the pillar of cloud by day and the pillar of fire by night, ever leading onward, the vision of the cross ought not to hinder our going forward. For one who has put his hand to the plough to look back is to become unfit for the Kingdom of Heaven. And equally so it must be to disobey God, if distrust of His upholding us in the course along which He would guide our steps, whatever trial may meet us in the path, becomes a stumbling-block or hindrance to our faith.

T. T. CARTER

What time I am afraid, I will trust in Thee.

PSALMS lvi. 3

They commended them to the Lord, on whom they believed.

ACTS xiv. 23

A CONSTANT anticipation of evils which perhaps never will come, a foreboding which takes away life and energy from the present, will simply hinder and cloud the soul, and make it timid and sad. If troublous thoughts as to the future will press, darkening a bright present, or hurrying on coming clouds, the safest thing is to offer them continually as they arise to God, offering too the future which they contemplate, and asking for grace to concentrate our energies on the immediate duties surrounding us. Many have dreaded troubles which they thought must come; and while they went on ever expecting to make the turn in their path which was to open out fully the evil, lo! they found that they had reached the journey's end, and were at the haven where they would be. Even for others it is not wise to indulge in overmuch looking forward in fearfulness. Come what may to the dearest ones we have on earth, God and His upholding grace will be there, and He cares for them more than even we can do. An earnest commendation to His love will avail them more than all our fretting.

H. L. SIDNEY LEAR

FEBRUARY 5

Fear thou not; for I am with thee; be not dismayed; for I am thy God; I will strengthen thee, yea, I will help thee; yea, I will uphold thee with the right hand of my righteousness.

ISAIAH xli. 10

> Do like a child and lean and rest
>   Upon thy Father's arm;
> Pour out thy troubles on His breast,
>   And thou shalt know no harm;
> Then shalt thou by His hand be brought,
> By ways which now thou knowest not,
> Up through a well-fought fight,
> To heavenly peace and light.

PAUL GERHARDT

USE thy utmost endeavor to attain such a disposition of spirit that thou mayest become one with Me, and thy will may become so entirely conformed to My all-perfect will, that not only shalt thou never desire that which is evil, but not even that which is good, if it be not according to My will; so that whatever shall befall thee in this earthly life, from whatsoever quarter it may come, whether in things temporal or things spiritual, nothing shall ever disturb thy peace, or trouble thy quietness of spirit; but thou shalt be established in a firm belief that I, thine omnipotent God, love thee with a dearer love and take of thee more watchful care than thou canst for thyself.

ST. CATHARINE OF SIENA

Let not your hearts faint; fear not, and do not tremble.

DEUTERONOMY xx. 3

THOU wilt be near me, Father, when I fail,
  For Thou hast called me now to be Thy son,
And when the foe within me may assail,
  Help me to say in Christ, "Thy will be done;"
This ever calms, this ever gives me rest;
  There is no fight in which I may not stand,
When Christ doth dwell supreme within my breast,
  And Thou uphold'st me with Thy mighty hand.

JONES VERY

THOU must begin low, and be glad of a little light to travel with, and be faithful thereunto; and in faithfulness expect additions of light, and so much power as may help thee to rub on. And though thou may be long weak and little and ready to perish; yet the Father will help thee, and cause His life to shoot up in thee. Thankfully receive the smallest visitation that comes from Him to thy soul; for there is life and peace in it, and death and perplexity in turning from it.

ISAAC PENINGTON

All the evil we do not commit, all the temptations to which we do not consent or which never visit us; all our holy thoughts and good intentions, all our longings after that which is right,—are so many witnesses of His loving kindness towards us. How could He help you thus unless He cared for you?

CHARLES DE CONDREN

Ye are not in the flesh, but in the Spirit, if so be that the Spirit of God dwell in you.

ROMANS xvii. 9

THAT life is carnal in which our spirit, meant for God, is dragged at the chariot-wheels of our lower life; and that is spiritual which is ruled and mastered by the Spirit. Secular business is spiritual if it is ruled by the divine Spirit according to the law of righteousness. Politics are spiritual, commercial and municipal life are spiritual, art and science are spiritual, and everything that develops our faculties is spiritual, if we will allow the divine Spirit to rule in all according to the law of righteousness, truth, and beauty. For the whole of our being, with all its sum of faculties, is made by God and meant for God.

CHARLES GORE

It is the very business of your life to cultivate every faculty you have (the highest most, and most in the highest directions), in the belief that He has given them to you that you may become His intruments for usefulness; and that He asks this of you, because, if you grant it, you enable Him to give you more of His own happiness than you can otherwise receive, and far more than you can imagine.

THEOPHILUS PARSONS

In the shadow of His hand hath He hid me, and made me a polished shaft; in His quiver hath He hid me; and said unto me, Thou art my servant, O Israel, in whom I will be glorified.

ISAIAH xlix 2, 3

THE glory is not in the task, but in
The doing it for Him.

JEAN INGELOW

IT is wholly impossible to live according to Divine order, and to make a proper application of heavenly principles, as long as the necessary duties which each day brings seem only like a burden grievous to be borne. Not till we are ready to throw our very life's love into the troublesome little things can we be really faithful in that which is least and faithful also in much. Every day that dawns brings something to do, which can never be done as well again. We should, therefore, try to do it ungrudgingly and cheerfully. It is the Lord's own work, which He has given us as surely as He gives us daily bread. We should thank Him for it with all our hearts, as much as for any other gift. It was designed to be our life, our happiness. Instead of shirking it or hurrying over it, we should put our whole heart and soul into it.

JAMES REED

FEBRUARY 9

Pray without ceasing. In everything give thanks:
for this is the will of God in Christ Jesus concern-
ing you.

1 THESSALONIANS v. 17, 18

As Thou, Lord, an immortal soul
Hast breathed into me,
So let my soul be breathing forth
Immortal thanks to Thee.
JOHN MASON

LET us not be content to pray morning and
evening, but let us live in prayer all day long. Let
this prayer, this life of love, which means death to
self, spread out from our seasons of prayer, as from
a centre, over all that we have to do. All should become prayer, that is, a loving consciousness of God's
presence, whether it be social intercourse or business.
Such a course as this will ensure you a profound
peace.

FRANÇOIS DE LA MOTHE FÉNELON

How are we to fulfil our Lord's injunction, "that
men ought always to pray, and not to faint"? By the
heart's prayer, which consists in a constant habitual
love of God, trusting Him, submitting in all things to
His will; and by giving a never failing heed to His
voice, as heard within the conscience.

JEAN NICOLAS GROU

40

It is good that a man quietly wait for the salvation of the Lord.

LAMENTATIONS iii. 26

IN to Thy silent place of prayer
  The anxious, wandering mind recall—
Dwell 'mid Thy own creation there,
  Restoring, claiming, hallowing all.
Then the calm spirit, won from sin,
  Thy perfect sacrifice shall be,
And all the ransomed powers therein
  Shall go forth, glorifying Thee.

ANNA L. WARING

TAKE time to be separate from all friends and all duties, all cares and all joys; time to be still and quiet before God. Take time not only to secure stillness from man and the world, but from self and its energy. Let the Word and prayer be very precious; but remember, even these may hinder the quiet waiting. The activity of the mind in studying the Word, or giving expression to its thoughts in prayer, the activities of the heart, with its desires and hopes and fears, may so engage us that we do not come to the still waiting on the All-Glorious One. Though at first it may appear difficult to know how thus quietly to wait, with the activities of mind and heart for a time subdued, every effort after it will be rewarded; we shall find that it grows upon us, and the little season of silent worship will bring a peace and a rest that give a blessing not only in prayer, but all the day.

ANDREW MURRAY

FEBRUARY 11

Be ye kind one to another.

EPHESIANS iv. 32

THE remedy for sadness is prayer. But as sadness broods in selfishness, and is inclined to rest rather in our own unhappy thoughts than on God, the soul turns to prayer with reluctance. Hence the saddened one must first turn to God by vocal prayer, persevering in which that reluctance will be overcome; and as the sadness subsides, the spirit will enter anew into the heart of prayer. The second remedy against sadness is to break out of it by some external act of kindness or generosity. For the malady consists in a morbid concentration upon one's self, and a brooding within one's self that repels sympathy and kindness, as being adverse to this melancholy mood, a mood that can only be cherished in isolation of spirit. But let the will make a little effort to be kind and considerate towards another; and it is amazing how soon that malignant charm is broken that held the soul spellbound to her saddened thoughts and imaginary grievances. A smile, a kind look, a few gentle words, a considerate action, though begun with effort, will suffice to open the soul, and set the spirit free from its delusion.

WILLIAM BERNARD ULLATHORNE

To cultivate kindness is a great part of the business of life.

SAMUEL JOHNSON

Search me, O God, and know my heart; try me, and know my thoughts; and see if there be any wicked way in me, and lead me in the way everlasting.

PSALMS CXXXIX. 23, 24

"AM I really what I ought to be? Am I what, in the bottom of my heart, I honestly wish to be? Am I living a life at all like what I myself approve? My secret nature, the true complexion of my character, is hidden from all men, and only I know it. Is it such as I should be willing to show? Is my soul at all like what my kindest and most intimate friends believe? Is my heart at all such as I should wish the Searcher of Hearts to judge me by? Is every year adding to my devotion, to my unselfishness, to my conscientiousness, to my freedom from the hypocrisy of seeming so much better than I am? When I compare myself with last year, am I more ready to surrender myself at the call of duty? am I more alive to the commands of conscience? have I shaken off my besetting sins?" These are the questions which this season of Lent ought to find us putting fairly and honestly to our hearts.

FREDERICK TEMPLE

FEBRUARY 13

Seeing ye have purified your souls in obeying the truth through the Spirit.

1 PETER i. 22

THY wonderful grand will, my God!
  Triumphantly I make it mine;
And faith shall breathe her glad "Amen"
  To every dear command of Thine.

JEAN SOPHIA PIGOTT

YOU little think how much the life of all your graces depends upon your ready and cordial obedience to the Spirit. When the Spirit urgeth thee to secret prayer, and thou refusest obedience; when He forbids thee a known transgression, and yet thou wilt go on; when He telleth thee which is the way, and which not, and thou wilt not regard,—no wonder if heaven and thy soul be strange.

RICHARD BAXTER

Whatever the particular call is, the particular sacrifice God asks you to make, the particular cross He wishes you to embrace, whatever the particular path He wants you to tread, will you rise up, and say in your heart, "Yes, Lord, I accept it; I submit, I yield, I pledge myself to walk in that path, and to follow that Voice, and to trust Thee with the consequences"? Oh! but you say, "I don't know what He will want next." No, we none of us know that, but we know we shall be safe in His hands.

CATHERINE BOOTH

Walk worthy of God, who hath called you unto His kingdom and glory.

1 THESSALONIANS ii. 12

AMID our most trivial duties, on days which are passing in the usual round of uneventful routine, He may speak to us as never before. A quiet word may be dropped by a friend,—a sentence read in a book,—a thought lodged, we know not how or why, in the mind. We are laid under obligations to a new and more imperious view of life and duty. There is, of course, room for self-delusion of many kinds in the supposed visit of the heavenly call. But we are tolerably safe if two conditions are observed,—if, first, the duty or line of life prescribed is unwelcome to our natural inclinations; and if, secondly, it does not contradict what we know God has taught us hitherto. To listen for the footsteps of the divine Redeemer passing by us in the ordinary providences of life is a most important part of the probation of every man. How much may depend upon following when He beckons us to some higher duty, to some more perfect service, we shall only know when we see all things as they really are in the light of His eternity.

H. P. LIDDON

I will charge my soul to believe and wait for Him, and will follow His providence, and not go before it, nor stay behind it.

SAMUEL RUTHERFORD

I therefore so run, not as uncertainly; so fight I, not as one that beateth the air; but I keep under my body, and bring it into subjection.

1 CORINTHIANS ix. 26, 27

THE slack, indolent temperament, disposed to self-indulgence and delay, will find a very practical and helpful discipline in strict punctuality, a fixed habit of rising to the minute, when once a time is settled on; in being always ready for meals, or the various daily matters in which our unpunctuality makes others uncomfortable. Persons have found their whole spiritual life helped and strengthened by steadfastly conquering a habit of dawdling, or of reading newspapers and desultory bits of books, when they ought to be settling about some duty.

H. L. SIDNEY LEAR

Let us "redeem the time." Desultory working, fitful planning, irregular reading, ill-assorted hours, perfunctory or unpunctual execution of business, hurry and bustle, loitering and unreadiness,—these, and such like, are the things which take out the whole pith and power from life, which hinder holiness, and which eat like a canker into our moral being.

HORATIUS BONAR

*I therefore, the prisoner of the Lord, beseech you
that ye walk worthy of the vocation wherewith ye
are called.*

EPHESIANS iv. 1

KNOWING Thou needest this form, as I Thy divine inspiration,
Knowing Thou shapest the clay with a vision and purpose divine,
So would I answer each touch of Thy hand in its loving creation,
That in my conscious life Thy beauty and power may shine.
CHRISTOPHER P. CRANCH

LET us examine our capacities and gifts, and then
put them to the best use we may. As our own view
of life is of necessity partial, I do not find that we can
do better than to put them absolutely in God's hand,
and look to Him for the direction of our life-energy.
God can do great things with our lives, if we but give
them to Him in sincerity. He can make them useful,
uplifting, heroic. God never wastes anything. God
never forgets anything. God never loses anything. As
long as we live we have a work to do. We shall never
be too old for it, nor too feeble. Illness, weakness,
fatigue, sorrow,—none of these things can excuse us
from this work of ours. That we are alive to-day is
proof positive that God has something for us to do
to-day.

ANNA R. B. LINDSAY

I the Lord have called thee in righteousness, and will hold thine hand, and will keep thee.

ISAIAH xlii. 6

Don'T be content with spending all your time on your faults, but try to get a step nearer to God. It is not He who is far away from us, but we from Him. If you ask me the best means to persevere, I would say, if you have succeeded in getting hold of Almighty God's hand, *don't let it go.* Keep hold of Him by constantly renewing ejaculatory prayers to Him, acts of desire, and the seeking to please Him in little things.

MOTHER FRANCIS RAPHAEL

Strive to be as a little child who, while its mother holds its hand, goes on fearlessly, and is not disturbed because it stumbles and trips in its weakness. So long as God holds you up by the will and determination to serve Him with which He inspires you, go on boldly and do not be frightened at your little checks and falls, so long as you can throw yourself into His arms in trusting love. Go there with an open, joyful heart as often as possible; if not always joyful, at least go with a brave and faithful heart.

ST. FRANCIS DE SALES

Acquaint now thyself with Him, and be at peace: thereby good shall come unto thee.

DON'T be unwise enough to think that we are serving God best by constant activity at the cost of headaches and broken rest. I am getting to be of the opinion that we may be doing too much. We want—at least this is my own want—a higher quality of work. Our labor should be to maintain unbroken communion with our blessed Lord; then we shall have entire rest, and God abiding in us; that which we do will not be ours, but His.

JOHN KENNETH MACKENZIE

Our object in life should not be so much to get through a great deal of work, as to give perfect satisfaction to Him for whom we are doing the work.

WM. HAY M. H. AITKEN

Let me not seek out of Thee what I can only find in Thee, peace and rest and joy and bliss, which abide only in Thy abiding joy. Lift up my soul above the weary round of harassing thoughts to Thy eternal Presence. Lift up my soul to the pure, bright, clear, serene, radiant atmosphere of Thy Presence, that there I may breathe freely, there repose in Thy love, there be at rest from myself and from all things that weary me; thence return, arrayed with Thy peace, to do and bear what shall please Thee.

E. B. PUSEY

FEBRUARY 19

*God is able to make all grace abound toward you:
that ye always having all sufficiency in all things,
may abound to every good work.*

2 CORINTHIANS ix. 8

O LOVE, Thy sovereign aid impart
    To save me from low-thoughted care;
Chase this self-will through all my heart,
    Through all its latent mazes there;
Make me Thy duteous child, that I
    Ceaseless may "Abba, Father" cry.

GERHARD TERSTEEGEN

T HE grace which keeps me from falling one inch
further, irrecoverably, and is not worn out by my
provocations in this wilderness, is simply more visibly
alive and active in my most certain experiences, more
prompt, more steady, than I have any experience of
among material things and persons. Everything material is simply feeble; and everything personal is
shadowy, as compared with this personality under
whose shadow I am allowed to dwell. And all this is
the more extraordinary because of the hurry, hotness,
dryness, aridity of the life I am obliged to live in
London, if correspondence, interviews, letters, are to
be kept down and dealt with at all. The want of time
to read and think, the shortness and distractions of
prayer, seem to threaten one's very existence as a
conscious child of God. And yet He is on my right
hand and I know it.

EDWARD WHITE BENSON

*My brethren, count it all joy when ye fall into
divers temptations; knowing this, that the trying
of your faith worketh patience.*

JAMES i. 2, 3

TEMPTATION is surely an assault to be withstood,
but at the same time it is an opportunity to be seized.
Viewed in this light, life becomes inspiring, not in
spite but because of its struggles, and we are able to
greet the unseen with a cheer, counting it unmixed
joy when we fall into the many temptations which,
varied in form, dog our steps from the cradle to the
grave. The soldier who is called to the front is stimu-
lated, not depressed; the officer who is bidden by his
general to a post of great responsibility, and so of
hardship and peril, is thrilled with the joy of his task.
An opportunity has been given him to prove himself
worthy of great trust, which can be done only at the
cost of great trouble.

This is a true picture of temptation. And the result
of it all is a nature invigorated and refined, a character made capable of close friendship with God, to say
nothing of the unmeasured joy that is the attendant
of nobility of soul and stalwart Christian manhood.

CHARLES H. BRENT

Every trial that we pass through is capable of being
the seed of a noble character. Every temptation that
we meet in the path of duty is another chance of
filling our souls with the power of Heaven.

FREDERICK TEMPLE

FEBRUARY 21

*I will delight myself in Thy commandments, which
I have loved.*

PSALMS cxix. 47

THIS everlasting and compunctious study of duty,
—duty to everybody, everywhere, every day,—it keeps
you questioning all the while, rasping in a torment of
debates and compunctions, till you almost groan aloud
for weariness. It is as if your life itself were slavery.
And then you say, with a sigh, "Oh, if I had nothing
to do but just to be with Christ personally, and have
my duty solely as with Him, how sweet and blessed
and secret and free would it be." Well, you may have
it so; exactly this you may do and nothing more! Sad
mistake that you should ever have thought otherwise!
what a losss of privilege has it been! Come back then
to Christ, retire into the secret place of His love, and
have your whole duty personally as with Him. Only
then you will make this very welcome discovery, that,
as you are personally given up to Christ's person, you
are going where He goes, helping what He does,
keeping ever dear, bright company with Him, in all
His motions of good and sympathy, refusing even to
let Him suffer without suffering with Him. And so you
will do a great many more duties than you even think
of now; only they will all be sweet and easy and free,
even as your love is.

HORACE BUSHNELL

Glory ye in His holy name; let the heart of them rejoice that seek the Lord.

PSALMS CV. 3

Fear not, little flock; for it is your Father's good pleasure to give you the kingdom.

LUKE xii. 32

> I KNOW not what it is to doubt,
>   My heart is ever gay;
> I run no risk, for come what will,
>   Thou always hast Thy way.

FREDERICK WM. FABER

THIS way of seeing our Father in everything makes life one long thanksgiving and gives a rest of heart, and, more than that, a gayety of spirit, that is unspeakable. Some one says, "God's will on earth is always joy, always tranquillity." And since He must have His own way concerning His children, into what wonderful green pastures of inward rest, and beside what blessedly still waters of inward refreshment is the soul led that learns this secret. If the will of God is our will, and if He always has His way, then we always have our way also, and we reign in a perpetual kingdom. He who sides with God cannot fail to win in every encounter; and, whether the result shall be joy or sorrow, failure or success, death or life, we may, under all circumstances, join in the Apostle's shout of victory, "Thanks be unto God which always causeth us to triumph in Christ!"

HANNAH WHITALL SMITH

For this is the love of God, that we keep His commandments; and His commandments are not grievous.

1 JOHN v. 3

HIS commandments grievous are not,
Longer than men think them so;
Though He send me forth, I care not,
Whilst He gives me strength to go.

FRANCIS QUARLES

FOR nothing is grievous or burdensome to him who loves. They are not grievous, because love makes them light; they are not grievous, because Christ gives strength to bear them. Wings are no weight to the bird, which they lift up in the air until it is lost in the sky above us, and we see it no more, and hear only its note of thanks. God's commands are no weight to the soul which, through His Spirit, He upbears to himself; nay, rather, the soul, through them, the more soars aloft and loses itself in the love of God. "The commandments of God are not grievous," because we have a power implanted in us mightier than all which would dispute the sway of God's commandments and God's love, a power which would lift us above all hindrances, carry us over all temptations, impel our listlessness, sweep with it whatever opposes it, sweep with it even the dulness or sluggishness of our own wills,—the almighty power of the grace of God.

EDWARD B. PUSEY

*Jesus Christ Himself being the chief cornerstone;
in whom all the building fitly framed together
groweth unto an holy temple in the Lord: in whom
ye also are builded together for an habitation of
God through the Spirit.*

EPHESIANS ii. 20-22

WHEN God afflicts thee, think He hews a rugged stone,
Which must be shaped, or else aside as usless thrown.

RICHARD CHENEVIX TRENCH

WHAT comforts me is the thought that we are
being shaped here below into stones for the heavenly
temple,—that to be made like Him is the object of
our earthly existence. He is the shaper and carpenter
of the heavenly temple. *He* must *work* us into shape,
our part is to be still in His hands; every vexation is a
little chip; also we must not be in a hurry to go out
of the quarry, for there is a certain place for each
stone, and we must wait till the building is ready for
that stone; it would put out the building if we were
taken pell-mell.

CHARLES GEORGE GORDON

Oh, thrice fools are we, who like new-born princes
weeping in the cradle, know not that there is a kingdom before them; then, let our Lord's sweet hand
square us, and hammer us, and strike off the knots of
pride, self-love, and world-worship, and infidelity, that
He may make us stones and pillars in His Father's
house.

SAMUEL RUTHERFORD

Grow in the grace and knowledge of our Lord and Saviour Jesus Christ. To Him be the glory both now and for ever. Amen.

2 PETER iii. 18

Did not our heart burn within us, while He talked with us by the way, and while He opened to us the Scriptures?

LUKE xxiv. 32

NOTHING could make the period of Lent so much of a reality as to employ it in a systematic effort to fix the mind on Jesus. The history in the Gospels is so well worn that it often slips through the head without affecting the heart. But if, retiring into solitude for a portion of each day, we should select some one scene or trait or incident in the life of Jesus, and with all the helps we can get seek to understand it fully, tracing it in the other evangelists, comparing it with other passages of Scripture, etc., we should find ourselves insensibly interested, and might hope that, in this effort of our souls to understand Him, Jesus Himself would draw near, as He did of old to the disciples on the way to Emmaus. This looking unto Jesus and thinking about Him is a better way to meet and overcome sin than any physical austerities or spiritual self-reproaches. It is by looking at Him, the Apostle says, "as in a glass," that we are "changed into the same image, as from glory to glory."

HARRIET BEECHER STOWE

Do not I fill heaven and earth, saith the Lord.

JEREMIAH xxiii. 24

LET me not dwell so much within
My bounded heart, with anxious heed—
Where all my searches meet with sin,
And nothing satisfies my need—
It shuts me from the sound and sight
Of that pure world of life and light.

ANNA L. WARING

Do you think that the infinite God cannot fill and satisfy your heart?

FRANÇOIS DE LA MOTHE FÉNELON

Let not cares, riches, pleasures of this world, choke the heart, which was formed to contain the love of God. Pray, and all is thine. Thine is God Himself, who teacheth thee to pray for Himself. To pray is to go forth from earth, and to live in Heaven.

EDWARD B. PUSEY

The vision of God is indeed the transfiguration of the world; communion with God is the inspiration of life. That vision, that communion, Christ by His coming had made our abiding inheritance. As often as the Christian touches heaven, the heaven which lies about us though our eyes are holden that we should not see it, he is again filled with the powers of the world to come. Then reverence finds its perfect satisfaction; then devotion finds its invincible strength.

BROOKE FOSS WESTCOTT

57

FEBRUARY 27

Wherefore take unto you the whole armor of God, that ye may be able to withstand in the evil day, and, having done all, to stand.

EPHESIANS vi. 13

That he may please him who hath chosen him to be a soldier.

2 TIMOTHY ii. 4

SOLDIERS of Christ, arise,
  And put your armor on,
Strong in the strength which God supplies
  Through His eternal Son.

CHARLES WESLEY

WHITHER goest thou?

Where is thy soul?

Is it in peace?

If troubled, why?

How art thou fulfilling the duties of thy position?

What are they?

What effort hast thou made to amend thy disposition, and conquer thy sins?

Hast thou been faithful to the light God has given thee?

What means shouldst thou use, especially with regard to thy most besetting sin or temptation?

Hast thou fought against it?

Hast thou thought about it at all?

What hast thou done with the circumstances of the last month?

Have they wrought God's work in thee?

PÈRE RAVIGNAN

Mercy unto you, and peace, and love be multiplied.

JUDE 2

He that loveth not knoweth not God; for God is love.

1 JOHN iv. 8

> HE rests in God and He in him,
>   Who still abides in love;
> In love the saints and seraphim
>   Obey and praise above;
> For God is love; the loveless heart
> Hath in His life and joy no part.
>
> C. F. GELLERT

DIVINE love is perfect peace and joy, it is a freedom from all disquiet, it is all content and happiness; and makes everything to rejoice in itself. Love is the Christ of God; wherever it comes, it comes as the blessing and happiness of every natural life, a redeemer from all evil, a fulfiller of all righteousness, and a peace of God, which passeth all understanding. Through all the universe of things, nothing is uneasy, unsatisfied, or restless, but because it is not governed by love, or because its nature has not reached or attained the full birth of the spirit of love. For when that is done, every hunger is satisfied, and all complaining, murmuring, accusing, resenting, revenging, and striving, are as totally suppressed and overcome, as the coldness, thickness, and horror of darkness are suppressed and overcome by the breaking forth of the light.

WILLIAM LAW

Unto whomsoever much is given, of him shall be much required.

LUKE xii. 48

GOD is ever seeking an entrance, and the avenue to the heart is closed against Him; He enters in, and is rudely thronged, or jostled, or civilly put off, or promised an audience at a more convenient season, if He is not, by deadly sin, cast out. How many calls by God's providence, by the tender austerity of His afflictions, by His compassion, His bounties, by the deaths of others, or our own prolonged lives when we seemed nigh unto death, by the beauty of truth, by the unsatisfactoriness of things present, by some sight, even if afar off, of things eternal, by the sense of *His* presence by the ocean of whose love we are encompassed, by some sensible sweetness over-streaming us, —any one of these might have been a lasting conversion to God, and where have they left us? Above the common gifts to all, our creation, preservation, and all the blessings of this life; besides that universal gift of "the redemption of the world by our Lord Jesus Christ," we thank Him for that which is varied to each, "the means of grace." What we have had might have made glorious saints of those who have had less.

E. B. PUSEY

*For to me to live is Christ and to die is gain . . .
having a desire to depart and to be with Christ
which is far better.*

PHILIPPIANS i. 21, 23

IF I were annihilated this moment, I should bless
God for having been allowed to live. Far more, if I
were to have to toil and suffer in this sorrowful but
glorious earth-life through unnumbered ages, and the
sorrow and suffering continued to bring the living
life with it that it has brought, I would gladly accept
sorrow and suffering here on earth. How much more,
then, when I expect, and am sure, that a very few
years more will place me with these precious life-
powers in a world fitted for highest life, with life in-
tensified, and all the pure great life of ages gathered
there, besides those whom I have dearly loved.

EDWARD THRING

Our present life in Christ may be compared to that
of the seed; a hidden life, contending underground
against cold and darkness and obstructions, yet bearing within its breast the indestructible germ of
vitality. Death lifts the soul into the sunshine for
which a hidden, invisible work has prepared it.
Heaven is the life of the flower.

DORA GREENWELL

MARCH 2

To give knowledge of salvation unto His people by the remission of their sins, through the tender mercy of our God; whereby the dayspring from on high hath visited us, to give light to them that sit in darkness and in the shadow of death, to guide our feet into the way of peace.

LUKE i 77-79

I BELIEVE that love reigns, and that love will prevail. I believe that He says to me every morning, "Begin again thy journey and thy life; thy sins, which are many, are not only forgiven, but they shall be made, by the wisdom of God, the basis on which He will build blessings."

THOMAS ERSKINE

There is no thirst of the soul so consuming as the desire for pardon. The sense of its bestowal is the starting-point of all goodness. It comes bringing with it, if not the freshness of innocence, yet a glow of inspiration that nerves feeble hands for hard tasks, a fire of hope that lights anew the old high ideal, so that it stands before the eye in clear relief, beckoning us to make it our own. To be able to look into God's face, and know with the knowledge of faith that there is nothing between the soul and Him, is to experience the fullest peace the soul can know. Whatever else pardon may be, it is above all things admission into full fellowship with God.

CHARLES H. BRENT

Hungry and thirsty, their soul fainted in them. Then they cried unto the Lord in their trouble, and He delivered them out of their distresses.

PSALMS cvii. 5, 6

Blessed are they which do hunger and thirst after righteousness, for they shall be filled.

MATTHEW v. 6

THOU hear'st the hungry ravens when they cry,
   And to Thy children shalt thou not send bread,
Who on Thy aid alone for help rely,
   And in the steps of Christ alone would tread?
They shall not cry for righteousness in vain,
But bread from heaven Thy hand shall soon supply.

JONES VERY

IF God had not said, Blessed are those that hunger, I know not what could keep weak Christians from sinking in despair; many times all I can do is to find and complain that I want Him, and wish to recover Him; now this is my stay, that He in mercy esteems us not only by having, but by desiring also; and, after a sort, accounts us to have that which we want and desire to have.

JOSEPH HALL

Honest sighing is faith breathing and whispering in the ear; the life is not out of faith, where there is sighing, looking up with the eyes, and breathing toward God.

SAMUEL RUTHERFORD

He never yet rejected the feeble soul which clung to Him in love.

H. L. SIDNEY LEAR

God, who commanded the light to shine out of darkness, hath shined in our hearts, to give the light of the knowledge of the glory of God in the face of Jesus Christ.

2 CORINTHIANS iv. 6

Surely, He hath borne our griefs, and carried our sorrows.

ISAIAH liii. 4

THE way to think of God so as to know Him, is to think of Christ. Then we see Him, and can understand how tender and merciful and good He is. We see that if He sends us sorrows and difficulties, He only sends them because they are the true blessings, the things that are truly good. He would have us like Himself, with a happiness like His own, and nothing below it; and so as His own happiness is in taking sorrow and infirmity, and ever assisting, and giving and sacrificing Himself, He gives us sorrows too, and weaknesses, which are not the evils that we think them, but are what we should be most happy in, if we were perfect and had knowledge like Him. So there is a use and a service in all we bear, in all we do, which we do not know, but which He knows, and which in Christ He shows to us. It is a use *for others*, a hidden use, but one which makes all our life rich, and that richest which is most like Christ's.

JAMES HINTON

Thy God hath commanded thy strength; strengthen, O God, that which Thou hast wrought for us.

PSALMS lxviii. 28

Fear not, nor be dismayed; be strong, and of good courage.

JOSHUA x. 25

> THEN combat well, of naught afraid,
> For thus His follower thou art made,
> Each battle teaches thee to fight,
> Each foe to be a braver knight,
>   Armed with His might.

J. H. BOHMER, 1704

HENCEFORTH my soul should fight with the prestige of victory, with the courage that comes of having striven and won, trusted and not been confounded.

JULIANA H. EWING

They have had their victories; and when the stress is hardest, it is wise to look back on these for encouragement, as songs of joy and triumph bring strength and support along a way beset with pain and sorrow and disappointments; which, when seen in their true proportions, are only as faint specks showing in a universe of infinite light.

LAURENCE OLIPHANT

According to your faith be it unto you.

MATTHEW ix. 29

Said I not unto thee, that, if thou wouldest believe, thou shouldest see the glory of God?

JOHN xi. 40

I FIND that while faith is steady nothing can disquiet me, and when faith totters nothing can establish me. If I ramble out among means and creatures, I am presently lost, and can come to no end. But if I stay myself on God, and leave Him to work in His own way and time, I am at rest, and can lie down and sleep in a promise, though a thousand rise up against me. Therefore my way is not to cast beforehand, but to walk with God by the day. Keep close to God, and then you need fear nothing. Maintain secret and intimate acquaintance with Him, and then a little of the creature will go a great way. Crowd not religion into a corner of the day. Would men spend those hours they wear out in plots and devices in communion with God, and leave all on Him by venturesome believing, they would have more peace and comfort.

JOSEPH ELIOT, 1664

Faith is the better of the free air, and of the sharp winter storm in its face.

SAMUEL RUTHERFORD

Fear not, neither be discouraged.

DEUTERONOMY i. 21

> HAPPY are they that learn, in Thee,
>   Though patient suffering teach,
> The secret of enduring strength,
>   And praise too deep for speech,—
> *Peace* that no pressure from without,
>   No strife within, can reach
>   ANNA L. WARING

ONE of the greatest trials and miseries of this life seems to me to be the absence of a grand spirit to keep the body under control; illnesses and grievous afflictions, though they are a trial, I think nothing of, if the soul is strong, for it praises God, and sees that everything comes from His hand.

ST. TERESA

Many say they have no peace nor rest, but so many crosses and trials, afflictions and sorrows, that they know not how they shall ever get through them. Now he who in truth will perceive and take note, perceiveth clearly that true peace and rest lie not in outward things. There liveth no man on earth who may always have rest and peace without troubles and crosses. Wherefore yield thyself willingly to them, and seek only that true peace of the heart, which none can take away from thee, that thou mayest overcome all assaults.

THEOLOGIA GERMANICA

MARCH 8

*Nay, in all these things we are more than con-
querors through Him that loved us.*

ROMANS viii. 37

> LORD, in this awful fight with Sin
>   I would not just prevail;
> Against each lust so strong within
>   I would not almost fail.
> Full, gladsome, glorious victory
>   Should crown the Holy War;
> Lord! I would triumph well—would be—
>   A more than conqueror.

THOMAS H. GILL

DO not try only to abstain from sin, but strive, by
God's grace, to gain the opposite grace. If thou
wouldest not slip back into sin, thou must stretch forward to Christ and His holiness. It is a dull, heavy,
dreary, toilsome way, just to avoid sin. Thou wouldest
not simply not be impatient; thou wouldest long to be
like thy Lord, who was meek and lowly of heart. Thou
wouldest not only not openly murmur; thou wouldest
surely long, like the beloved Apostle, to rest on
Jesus' breast, and will what He wills.

EDWARD B. PUSEY

The only real relief is in absolute conquest; and the
earlier the battle begins, the easier and the shorter it
will be. If one can keep irritability under, one may
escape a struggle to the death with passion.

JULIANA H. EWING

*The Lord is my light and my salvation; whom shall
I fear? the Lord is the strength of my life; of
whom shall I be afraid?*

PSALMS XXVII. 1

GOD is my strong salvation,
  What foe have I to fear?
In darkness and temptation,
  My light, my help, is near.
Though hosts encamp around me,
  Firm to the fight I stand,
What terror can confound me
  With God at my right hand?

JAMES MONTGOMERY

ALL the spiritual enemies, all the enemies of a
man's own house, are to be destroyed by the power of
the Lord Jesus Christ, working by His grace in the
heart. And when salvation is brought home to the
heart, and wrought out there by the Lord, it is to be
enjoyed and abode in, and the soul is not to return
back again into captivity; but, being delivered out of
the hands of its inward and spiritual enemies, is to
serve God in the dominion of His Son's life, in holiness and righteousness all its days here upon the
earth.

ISAAC PENINGTON

Who does not know what it is to rise up from a
fault—perceived, confessed, and forgiven—with an almost joyous sense of new energy, strength, and will to
persevere?

H. L. SIDNEY LEAR

Thou art my hiding-place; Thou shalt preserve me from trouble; Thou shalt compass me about with songs of deliverance.　　PSALMS xxxii. 7

FEAREST sometimes that thy Father
　　Hath forgot?
When the clouds around thee gather,
　　Doubt Him not.
Always hath the daylight broken,—
Always hath He comfort spoken,—
Better hath He been for years
　　Than thy fears.

KARL RUDOLPH HAGENBACH

IT is the indwelling Presence of God, believed in trusted, reverenced, recollected, which ought to become the support to meet every case of trouble. The soul finds rest from its perplexities, as it turns from what perplexes and disturbs it, to fix its gaze and hope and purpose on Him. If there be a pressure of distress, or anxiety, or care, or perplexity of any kind, a heavy burden weighing down the spirits, then let the soul look off for a moment from itself, and from the trying object, to God. The recollection of His presence within, ever abiding, continually renewed by perpetual communion, would secure to the soul, if duly and constantly cherished, an habitual life of rest.

T. T. CARTER

What harm can happen to him who knows that God does everything, and who loves beforehand everything that God does?　　MADAME SWETCHINE

Thou, therefore, my son, be strong in the grace that is in Christ Jesus.

2 TIMOTHY ii. 1

I WOULD arise in all Thy strength
My place on earth to fill,
To work out all my time of war
With love's unflinching will.
Firm against every doubt of Thee
For all my future way—
To walk in Heaven's eternal light
Throughout the changing day.
ANNA L. WARING

EVERY trouble is an opportunity to win the grace of strength. Whatever else trouble is in the world for, it is here for this good purpose: to develop strength. For a trouble is a moral and spiritual task. It is something which is hard to do. And it is in the spiritual world as in the physical, strength is increased by encounter with the difficult. A world without any trouble in it would be, to people of our kind, a place of spiritual enervation and moral laziness. Fortunately, every day is crowded with care. Every day to every one of us brings its questions, its worries, and its tasks, brings its sufficiency of trouble. Thus we get our daily spiritual exercise. Every day we are blessed with new opportunities for the development of strength of soul.

GEORGE HODGES

MARCH 12

For their sakes I consecrate Myself.

JOHN xvii. 19 (R. V. MARGIN)

THE thought may help us in regard to all the temptations of our life, even the most hidden and solitary. It may help us to do battle with our despondency and sadness, with our restlessness and resentment, with the perverting and corrupting misery of ambition. We must be watchful and uncompromising, if the self-consecration is to do its work. One sin alone indulged, condoned, domesticated, may spoil it all; may cripple all our hope of helpfulness; may baffle the willingness of God to use us in His work for others. "For their sakes I consecrate myself." This, then, is our constant hope, that God will so cleanse and purify our hearts that they may not hinder the transmission to others of that light and truth which issue from His Presence. For that hope we would cast out all that defiles and darkens us; we would freely give ourselves to Christ, that He may enter in and rule and animate us; so that, through all our unworthiness, something of His brightness and peace may be made known to men.

FRANCIS PAGET

Did I but live nearer to God, I could be of so much more help.

GEORGE HODGES

72

God so loved the world, that He gave His only begotten Son that whosoever believeth in Him should not perish, but have everlasting life.

JOHN iii. 16

LET your love be wide as His,
With the whole world around His knees;
Gather into your warm heart
All His creatures,—not a part;
So your love shall be like His.

KATHARINE TYNAN HINKSON

GOD hath made all that is made, and God loveth all that He hath made; and he that loveth all his fellow Christians, for God's sake, he loveth all that is.

MOTHER JULIANA

Your God is love; love Him and in Him all men, as His children in Christ. Your Lord is a fire; do not let your heart be cold, but burn with faith and love. Your Lord is light; do not walk in darkness. Your Lord is a God of mercy and bountifulness; be also a source of mercy and bountifulness to your neighbors.

FATHER JOHN

"Love the Lord thy God with all thy heart, and thy neighbor as thyself;" and then go on thy way. The way in which God shall lead thee may be over rocks and deserts, over mountains and oceans, amid things perilous to the sight and the touch; but still go on thy way rejoicing.

THOMAS C. UPHAM

Let all those that seek Thee rejoice and be glad in Thee.

PSALMS lxx. 4

> LORD! along this earthly way
>   Thou Thy pilgrim greetest;
> To Thy thankful child each day
>   Thou Thy love repeatest;
> Thou dost bid me weep no more,
> Thou dost teach this song to soar,
> Thou dost all the sweetness pour
>   When my life is sweetest.
>
> THOMAS H. GILL

I AM thankful that I have learned, not only to see that I ought to say, but to feel what it is truly to say, "good is the will of the Lord" in little things as well as in great things. Many who seek to be enabled, and are in measure enabled, to say this in great things, have yet to learn what it is to say it in little things; and, in consequence, they are often heard complaining of what in little matters God appoints for them, in a way that contradicts the faith that "all things work together for good to them that love God," and that, therefore, there is a good in all things, to be extracted from each thing as it comes, by receiving it in the light of love. Love to God, that love which receives God Himself as the portion of the soul in every cup, its sweetest ingredient, whatever other sweet ingredients may be in it, is as essential to the right understanding of what God does in providence as the faith that He is love in what He does.

JOHN MCLEOD CAMPBELL

Let all that ye do be done in love.

1 CORINTHIANS xvi. 14 (R. V.)

> If thou art blessed,
> Then let the sunshine of thy gladness rest
> On the dark edges of each cloud that lies
> Black in thy brother's skies.
> If thou art sad,
> Still be thou in thy brother's gladness glad.
>
> ANNA E. HAMILTON

WHAT can be more unkind than to communicate our low spirits to others, to go about the world like demons, poisoning the fountains of joy? Have I more light because I have managed to involve those I love in the same gloom as myself? Is it not pleasant to see the sun shining on the mountains, even though we have one of it down in our valley? Oh, the littleness and the meanness of that sickly appetite for sympathy, which will not let us keep our sorrows to ourselves! Let us hide our pains and sorrows. But, while we hide them, let them also be spurs within us to urge us on to all manner of overflowing kindness and sunny humor to those around us. When the very darkness within us creates a sunshine around us, then has the spirit of Jesus taken possession of our souls.

FREDERICK WM. FABER

She now rarely lost the sacred opportunity of giving pleasure.

SARAH W. STEPHEN

Yea, I have loved thee with an everlasting love:
therefore with lovingkindness have I drawn thee.
JEREMIAH xxxi. 3

MY song is love unknown;
My Saviour's love to me;
Love to the loveless shown,
That they might lovely be.
SAMUEL CROSSMAN

HE so governs and shapes all the circumstances of life, that if we use them aright we may draw near to Him here, and prepare to be near Him in the Forever after. He longs for our love,—our love, which is so feeble and faint, and yet so precious in His sight when we give it to Him freely. And why does He so desire it? Ah! I have told you many times before, and yet we cannot too often remember it, that it is because, if we love Him, He can make us supremely happy. All that belongs to us, or occurs to us, in this life, is so ordered that we may find in it the means of putting far from us those obstructions of evil which prevent us from seeing Him as He is, and as He has revealed Himself to us; for if we did but so see Him, how could we fail to love Him with the whole heart and soul?

THEOPHILUS PARSONS

How shall we become lovely? By loving Him who is ever lovely.

ST. AUGUSTINE

Who is made unto us wisdom, and righteousness, and sanctification and redemption.

1 CORINTHIANS i. 30

> CHRIST with me, Christ before me,
> Christ behind me, Christ within me,
> Christ beneath me, Christ above me,
> Christ at my right hand, Christ at my left.
>
> . . . .
>
> Christ in the heart of every man who thinks of me,
> Christ in the mouth of every man who speaks to me,
> Christ in every eye that sees me,
> Christ in every ear that hears me.

ST. PATRICK

CHRIST is in all His redeemed, as the soul of their soul, the life of their life. He is the pitying heart and the helping hand of God with every needy, praying spirit in the world. He is the sweet light of the knowledge of God that breaks in upon every penitent heart. He is not only with those who believe in Him and love Him, but also with those who neither believe in Him nor love Him, that He may be to them also *Jesus their Saviour*. The Christ of God is in thy heart, waiting and aiming to get the consent of thy will, that He may save thee. Wherever man is, there also is Christ, endeavoring to free him from the law of sin and death, by becoming Himself the law of the spirit of his life.

JOHN PULSFORD

MARCH 18

Ye that love the Lord, hate evil.

PSALMS xcvii. 10

THERE is a general stock of evil in the world to which we all contribute, or which, by God's grace, some may diminish; a vast and fertile tract of ungodliness, of low motives, of low aims, of low desires, of low sense of duty or no sense at all. It is the creation of ages, that tradition; but each age does something for it, and each individual in each age does, if he does not advisedly refuse to do, his share in augmenting it, just as the chimney of every small house does something to thicken and darken the air of London. And this general fund or stock of evil touches us all like the common atmosphere which we breathe. And thus it is that when you or I, even in lesser matters, do or say what our conscience condemns, we do really make a contribution to that general fund of wickedness which, in other circumstances and social conditions than ours, produces flagrant crime. Especially if it should happen that we defend what we do, or make light of it, or make a joke of the misdeeds of others, we do most actively and seriously augment this common fund or tradition of wickedness.

HENRY PARRY LIDDON

From thence, when the brethren heard of us, they came to meet us as far as Appii Forum, and The Three Taverns; whom when Paul saw, he thanked God, and took courage.

ACTS xxviii. 15

THROUGH the night of doubt and sorrow
  Onward goes the pilgrim band,
Singing songs of expectation,
  Marching to the promised land.
Clear before us through the darkness
  Gleams and burns the guiding light;
Brother clasps the hand of brother,
  Stepping fearless through the night.

BERNARD S. INGEMANN

WE fight not for ourselves alone. These are they—our brethren—the cloud wherewith we walk encompassed; it is for them that we wrestle through the long night; they count on the strength that we might bring them, if we so wrestle that we prevail. The morning that follows the night of our lonely trial would, if we be faithful, find us new men, with a new name of help, and of promise, and of comfort, in the memory of which others would endure bravely, and fight as we had fought. Oh! turn to God in fear, lest through hidden disloyalty we have not a cup of cold water to give those who turn to us for succor in their sore need!

HENRY SCOTT HOLLAND

*The law of the Spirit of life in Christ Jesus hath
made me free from the law of sin and death.*

ROMANS viii. 2

NOT yet thou knowest what I do
  Within thine own weak breast,
To mould thee to My image true,
  And fit thee for My rest.
But yield thee to My loving skill;
  The veiled work of grace,
From day to day progressing still,
  It is not thine to trace.

FRANCES R. HAVERGAL

GOD will have the service which comes of a sound
mind and a joyous heart; and nothing more impedes
and impairs soundness of mind and joyousness of
heart than petty scruples.

EDWARD M. GOULBURN

Be content to go on quietly. When you discover
somewhat in yourself which is earthly and imperfect,
be patient while you strive to cast it out. Your per-
ceptions will grow,—at first God will show you very
obvious stumbling-blocks;—be diligent in clearing
these away, and do not aim at heights to which you
are not yet equal. Leave all to God, and while you
earnestly desire that He would purify your intention,
and seek to work with Him to that end, be satisfied
with the gradual progress He sets before you; and
remember that He often works in ways unseen by us.

JEAN NICOLAS GROU

Inasmuch as ye did it not to one of the least of these, ye did it not to me.

MATTHEW xxv. 45

Abide ye here, and watch with me.

MATTHEW xxvi. 38 (R. V.)

If to-day thou turn'st aside
In thy luxury and pride,
Wrapped within thyself, and blind
To the sorrows of thy kind,
Thou a faithless watch dost keep,
Thou art one of those who sleep.

ANNA C. LYNCH BOTTA

I HAVE been sorrowfully convinced that in what I thought necessary attention to home duties, my time and strength have been engrossed to a degree that I fear has interfered with my duty to others. It is a serious consideration, how much good we miss of doing by our want of watchfulness for opportunities, and our engrossment even in our lawful and necessary cares; and there is another way, too, in the influence we might continually exert over all who come in contact with us, and through them over others, to an extent of which we are probably not aware, if we continually kept in a meek and quiet spirit. Ah, it may be with some of us that it is more for what we leave undone than for what we do, that we shall be called to an account.

ELIZABETH TABER KING

Ye shall diligently keep the commandments of the Lord your God, and His testimonies, and His statutes, which He hath commanded thee. And thou shalt do that which is right and good in the sight of the Lord, that it may be well with thee.

DEUTERONOMY vi. 17, 18

WE ought to become holy in the state in which Providence has placed us, instead of making projects of goodness in the future; and we need the greatest faithfulness to God in the smallest things. That state of life to which God has called us is safe for us, if we fulfil all our duties therein. Accustom yourself to adore His holy will frequently, by humbly submitting your own to His orders and His Providence. Let us do what we know He requires of us, and, as soon as we know His will, let us not spare ourselves, but be very faithful to Him. Such faithfulness ought not merely to lead us to do great things for His service, but whatever our hand finds to do, and which belongs to our state of life. The smallest things become great when God requires them of us; they are small only in themselves; they are always great when they are done for God, and when they serve to unite us with Him eternally.

FRANÇOIS DE LA MOTHE FÉNELON

*He calleth His own sheep by name, and leadeth
them out. When He hath put forth all His own,
He goeth before them, and the sheep follow Him;
for they know His voice.*

JOHN X. 3, 4 (R. V.)

H E only asks thee to yield thyself to Him, that He
may work in thee to will and to do by His own mighty
power. Thy part is to yield thyself, His part is to work;
and never, never will He give thee any command
which is not accompanied by ample power to obey it.
Take no thought for the morrow in this matter; but
abandon thyself with a generous trust to thy loving
Lord, who has promised never to call His own sheep
out into any path without Himself going before them
to make the way easy and safe. Take each little step
as He makes it plain to thee. Bring all thy life in each
of its details to Him to regulate and guide. Follow
gladly and quickly the sweet suggestions of His Spirit
in thy soul. And day by day thou wilt find Him bringing thee more and more into conformity with His will
in all things; moulding thee and fashioning thee, as
thou art able to bear it, into a vessel unto His honor,
sanctified and meet for His use, and fitted to every
good work.

HANNAH WHITALL SMITH

MARCH 24

Being confident of this very thing that He which hath begun a good work in you will perform it until the day of Jesus Christ.

PHILIPPIANS i. 6

Ye are of God, little children, and have overcome them; because greater is He that is in you, than he that is in the world.

1 JOHN iv. 4

WHY is it that we, in the very kingdom of grace, surrounded by angels, and preceded by saints, nevertheless, can do so little, and, instead of mounting with wings like eagles, grovel in the dust, and do but sin, and confess sin alternately? Is it that the *power* of God is not within us? Is it literally that we are *not able* to perform God's commandments? God forbid. We are able. We have that given us which makes us able. We do have a power within us to do what we are commanded to do. What is it we lack? The power? No; the will. What we lack is the simple, earnest, sincere inclination and aim to use what God has given us, and what we have in us.

JOHN HENRY NEWMAN

God is on my side. He makes Himself responsible for my being. If I will only entrust myself to Him with the cordial return of trustful love, then all that He has ever breathed into my heart of human possibility He will realize and bring to perfection.

CHARLES GORE

Behold the handmaid of the Lord; be it unto me according to thy word.

LUKE i. 38

> OH, let my thought, my actions, and my will
>   Obedient solely to Thy impulse move,
> My heart and senses keep Thou blameless still,
>   Fixed and absorbed in Thine unbounded love.
> Thy praying, teaching, striving, in my heart,
> Let me not quench, nor make Thee to depart.
>
> GERHARD TERSTEEGEN

WE can see plainly how her ready self-surrender in faith, in trust, to her unknown, her mysterious destiny; how her instant expression of entire self-oblation to the Divine Will, to all that she was called to be and to do, to bear all that might in the future be required of her, is a constant witness of the mind that ought to animate and pervade the whole action of the soul. Life, if true, should be always the offering up of what we are, to do our best for Him who has called us. The responsibilities, the ventures, the conscious obligations which press on the soul, with all their conditions and unknown possibilities, supply the question that is to be solved; but the true response is the result of a habit formed through countless, nameless acts of conscientious obedience, which by use have become the bright and cheerful exercise of the one purpose of giving its best and purest to One most fully loved.

T. T. CARTER

I have given you an example, that ye should do as I have done to you.

JOHN xiii. 15

THERE are often bound to us, in the closest intimacy of social or family ties, natures hard and ungenial, with whom sympathy is impossible, and whose daily presence necessitates a constant conflict with an adverse influence. There are, too, enemies,—open or secret,—whose enmity we may feel yet cannot define. Our Lord, going before us in this hard way, showed us how we should walk. It will be appropriate to the solemn self-examination of the period of Lent to ask ourselves, Is there any false friend or covert enemy whom we must learn to tolerate, to forbear with, to pity and forgive? Can we in silent offices of love wash their feet as our Master washed the feet of Judas? And, if we have no real enemies, are there any bound to us in the relations of life whose habits and ways are annoying and distasteful to us? Can we bear with them in love? Can we avoid harsh judgments, and harsh speech, and the making known to others our annoyance? The examination will probably teach us to feel the infinite distance between us and our divine Ideal, and change censoriousness of others into prayer for ourselves.

HARRIET BEECHER STOWE

Not as I will, but as Thou wilt.

MATTHEW xxvi. 39

THY will, not mine, O Lord,
However dark it be!
Lead me by Thine own hand,
Choose out the path for me.
I dare not choose my lot;
I would not, if I might;
Choose Thou for me, my God;
So shall I walk aright.

HORATIUS BONAR

CHOOSE but the will of God, and thou willest with His wisdom, thou choosest with His all-perfect choice; thou enterest into His counsels; thou lovest with His love. Be this our watch-word, brethren, for the Church, for those we love, for our own souls. Be this our rule in action, "not what I will, but what Thou"; this, in suffering; "not what I, but what Thou." This shall hallow our hopes; this shall hush our fears; this shall ward off disquiet; this shall preserve our peace; this shall calm anxieties; this (if so it must be) shall soothe our heart-aches; this shall give repose to our weariness; this, the deeper our trouble, shall be the deeper foretaste of everlasting peace and rest. "Lord, not what I will, but what Thou"; not what I, in my misery, and ignorance, and blindness, and sin, but what Thou, in Thy mercy, and holiness, and wisdom, and love.

E. B. PUSEY

Hereby know we love, because He laid down His life for us.

1 JOHN iii. 16 (R. V.)

LOVE which outlives
All sin and wrong, Compassion which forgives
To the uttermost, and Justice whose clear eyes
Through lapse and failure look to the intent,
And judge our frailty by the life we meant.

JOHN G. WHITTIER

IN return for the love which brought the Son of Man down from heaven, in return for the love which led Him to die for us on the cross, we cannot give Him holy lives, for we are not holy; we cannot give Him pure souls, for our souls are not pure; but this one thing we can give, and this is what He asks, hearts that shall never cease from this day forward, till we reach the grave, to strive to be more like Him; to come nearer to Him; to root out from within us the sin that keeps us from Him. To such a battle I call you in His name. And even if at the last day you shall not be able to show any other service, yet be sure that when thousands of His saints go forth to meet Him, and to show His triumph, He will turn to embrace with arms of tenderness the poor penitent who has nothing to offer but a life spent in one never-ceasing struggle with himself, an unwearied battle with the faults that had taken possession of his soul.

FREDERICK TEMPLE

Let the peace of Christ rule in your hearts, to the which also ye were called in one body; and be ye thankful.

COLOSSIANS iii. 15 (R. V.)

MAY faith, deep rooted in the soul,
Subdue our flesh, our minds control;
May guile depart, and discord cease,
And all within be joy and peace.

ST. AMBROSE

THE repose, the quiet balanced rest which marks our Lord's perfected life, is intended to grow more and more steadfast in those who are truly His; not the repose of indolence, not the calm arising from absence of trial and lack of temptation, a mere accidental freedom from inward struggle or difficulty, but the repose which lives in the conquest of passion, in the crucifixion of self, in a subdued will, in the reconciliation of every thought with a perfected obedience, as the whole inner being, entranced in God, yields itself in delighted harmony with His perfect mind. Such repose is attained through the continual progress of a life of grace, as it gradually overcomes the restlessness of nature, the excitements of self, the disturbance of temper or passion, the fruitless impatience of the will.

T. T. CARTER

Peace, when "ruling" the heart and "ruling" the mind, opens in both every avenue of joy.

SARAH W. STEPHEN

He died for all, that they which live should no longer live unto themselves, but unto Him who for their sakes died and rose again.

2 CORINTHIANS v. 15 (R. V.)

I will see you again, and your heart shall rejoice, and your joy no man taketh from you.

JOHN xvi. 22

THEN let thy life through all its ways
One long thanksgiving be,
Its theme of joy, its song of praise,
"Christ died, and rose for me."

J. B. S. MONSELL

IF you come to seek His face, not in the empty sepulchre, but in the living power of His presence, as indeed realizing that He has finished His glorious work, and is alive for evermore, then your hearts will be full of true Easter joy, and that joy will shed itself abroad in your homes. And let your joy not end with the hymns and the prayers and the communions in His house. Take with you the joy of Easter to the home, and make that home bright with more unselfish love, more hearty service; take it into your work, and do all in the name of the Lord Jesus; take it to your heart, and let that heart rise anew on Easter wings to a higher, a gladder, a fuller life; take it to the dear grave-side and say there the two words "Jesus lives!" and find in them the secret of calm expectation, the hope of eternal reunion.

JOHN ELLERTON

Behold what manner of love the Father hath bestowed upon us, that we should be called the sons of God.

1 JOHN iii. 1

> DOST think thy prayers He doth not heed?
> He knows full well what thou dost need,
>   And heaven and earth are His;
> My Father and my God, who still
> Is with my soul in every ill.
>
> HANS SACHS

BEHOLD and see thy Lord thy God that is thy Maker, and thy endless joy. See thine own Brother, thy Saviour, my child; behold and see what liking and bliss I have in thy salvation; and for my love, rejoice with me. How should it now be, that thou shouldst anything pray me that pleased me, but that I should full gladly grant it thee; for my pleasure is thy holiness, and thy endless joy and bliss with me.

MOTHER JULIANA

Did not Jesus say, "I am the door of the sheepfold"? What to us is the sheepfold, dear children? It is the heart of the Father, whereunto Christ is the Gate that is called Beautiful. O children, how sweetly and how gladly has He opened that door into the Father's heart, into the treasure-chamber of God! And there within He unfolds to us the hidden riches, the nearness and the sweetness of companionship with Himself.

JOHN TAULER

APRIL 1

A vessel unto honor, sanctified, and meet for the Master's use, and prepared unto every good work.
2 TIMOTHY ii. 21

AM an instrument for His use; perhaps to bear burdens, as of pain, sorrow, or shame; perhaps to convey messages, writing, speaking, conversing; perhaps simply to reflect light, showing His mind in the commonest of all daily rounds. In only one way can I truly do anything of these; in the way of inner harmony with Him, and peace and joy in Him.

HANDLEY C. G. MOULE

Mould us, great God, into forms of beauty and usefulness by the wheel of Providence and by the touch of Thy hand. Fulfil Thine ideal, and conform us to the image of Thy Son. In Thy great house may we stand as vessels meet for Thy use. We are little better than common earthenware, but may we be cleansed, and purified, and filled with Thy heavenly treasure. Dip us deep into the River of Life, and give refreshment by us to many parched and weary hearts.

F. B. MEYER

The soul which gives itself wholly and without reserve to God, is filled with His own peace; and the closer we draw to our God so much the stronger and more steadfast and tranquil shall we become.

JEAN NICOLAS GROU

He that is faithful in that which is least is faithful also in much; and he that is unjust in the least is unjust also in much.

LUKE xvi. 10

Be ye therefore perfect, even as your Father which is in heaven is perfect.

MATTHEW v. 48

PERFECTION in outward conduct consists not in extraordinary things; but in doing common things extraordinarily well. Neglect nothing; the most trivial action may be performed to ourselves, or performed to God. If love be in your heart, your whole life may be one continual exercise of it. Oh, if we did but love others! How easily the least thing, the shutting of a door gently, the walking softly, speaking low, not making a noise, or the choice of a seat, so as to leave the most convenient to others, might become occasions of its exercise.

MÈRE ANGÉLIQUE ARNAULD

He is wont to carry on His hidden dealings with the soul by means of what we should call very little things. He requires an absolute purity of heart in those with whom He vouchsafes to dwell, and a spirit of self-sacrifice which is ever ready to offer all things, however seemingly small, to Him.

ABBÉ GUILLORÉ

APRIL 3

Thou owest to me even thine own self.

According to Christ's teaching, the priest and Levite did not pay their debt to their Samaritan neighbor, because they thought him a stranger with no claim on them. Dives ignored his rich man's debt to Lazarus. We can all think of manifold debts—to the lonely whom we might visit, the misunderstood whom we might sympathize with, the ignorant whom we might teach. Is it not bewildering even to attempt to realize our debts? And yet, let a man make a beginning, and all will be well. Let him steadily set himself to behave towards those whom he employs, or those who employ him, towards railway porters and shop assistants and others who minister to his convenience, as being men and women with the same right to courteous treatment, and to a real opportunity to make the best of themselves, as he has himself; let him thus realize his debts to his nearest "neighbors," and the whole idea of humanity, of brotherhood, will be deepened and made real to him. He will get a habit of considerateness and thoughtfulness for others, as belonging to Christ, which will express itself habitually towards all, and especially the weak.

CHARLES GORE

*Let all those that put their trust in Thee rejoice;
let them also that love Thy name be joyful in Thee.*

PSALMS vi. 11

That they might have My joy fulfilled in themselves.

JOHN xvii. 13

GOD desires us to live as close as we can to the life
that Jesus Christ lived. That is the broad avenue to
perfect happiness. Most of us know by experience that
in proportion as we have followed Him, we have
found happiness. And we know by still larger experience that as we turn away from Him the world gets
dark, and life ceases to be worth living.

GEORGE HODGES

Each soul has its own faculty; it can help in some
way to make the world more cheerful and more
beautiful. This it is which makes life worth living.
If we are living only for ourselves, our own amusement, luxury, advancement, life is not worth living.
But if we are living as co-workers with Christ, as
fellow-helpers with God, as part of the noble army of
martyrs who bear witness to the truth in all time, then
our lives are full of interest. This gives sweetness and
strength to all our days.

JAMES FREEMAN CLARKE

APRIL 5

It is good for me to draw near to God.

PSALMS lxxiii. 28

—AND the sea of care grows still
In the shining of Thy smile;
And Thy love's all-quickening ray
Chases night and pain away,
That my heart grows light the while.
WOLFGANG CHRISTOPH DESSLER

IF we believe that God is always at hand, always ready to hear, surely we should take delight in telling Him all our little cares, and woes, and hopes, as they flit by.

H. L. SIDNEY LEAR

If you have not much time at your disposal, do not fail to profit by the smallest portions of time which remain to you. We do not need much time in order to love God, to renew ourselves in His Presence, to lift up our hearts towards Him, to worship Him in the depths of our hearts, to offer Him what we do and what we suffer.

FRANÇOIS DE LA MOTHE FÉNELON

There is always time to look up to Him for His smile.

F. B. MEYER

These frequent looks of the heart exceedingly sweeten and sanctify our other employments, and diffuse somewhat of heaven through all our actions.

ROBERT LEIGHTON

We know not what we should pray for as we ought.
ROMANS viii. 26

O Lord, hear; O Lord, forgive; O Lord, hearken and do.
DANIEL ix. 19

GRANT us not the ill
We blindly ask; in very love refuse
Whate'er Thou know'st our weakness would abuse.
JOHN KEBLE

WE know not precisely what is best for us. We know not what will make us truly happy. We know not what will help us best in our struggle against temptations. And if *we* were to try to make a distinction between our mere passing wishes and that which our souls really needed, we should utterly fail. But we need not try. Let us take all our wishes, all our longings, all the promptings of our consciences, to the feet of our Father. He will hear and He will do. He will hear all we say. He will know what parts of our prayer are best for us to have, and what are not. And He will give us what His fatherly love will choose. And therefore to all our prayers we will add, "Thy will be done in earth, as it is in heaven."
FREDERICK TEMPLE

APRIL 7

When my spirit was overwhelmed within me, then Thou knewest my path.

PSALMS cxlii. 3

THE work which we count so hard to do,
He makes it easy, for He works too;
The days that are long to live are His,—
A bit of His bright eternities;
And close to our need His helping is.

SUSAN COOLIDGE

DO not yield to the temptation of looking at everything *at once*, as if everything would happen at once, and all the events of the day be crowded into an hour. Do not thus forecast, but take each thing as it comes to you, and look upon it as the present expression of the will of God concerning you; then regard the next in the same way, and thus receive your day piece by piece from Him who will remember always when He gives you work to do, that you need strength to do it.

Often, when you have almost fainted in spirit, the thought comes, "If thou hast run with the footmen, and they have wearied thee, what shalt thou do with the horsemen?" Put it from you, it is a faithless thought; if you need more strength, you will have it, be sure of that; or the call to greater exertion may never come to you. Your business is with the present; leave the future in His hands who will be sure to do the best, the very best for you.

PRISCILLA MAURICE

He is the Rock, His work is perfect; for all His ways are judgment; a God of truth, and without iniquity, just and right is He.

DEUTERONOMY xxxii. 4

We are His people, and the sheep of His pasture.

PSALMS c. 3

The Lord is my shepherd, I shall not want. Yea, though I walk through the valley of the shadow of death, I will fear no evil; for Thou art with me; Thy rod and Thy staff they comfort me.

PSALMS xxiii. 1, 4

DUTIES are ours, events are the Lord's; when our faith goeth to meddle with events, and to hold a court (if I may so speak) upon God's Providence, and beginneth to say, "How wilt Thou do this or that?" we lose ground; we have nothing to do there; it is our part to let the Almighty exercise His own office, and steer His own helm; there is nothing left us, but to see how we may be approved of Him, and how we may roll the weight of our weak souls, in well-doing, upon Him who is God omnipotent, and when what we thus essay miscarrieth, it shall neither be our sin nor cross.

SAMUEL RUTHERFORD

Shall there be a mutiny among the flocks and herds, because their lord or their shepherd chooses their pastures, and suffers them not to wander into deserts and unknown ways?

JEREMY TAYLOR

APRIL 9

And ye know that He was manifested to take away our sins; and in Him is no sin.

1 JOHN iii. 5

They that sin are enemies to their own life.

TOBIT xii. 10

To choose sin is to reject Christ; to be ashamed, for fear of man, to do what Christ commands, is to deny Christ; to do, for fear of man, what Christ forbids, what is it but, with Pilate, to condemn Christ? for a Christian to be guilty of wilful deadly sin, what is it, but to crucify Christ afresh, and put Him to an open shame? Do what ye know to be pleasing to God, and avoid, by the grace of God, what ye know will displease Him, and God will enliven your penitence, and enlarge your faith, and brighten your hopes, and kindle your love. Only be *very* diligent, not knowingly to do anything which displeases God; be very diligent not to tamper with your conscience and do what you suspect may displease God.

EDWARD B. PUSEY

We can never cling to a besetting sin with one hand, and grasp Jesus Christ with the other. Until thou art content to reckon thyself dead indeed to every known form of sin, whether thou thinkest it small or great, thou never canst follow Jesus.

WM. HAY M. H. AITKEN

100

Choose you this day whom ye will serve.
JOSHUA xxiv. 15

BARABBAS and Jesus cannot both live within us. One must die. Yes, every emotion of selfishness or worldliness in every soul plays the part of Barabbas. Good influences may have prevailed for a time, and they, or perhaps motives of worldly regard, may have put Barabbas in prison, and under some restraint; but the decisive, the fatal question, remains, Shall he die? Yes, he or Jesus. Nor is it only on great occasions and in fearful crises that this question comes to us. Every hour, every moment, when we resist what we must know to be the influence of our Lord, and, casting that aside, give the victory, under whatever pretence or name, to that which is indeed our own Barabbas, we then do all that we are able to do to crucify our Lord afresh. Every emotion which tempts us to refuse obedience to Him, "to make insurrection," to suppress and overcome whatever sense of right conscience gives—is not that the robber, rebel, murderer, Barabbas? We may have, indeed, imprisoned him, we may have resolved that he should die—shall we now release him from restraint, and let him go free? If we do, we know now what must happen—we know between what alternatives we choose.

THEOPHILUS PARSONS

APRIL 11

In Thy name shall they rejoice all the day.

PSALMS lxxxix. 16

> Now first to souls who thus awake
>   Seems earth a fatherland:
> A new and endless life they take
>   With rapture from His hand.
> The fears of death and of the grave
>   Are whelmed beneath the sea,
> And every heart, now light and brave,
>   May face the things to be.
>
> FRIEDRICH VON HARDENBERG

HAPPINESS, let us understand this well, is as truly our portion here as above; it cannot fail to fall within the lot of those who have chosen for their portion Him whose nature is one with infinite, unalienable Joy. God, in communicating Himself to the soul, of necessity communicates happiness; and all souls in union with Him have returned to their central rest, and are happy, in exact proportion to the closeness and fulness of their union,—happy, in other words, by so much as they have within them of God.

DORA GREENWELL

Happiness, Heaven itself, is nothing else but a perfect conformity, a cheerful and eternal compliance of all the powers of the soul with the Will of God.

SAMUEL SHAW, 1669

Fear not; I am the first and the last, and the Living One; and I was dead, and behold, I am alive for evermore, and I have the keys of death and of Hades.

REVELATION i. 18 (R. V.)

LET all things seen and unseen,
Their notes of gladness blend,
For Christ the Lord is risen,
Our Joy that hath no end.

ST. JOHN OF DAMASCUS A. D. 760

"THE time of the singing of birds is come,"—the time when nature calls aloud to us and bids us awaken out of the deadness of personal grief, and rejoice in the new manifestation of His beauty that God is making to the world. "Behold, *I* am alive for evermore, and the dead live to *Me*." Was not this the secret saying which the new verdure was writing all over the hills, and which the young pattering leaves and singing-birds were repeating in music? It must be well to have ears to hear and a heart that could respond with a little flutter of returning joy and thankfulness.

ANNIE KEARY

The return of Easter should be to the Christian life the call of a trumpet. It is the news of a great victory. It is the solution of a great perplexity. It is the assurance of a great triumph.

FREDERICK TEMPLE

Now if any man have not the Spirit of Christ, he is none of His.

ROMANS viii. 9

WHAT profits it that He is risen,
    If dead in sins thou yet dost lie?
If yet thou cleavest to thy prison,
    What profit that He dwells on high?
His triumph will avail thee nought,
If thou hast ne'er the battle fought.

LYRA GERMANICA

MANY, who often hear the gospel of Christ, are yet but little affected, because they are void of the Spirit of Christ.

But whosoever would fully and feelingly understand the words of Christ, must endeavor to make all his life like in its beauty unto His.

What will it avail thee to dispute profoundly of the Trinity, if thou be void of humility, and art thereby displeasing to the Trinity?

Surely, high words do not make a man holy and just; but a virtuous life maketh him dear to God.

I had rather feel compunction, than understand the definition thereof.

If thou didst know the whole Bible by heart, and the sayings of all the philosophers, what would all that profit thee without the love of God and without grace?

THOMAS A. KEMPIS

*Whether therefore ye eat, or drink, or whatsoever
ye do, do all to the glory of God.*

1 CORINTHIANS x. 31

THY glory alone, O God, be the end of all that I say;
Let it shine in every deed, let it kindle the prayers that I pray;
Let it burn in my innermost soul, till the shadow of self pass
   away,
And the light of Thy glory, O God, be unveiled in the dawning of
   day.

FREDERICK GEORGE SCOTT

IT excepts nothing, "do all"; it instances only the
very least things, what our Lord includes under
"daily bread," that so we may stop at nothing short
of all, but our whole being, doing, thinking, willing,
longing, having, loving, may be wrapt up, gathered,
concentrated, in the One Will and Good Pleasure of
our God. Does any again ask, How can such little
things be done to the glory of God? Do them as thou
wouldest do them if thou sawest Christ by thee.

E. B. PUSEY

The time of labor does not with me differ from the
time of prayer; and, in the noise and confusion of the
kitchen where I am at work, while several persons are
at the same time calling for different things, I possess
God in as great tranquillity as if I were upon my knees
at the Blessed Sacrament.

BROTHER LAWRENCE

And I, if I be lifted up from the earth, will draw all men unto Me.

JOHN xii. 32

We know that, when He shall appear, we shall be like Him; for we shall see Him as He is.

1 JOHN iii. 2

> FOR if Christ be born within,
>   Soon that likeness shall appear
> Which the soul had lost through sin,
>   God's own image fair and clear,
> And the soul serene and bright
> Mirror back His heavenly light.
> LAURENTIUS LAURENTI 1700

LORD, never was a magnet so powerful to draw to itself the hard steel, as Thou, the Lord, lifted up on the cross, art powerful to draw unto Thee the hearts of men. O beloved Lord, draw me through joy and sorrow, from all that is in the world to Thee and to Thy cross; form me, and shape me into Thine image here below, that I may enjoy Thee eternally in the glory whither Thou art gone.

HENRY SUSO

Think who Christ is, and what Christ is,—and then think what His personal influence must be—quite infinite, boundless, miraculous. So that the very blessedness of heaven will not be merely the sight of our Lord; it will be the being made holy, and kept holy, by that sight.

CHARLES KINGSLEY

They are of those that rebel against the light; they know not the ways thereof, nor abide in the paths thereof.

JOB XXIV. 13

Thy people shall be willing in the day of Thy power.

PSALMS CX. 3

SEE, in Thy hands I lay them all—
My will that fails, my feet that fall;
My heart that wearies everywhere,
Yet finds Thy yoke too hard to bear.
KATHARINE T. HINKSON

THE way may at times seem dark, but light will arise, if thou trust in the Lord, and wait patiently for Him. That light may sometimes show hard things to be required, but do not be distressed if thy heart should rebel; bring thy unwillingness and disobedience to Him, in the faith that He will give thee power to overcome, for He cannot fail. "Greater is He that is in you, than he that is in the world," so keep close to Him, and the victory will be won. But do not, I beseech thee, neglect anything that is required, for disobedience brings darkness; and do not reason or delay, but simply follow the leadings of the Holy Spirit, and He will guide thee into all peace.

ELIZABETH T. KING

Thou shalt keep the commandments of the Lord thy God, to walk in His ways.

DEUTERONOMY viii. 6

And it came to pass, that, as they went, they were cleansed.

LUKE xvii. 14

GOD calls us to duty, and the only right answer is obedience. If it can be glad and willing and loving obedience, happy are we; but, in any case, whether we ourselves get enjoyment and blessing from the task or not, the call must be obeyed. The will of God must be done for the sake of God, not for the sake of ourselves. Undertake the duty, and step by step God will provide the disposition. We can at least obey. Ideal obedience includes the whole will and the whole heart. We cannot begin with that. But we can begin with what we have. God calls. It is better to obey blunderingly than not to obey at all.

GEORGE HODGES

The test of love is not feeling, but obedience.

WILLIAM BERNARD ULLATHORNE

If one fights for good behavior, God makes one a present of the good feelings.

JULIANA H. EWING

*Why art thou cast down, O my soul? and why art
thou disquieted within me? hope in God; for I
shall yet praise Him, who is the health of my
countenance, and my God.*

PSALMS xliii. 5

In prayer we own Thee, Father, at our side,
   Not always feel or taste Thee; and, 't is well,
So, hour by hour, courageous faith is tried,
   So, gladlier will the morn all mists dispel.

JOHN KEBLE

SOMETIMES we are disturbed because we have no
devout feelings; but what we want is a devout will.
We cannot always control the imagination, but we
can always do that which is our duty carefully and
patiently, with a view to pleasing God, and proving
our love to Him. We may feel cold and mechanical,
but we cannot fulfil our appointed duty without an
exercise of the will, and therefore all duties diligently
performed testify a desire to love, and prove our love.

H. L. SIDNEY LEAR

We must not allow ourselves to be cast down, nor
to despair, because our hearts seem colder at one time
than another. The test of the cold heart is the yielding
to sin, and, if we are clinging to Him, and to His will,
we may be quite sure that what we take for coldness
of heart is a trial, not a treason.

FREDERICK TEMPLE

To do good and to communicate forget not: for with such sacrifices God is well pleased.

HEBREWS xiii. 16

Freely ye have received, freely give.

MATTHEW x. 8

> SURELY Thou hast some work for me to do!
>   Oh, open Thou mine eyes,
> To see how Thou wouldst choose to have it done,
>   And where it lies!

ELIZABETH PRENTISS

THEN saw I that each kind compassion that man hath on his fellow-Christians with charity, it is Christ in him.

MOTHER JULIANA

Say not you cannot gladden, elevate, and set free; that you have nothing of the grace of influence; that all you have to give is at the most only common bread and water. Give yourself to your Lord for the service of men with what you have. Cannot He change water into wine? Cannot He make stammering words to be instinct with saving power? Cannot He change trembling efforts to help into deeds of strength? Cannot He still, as of old, enable you in all your personal poverty "to make many rich?" God has need of thee for the service of thy fellow men. He has a work for thee to do. To find out what it is, and then to do it, is at once thy supremist duty and thy highest wisdom. "Whatsoever He saith unto you, do it."

GEORGE BODY

The Lord of peace Himself give you peace at all times in all ways.   2 THESSALONIANS iii. 16 (R. V.)

Thou shalt hide them in the secret of Thy presence.   PSALMS xxxi. 20

LET my life be hid in Thee,
  Life of life and Light of light!
Love's illimitable sea,
  Depth of peace, of power the height!

Let my life be hid in Thee
  From vexation and annoy;
Calm in Thy tranquillity,
  All my mourning turned to joy.

JOHN BULL

IT is small things that, just because of their smallness, distress and overset us. I mean the weight of daily care, which in their small details of personal expenditure, and in the careful routine of a household, and in the rearing of children, and in the society of friends, and in the outside duty, and in private affairs, singly and separately is sufficiently burdensome; but altogether, and on one set of shoulders, is sometimes felt to be more than the strength can bear. Those anxious lives, tempted to be fretful, and hasty, and self-important, and fussed with their incessant activities, may, if rightly interpreted, and manfully grasped, settle down into round and sunny centres of regular, and peaceful, and fruitful activities. Where there is prayer, there is peace; and God, who makes every duty possible, knows, helps, and cares.   ANTHONY W. THOROLD

The Lord thy God in the midst of thee is mighty;
He will save, He will rejoice over thee with joy;
He will rest in His love; He will joy over thee
with singing. ZEPHANIAH iii. 17

> MADE for Thyself, O God!
> Made for Thy love, Thy service, Thy delight;
> Made to show forth Thy wisdom, grace and might;
> Made for Thy praise, whom veiled archangels laud;
> O strange and glorious thought, that we may be
> A joy to Thee.

F. R. HAVERGAL

I T is not of God's severity that He requires much
from man; it is of His great kindness that He will
have the soul to open herself wider, to be able to receive much, that He may bestow much upon her. Let
no one think that it is hard to attain thereunto.
Although it sound hard, and is hard at first, as
touching the forsaking and dying to all things, yet,
when one has reached this state, no life can be easier,
or sweeter, or fuller of pleasures; for God is right
diligent to be with us at all seasons, and to teach us,
that He may bring us to Himself, when we are like
to go astray. None of us ever desired anything more
ardently than God desires to bring men to the knowledge of Himself.

J. TAULER

God always fills in all hearts all the room which is
left Him there.

F. W. FABER

112

Behold, I stand at the door, and knock: if any man hear my voice, and open the door, I will come in to him, and will sup with him, and he with Me.

REVELATION iii. 20

O LOVE Divine!—whose constant beam
Shines on the eyes that will not see,
And waits to bless us, while we dream
Thou leavest us because we turn from Thee.

J. G. WHITTIER

UNHAPPY spirit, cast down under thy sins, multitudes of sins, years of sins!—heavily burdened as thou art, and pierced through with sorrows, *thou mayest look to God, and hope, for "HE delighteth in mercy."* His mercy can make *thee* a clean and beautiful, a happy and rejoicing spirit. God will be *"delighted"* to make thee "equal to the angels." So humble, so loving is thy God, and so earnestly does He long to bless thee, that behold, *He stands at thy door and knocks.*

JOHN PULSFORD

And if God knocks continually at the heart of man, desiring to enter in and sup there, and to communicate to him His gifts, who can believe that when the heart opens and invites Him to enter, He will become deaf to the invitation, and refuse to come in?

LORENZO SCUPOLI

And as thy servant was busy here and there, he was gone.

1 KINGS xx. 40

Blessed is he that considereth the weak; Jehovah will deliver him in the day of evil.

PSALMS xli. 1 (R. V. MARGIN)

Encourage the faint-hearted, support the weak, be long-suffering toward all.

1 THESSALONIANS v. 14 (R. V.)

IT is decreed in the providence of God that, although the opportunities for doing good, which are in the power of every man, are beyond count or knowledge; yet, the opportunity once neglected, no man by any self-sacrifice can atone for those who have fallen or suffered by his negligence. JULIANA H. EWING

Do not make life hard to any. R. W. EMERSON

Forgive us if this day we have done or said anything to increase the pain of the world. Pardon the unkind word, the impatient gesture, the hard and selfish deed, the failure to show sympathy and kindly help where we had the opportunity, but missed it; and enable us so to live that we may daily do something to lessen the tide of human sorrow, and add to the sum of human happiness. F. B. MEYER

O Lord my God, I cried unto Thee, and Thou hast healed me.

PSALMS XXX. 2

IT is sometimes a small matter that hindereth and hideth grace from us; at least if anything can be called small, and not rather a weighty matter, which obstructeth so great a good.

And, if thou remove this, be it great or small, and perfectly overcome it, thou wilt have thy desire.

For immediately, as soon as thou givest thyself to God from thy whole heart, and seekest neither this nor that, according to thine own pleasure or will, but settlest thyself wholly in Him, thou shalt find thyself united and at peace; for nothing can afford so sweet a relish, nothing be so delightful, as the good pleasure of the Divine Will.

THOMAS À. KEMPIS

If at any time this life of ours grows feeble, or low, or lonely, I know no other remedy than to return to its Eternal Source, to God Himself; and through Him all the means of grace become again living and true; and through Him all His creatures become again near and dear and accessible.

ELIZABETH RUNDLE CHARLES

Truly I am full of power by the Spirit of the Lord.

MICAH iii. 8

You, who are kept by the power of God through faith unto salvation.

1 PETER i. 4, 5

THOU must not look so much at the evil that is nigh, but rather at that which stands ready to pity and help,—and which hath pitied and helped thy distressed soul, and will pity and help it again. Why is there a mercy-seat, but for the sinner to look towards in time of need? Be patient till the Lord's tender mercy and love visit thee again; and then, look up to Him against this and such like snares, which would come between thee and the appearance of the Lord's love; that thou mayest feel more of His abidings with thee, and of the sweet effects thereof. For, these things are not to destroy thee, but to teach thee wisdom; which the Lord is able, through many exercises and sore trials, to bestow upon thee; that thy heart may be rid of all that burdeneth, and filled with all it rightly desires after, in the proper season and goodness of the Lord; to whose wise ordering and tender mercy I commit thee.

ISAAC PENINGTON

Oh, that I had wings like a dove! for then would I fly away, and be at rest.

PSALMS lv. 6

They that wait upon the Lord shall renew their strength; they shall mount up with wings as eagles.

ISAIAH xl. 31

I S there no way of escape for us when in trouble or distress? Must we just plod wearily through it all, and look for no relief? I rejoice to answer that there is a glorious way of escape for every one of us, if we will but mount up on wings, and fly away from it all to God. All creatures that have wings can escape from every snare that is set for them, if only they will fly high enough; and the soul that uses its wings can always find a sure "way to escape" from all that can hurt or trouble it. What then are these wings? Their secret is contained in the words "They that wait upon the Lord." The soul that waits upon the Lord is the soul that is entirely surrendered to Him, and that trusts Him perfectly. Therefore we might name our wings the wings of Surrender and of Trust. If we will only surrender ourselves utterly to the Lord, and will trust Him perfectly, we shall find our souls "mounting up with wings as eagles" to the "heavenly places" in Christ Jesus, where earthly annoyances or sorrows have no power to disturb us.

HANNAH WHITALL SMITH

APRIL 27

The words of a wise man's mouth are gracious.

ECCLESIASTES x. 12

*Heaviness in the heart of man maketh it stoop;
but a good word maketh it glad.*

PROVERBS xii. 25

IT would seem as if very few of us give this power
of kind words the consideration which is due to it. So
great a power, such a facility in the exercise of it,
such a frequency of opportunities for the application
of it, and yet the world still what it is, and we still
what we are! It seems incredible. Take life all
through, its adversity as well as its prosperity, its sickness as well as its health, its loss of its rights as well
as its enjoyment of them, and we shall find that no
natural sweetness of temper, much less any acquired
philosophical equanimity, is equal to the support of
a uniform habit of kindness. Nevertheless, with the
help of grace, the habit of saying kind words is very
quickly formed, and when once formed, it is not
speedily lost. Sharpness, bitterness, sarcasm, acute observation, divination of motives,—all these things
disappear when a man is earnestly conforming himself to the image of Christ Jesus. The very attempt
to be like our dearest Lord is already a well-spring of
sweetness within us, flowing with an easy grace over
all who come within our reach.

FREDERICK WM. FABER

Jesus stood still, and commanded him to be called.
MARK x. 49

—As we meet and touch, each day,
The many travellers on our way,
Let every such brief contact be
A glorious, helpful ministry;
The contact of the soil and seed,
Each giving to the other's need,
Each helping on the other's best,
And blessing, each, as well as blest.
SUSAN COOLIDGE

Do we not sometimes feel, in trial or perplexity, that others might help us if they would only stop and listen? But they will not, and in their constant hurry we know it is little use to speak. Let us note the lesson for ourselves, and give what we ask,—leisure to hear, attentive, concentrated, not divided,—calm, patient consideration. It may be our busy work, as we think, for the Master, which so overcrowds our lives that we have not time for this "standing still." Sad eyes meet ours, but we cannot stay to read their story. Some look to us for help in battles which we fought long ago, but we cannot turn aside to see how it fares with them in the strife, or to whisper the secret of victory. But He would have said, even though some plans of our own for His service were put aside, "Ye have done it unto Me."

H. BOWMAN

119

Thy will be done, as in heaven, so in earth.

LUKE xi. 2

THY Father reigns supreme above,
    The glory of His name
Is Grace and Wisdom, Truth and Love,
    His will must be the same.
And thou hast asked all joys in one,
In whispering forth, "Thy will be done."

FRANCES R. HAVERGAL

IN heaven God's will is *done,* and the Master teaches the child to ask that the will may be done on earth just as in heaven; in the spirit of adoring submission and ready obedience. Because the will of God is the glory of heaven, the doing of it is the blessedness of heaven. As the will is done, the kingdom of heaven comes into the heart.

ANDREW MURRAY

What is it thou wouldst have done, that He cannot do if He think fit? And if He think it not fit, if thou art one of His children, thou wilt think with Him; thou wilt reverence His wisdom, and rest satisfied with His will. This is believing indeed; the rolling all our desires and burdens over upon an almighty God; and where this is, it cannot choose but establish the heart in the midst of troubles, and give it a calm within in the midst of the greatest storms.

ROBERT LEIGHTON

Bless the Lord, O my soul: and all that is within me, bless His holy name: Who redeemeth thy life from destruction; who crowneth thee with loving-kindness and tender mercies.

PSALMS ciii. 1, 4

I DESIRE that thou shouldst consider with firm faith that I, thy most glorious God, who have created thee for eternal blessedness, am eternal, sovereign, omnipotent. I will that thou shouldst seriously meditate that in Me, thy God, dwell the most perfect knowledge and infinite wisdom; so that in My government of thee, the heavens, and the earth, and the entire universe, I cannot be deceived in any way, or misled by any error. Were it otherwise, I should neither be all wise, nor should I be God. Also consider attentively that, as I am thy God, so am I infinitely good, yea, love itself in My essence; that, therefore, I cannot will anything but that which is useful and salutary to thee and to all men; nor can I wish any evil to My creatures. Thus illuminated by the living light of faith, thou wilt perceive that I, thy God, have infinitely more knowledge, power, and will to advance thy happiness than thou hast. Therefore seek with all diligence to submit thyself totally to My will; so shalt thou abide in continual tranquillity of spirit, and shalt have Me forever with thee.

ST. CATHARINE OF SIENA

121

MAY 1

He that saith he abideth in Him ought himself also so to walk, even as He walked.

1 JOHN ii. 6

SINCE our way is troublesome and obscure, He commands us to mark His footsteps, tread where His feet have stood, and not only invites us forward by the argument of His example, but He hath trodden down much of the difficulty, and made the way easier and fit for our feet.

JEREMY TAYLOR

Do deeds of love for Him, to Him, following His steps. Believest thou in Christ? Do the works of Christ, that thy faith may live. Thou who sayest thou abidest in Christ, oughtest so to walk as He walked. If thou seekest thine own glory, enviest the prosperous, speakest ill of the absent, renderest evil to him who injureth thee, this did not Christ.

EDWARD B. PUSEY

To know Christ is the way to grow in holiness. Christianity is not a religion of rules. It is the religion of the divine example. Try to follow the blessed steps of the most holy life. Take His advice. Ask yourself, in the moment of perplexity or temptation, what would He do if He were here? Nothing else will so surely lead us into the way of holy living.

GEORGE HODGES

But when the young man heard that saying, he went away sorrowful, for he had great possessions.

MATTHEW xix. 22

WE too, in our own way, have often a quite impression that we are keeping all the commandments sufficiently, and inheriting the eternal life. One day a tremendous duty opens before us, and we are aghast at its hardness. What shall we do? What shall we answer? Is Christ deserving of everything from us, or only of part? It is a tremendous test which all cannot stand.

ANTHONY W. THOROLD

A great necessity is a great opportunity. Nothing is really lost by a life of sacrifice; everything is lost by failure to obey God's call. The opportunities of generously serving Jesus Christ are few; perhaps not more than one in a lifetime. They come, they do not return. What we do upon a great occasion will probably depend upon what we already are; what we are will be the result of previous years of self-discipline under the grace of Christ, or of the absence of it.

HENRY PARRY LIDDON

Things are not to be done by the effort of the moment, but by the preparation of past moments.

RICHARD CECIL

Who is among you that walketh in darkness and hath no light? let him trust in the name of the Lord, and stay upon his God.

ISAIAH l. 10

THE heart that yet can hope and trust,
And cry to Thee, though from the dust,
Is all unconquered still.

PAUL GERHARDT

PRESS this upon thy soul, for there is not such another charm for all its fears and disquiet; therefore repeat it still with David, sing this till it be stilled, and chide thy distrustful heart into believing: "Why art thou cast down, O my soul, and why art thou disquieted within me? Hope in God, for I shall yet praise Him." Though I am all out of tune for the present, never a right thing in my soul, yet He will put forth His hand and redress all, and I *shall yet once again praise*, and therefore, even now, I will hope.

ROBERT LEIGHTON

Oh, that we could breathe out new hope, and new submission, every day. Our waters are but ebb, and come neither to our chin, nor to the stopping of our breath. I may see (if I would borrow eyes from Christ) dry land, and that near: why then should we not laugh at adversity, and scorn our short-born and soon-dying temptations?

SAMUEL RUTHERFORD

Nothing shall by any means hurt you.

LUKE X. 19

When thou passest through the waters, I will be with thee; and through the rivers, they shall not overflow thee; when thou walkest through the fire, thou shalt not be burned; neither shall the flame kindle upon thee.

ISAIAH xliii. 2

JUST as soon as we turn toward Him with loving confidence, and say, "Thy will be done," whatever chills or cripples or enslaves our spirits, clogs their powers, or hinders their development, melts away in the sunshine of His sympathy. He does not free us from the pain, but from its power to dull the sensibilities; not from poverty and care, but from their tendency to narrow and harden; not from calumny, but from the maddening poison in its sting; not from disappointment, but from the hoplessness and bitterness of thought which it so often engenders. We attain unto this perfect liberty when we rise superior to untoward circumstances, triumph over the pain and weakness of disease, over unjust criticism, the wreck of earthly hopes, over promptings to envy, every sordid and selfish desire, every unhallowed longing, every doubt of God's wisdom and love and kindly care, when we rise into an atmosphere of undaunted moral courage, of restful content, of child-like trust, of holy, all-conquering calm.

WILLIAM W. KINSLEY

MAY 5

My soul is also sore vexed; but Thou, O Lord, how long? Return, O Lord, deliver my soul; oh, save me for Thy mercies' sake.

PSALMS vi. 3, 4

I LAY my head upon Thy infinite heart,
I hide beneath the shelter of Thy wing;
Pursued and tempted, helpless, I must cling
To Thee, my Father; bid me not depart,
For sin and death pursue, and Life is where Thou art!

ANONYMOUS

ACCUSTOM yourself to commune with God, not with thoughts deliberately formed to be expressed at a certain time, but with the feelings with which your heart is filled. If you enjoy His presence, and feel drawn by the attraction of His love, tell Him that you delight in Him, that you are happy in loving Him, and that He is very good to inspire so much affection in a heart so unworthy of His love. But what shall you say in seasons of dryness, coldness, weariness? Still say what you have in your heart. Tell God that you no longer find His love within you, that you feel a terrible void, that He wearies you, that His presence does not move you. Say to Him, "O God, look upon my ingratitude, my inconstancy, my unfaithfulness. Take my heart, for I cannot give it; and when Thou hast it, oh, keep it, for I cannot keep it for Thee; and save me in spite of myself."

FRANÇOIS DE LA MOTHE FÉNELON

Herein is love, not that we loved God, but that He loved us, and sent His Son to be the propitiation for our sins.

1 JOHN iv. 10

I SAW a little child, with bandaged eyes,
    Put up its hands to feel its mother's face;
She bent, and took the tender groping palms,
    And pressed them to her lips a little space.

I know a soul made blind by its desires,
    And yet its faith keeps feeling for God's face—
Bend down, O Mighty Love, and let that faith
    One little moment touch Thy lips of Grace.

ANNA J. GRANNIS

IF I felt my heart as hard as a stone; if I did not love God, or man, or woman, or little child, I would yet say to God in my heart, "O God, see how I trust Thee, because Thou are perfect, and not changeable like me. I do not love Thee. I love nobody. I am not even sorry for it. Thou seest how much I need Thee to come close to me, to put Thy arm round me, to say to me, *my child;* for the worse my state, the greater my need of my Father who loves me. Come to me, and my day will dawn; my love will come back, and, oh! how I shall love Thee, my God! and know that my love is Thy love, my blessedness Thy being."

GEORGE MACDONALD

Be persuaded, timid soul, that He has loved you too much to cease loving you.

FRANÇOIS DE LA MOTHE FÉNELON

MAY 7

*That the life also of Jesus might be made manifest
in our mortal flesh.*

2 CORINTHIANS iv. 11

THE fretting friction of our daily life,
  Heart-weariness with loving patience borne,
The meek endurance of the inward strife,
  The painful crown of thorn,

Prepare the heart for God's own dwelling-place,
  Adorn with sacred loveliness His shrine,
And brighten every inconspicuous grace,
  For God alone to shine.

                                    MARY E. ATKINSON

GOD has a purpose for each one of us, a work for
each one to do, a place for each one to fill, an influence for each one to exert, a likeness to His dear
Son for each one to manifest, and then, a place for
each one to fill in His holy Temple.

                                    ARTHUR C. A. HALL

The surest method of arriving at a knowledge of
God's eternal purposes about us is to be found in the
right use of the present moment. God's will does not
come to us in the whole, but in fragments, and generally in small fragments. It is our business to piece it
together, and to *live* it into one orderly vocation.

                                    F. W. FABER

And it came to pass, while He blessed them, He was parted from them, and carried up into heaven.

LUKE xxiv. 51

LIFT up our thoughts, lift up our songs,
And let Thy grace be given,
That while we linger here below,
Our hearts may be in heaven.

C. F. ALEXANDER

THE parting blessing of our Lord was changed in the moment of its utterance into a pledge of eternal love, of unfailing and ever-watchful care for the well-being of His people.

JOHN ELLERTON

When the living presence of Jesus was taken away from His own, it was not that they were to have Him less, but in a lovelier, in a diviner way. For when He rose up to heaven, He took there with Him, all their hearts, and all their minds, and all their love. So is it with us. He is gone up to heaven, into the bosom of the Father, into the Father's heart of love, and we ascend up there with Him, with all our hearts, and all our love, and rest where He resteth, in the Father's heart. *There* is there no separation, but one life, one existence, as He is one with the Father. And thus it is that being one with Him we can be as clear, bright mirrors that reflect His glory.

HENRY SUSO

MAY 9

If we live in the Spirit, let us also walk in the Spirit.

GALATIANS v. 25

He that followeth me shall not walk in darkness.

JOHN viii. 12

No, my dear Lord, in following Thee,
Not in the dark, uncertainly,
    This foot obedient moves;
'Tis with a Brother and a King,
Who many to His yoke will bring;
    Who ever lives and ever loves.

JOHN GAMBOLD

IF we are so led by the Spirit, where we go, and what we do, is of comparatively little moment; we may be forced by the circumstances of our life into surroundings that seem full of peril, but if God sent us there, such surroundings can do us no harm, though they may dull our *feeling* of happiness. Only let us remember that if, by God's mercy, we are free agents, and can choose our own way of life, then it is simple mockery to talk of aspirations for the higher life, if we deliberately indulge our lower nature, by living in an atmosphere of worldliness, or by doing something which is, perhaps, quite innocent for others, but consciously works us harm.

GEORGE H. WILKINSON

No one who has not tried it would believe how many difficulties are cleared out of a man's road by the simple act of trying to follow Christ.

ALEXANDER MACLAREN

They that say such things declare plainly that they seek a country.

HEBREWS xi. 14

For our citizenship is in heaven.

PHILIPPIANS iii. 20 (R. V.)

GREEN are the fields of the earth, holy and sweet her joys;
Take, and taste, and be glad—as fruit and blossom and bird,
But still as an exile, Soul; then, hey, with a singing voice,
For the stars and sun and sweet heaven, whose ultimate height
    is the Lord!
Ripe, lovely, and glad, you shall grow in the light of His face
    and His word.

KATHERINE TYNAN HINKSON

STAND still awhile, and seriously consider the noble end for which thou wast created, and for which God hath placed thee in this world! Thou wast not created for time and the creature, but for God and eternity, and to employ thyself with God and eternity. And thou art in the world, to the end that thou mayest again seek God, and His countenance which giveth blessedness, from which thou hast turned thyself away by sin; in order that thou mayest become thoroughly sanctified and enlightened, and that God may have joy, delight, peace, and pleasure in thee, and thou in God. GERHARD TERSTEEGEN

That prayer taught by the saint, "Make me reach, my God, the degree of holiness to which Thou didst call me in creating me!" LADY GEORGIANA FULLERTON

MAY 11

I know whom I have believed, and am persuaded that He is able to keep that which I have committed unto Him against that day.

2 TIMOTHY i. 12

LET me Thy power, Thy beauty see;
So shall the hopeless labor cease,
And my free heart shall follow Thee
Through paths of everlasting peace.
My strength Thy gift—my life Thy care,—
I shall forget to seek elsewhere
The wealth to which my soul is heir.

ANNA L. WARING

To give heart and mind to God, so that they are ours no longer—to do good without being conscious of it, to pray ceaselessly and without effort as we breathe—to love without stopping to reflect upon our feelings—such is the perfect forgetfulness of self, which casts us upon God, as a babe rests upon its mother's breast. JEAN NICOLAS GROU

Abiding in Jesus is not a work that needs each moment the mind to be engaged, or the affections to be directly and actively occupied with it. It is an entrusting of oneself to the keeping of the Eternal Love, in the faith that it will abide near us, and with its holy presence watch over us and ward off the evil, even when we have to be most intently occupied with other things. And so the heart has rest and peace and joy in the consciousness of being kept when it cannot keep itself. ANDREW MURRAY

Who gave Himself for us, that He might redeem us from all iniquity, and purify unto Himself a people for His own possession, zealous of good works.

TITUS ii. 14 (R. V.)

Love only can the conquest win,
The strength of sin subdue;
Come, O my Saviour, cast out sin,
And form my soul anew.
CHARLES WESLEY

LIVING and victorious faith is that whereby Christ dwelleth in our hearts. But Christ will not dwell in our hearts, if we fill our hearts with things which He hates. Yet is there then no victory, nor real faith, when the world holds a struggle with us, sometimes overcoming us, sometimes overcome? In some things victory should be complete at once. Sins of infirmity there may be; sins against light there should not be. To do wilfully and knowingly what God hates, destroys faith, and hope, and love. But so that thou art fighting against thy besetting sin, if thou art conquering thyself, thou art still Christ's soldier, even though in thought, word, or deed, thou be, from time to time, in lesser things surprised. This, then, is matter of faith, that if we will, we can, by the grace of God, prevail over every temptation.

EDWARD B. PUSEY

Thy testimonies have I taken as an heritage for ever; for they are the rejoicing of my heart.

PSALMS cxix. 111

GIRT with the love of God on every side,
Breathing that love as heaven's own healing air,
I work or wait, still following my Guide,
Braving each foe, escaping every snare.

HORATIUS BONAR

THE Lord preserve us near unto Himself, out of that which separates from Him and weakens; and nothing shall be able to interrupt our joy in the Lord, nor our delight and pleasure in His will.

ISAAC PENINGTON

It is easy to make great sacrifices when God does not ask them, but to give up our own will in each detail of life is something far harder. And this is what He *does* ask. To hold ourselves ever in readiness for His bidding—to count no token of it too slight—such is His call to each. Thus only shall we be ready for further service if He sees fit to lead us on to it.

H. BOWMAN

To live in the Spirit is the right condition of man, his normal condition; and to live in the Spirit is to live with God—hearing Him, and knowing Him, and loving Him, and delighting to do His will.

THOMAS ERSKINE

*Trust in Him at all times; ye people, pour out
your heart before Him; God is a refuge for us.*
PSALMS lxii. 8

FROM tedious toil, from anxious care,
Dear Lord, I turn again to Thee;
Thy presence and Thy smile to share
Makes every burden light to me.
RAY PALMER

IT is a good thing to have fixed seasons for lifting up
the heart to God, not merely the appointed hours of
prayer, but a momentary act before and after meals,
beginning any occupation, entering into society, leaving the house, etc. Especially it is a help to make
such brief acts after having said or done anything
either wrong or foolish, after any trifling vexation or
disappointment, when the spirit feels, it may be,
wounded and desolate, or when one's vanity is an-
noyed at having been guilty of some little folly or
unseemliness. Sometimes we are more really troubled
and sore at trifles of this sort than at far weightier
things. But if all such things were met with a momentary uplifting of the heart to God, all these little
frailties and worries would tend to mould the character more and more to God's pattern, and they would
assuredly lose their sting; for he who thinks much of
God will daily think less of himself.
H. L. SIDNEY LEAR

Thou hast been my defense and refuge in the day of my trouble.

PSALMS lix. 16

> COMMIT thy way to God,
>   The weight which makes thee faint;
> Worlds are to Him no load,
>   To Him breathe thy complaint.
> Up! up! the day is breaking,
>   Say to thy cares, good-night!
> Thy troubles from thee shaking,
>   Like dreams in day's fresh light.
>
> PAUL GERHARDT

WHEN you find yourself, as I dare say you sometimes do, overpowered as it were by melancholy, the best way is to go out, and do something kind to somebody or other.

JOHN KEBLE

Do not give way to depression,—but resign yourself to our dear Lord with the object of bearing bravely the discomforts and petty contradictions of this life.

CHARLES DE CONDREN

Never suffer yourself to be subdued by melancholy; it is amongst the things that will most injure you. It is impossible to persevere in the path of holiness, if we give not ourselves to it with joy. The love of God should impart peace to the soul.

MADAME DE GUYON

My flesh and my heart faileth; but God is the strength of my heart, and my portion for ever.
PSALMS lxiii. 26

O, LITTLE heart of mine! shall pain
Or sorrow make thee moan,
When all this God is all for thee,
A Father and thine own?
FREDERICK W. FABER

MAKE allowance for infirmities of the flesh, which are purely physical. To be fatigued, body and soul, is not sin; to be in "heaviness" is not sin. Christian life is not a feeling; it is a principle: when your hearts will not *fly*, let them *go*, and if they "will neither fly nor go," be sorry for them and patient with them, and take them to Christ, as you would carry your little lame child to a tender-hearted, skilful surgeon. Does the surgeon, in such a case, upbraid the child for being lame?

ELIZABETH PRENTISS

When you feel ill and indisposed, and when in this condition your prayer is cold, heavy, filled with despondency, and even despair, do not be disheartened or despairing, for the Lord knows your sick and painful condition. Struggle against your infirmity, pray as much as you have strength to, and the Lord will not despise the infirmity of your flesh and spirit.

FATHER JOHN

137

Through God we shall do valiantly, for He it is that shall tread down our enemies.

PSALMS lx. 12

Create in me a clean heart, O God; and renew a right spirit within me.

PSALMS li. 10

IF any man compares his own soul with the picture drawn in the New Testament of what a Christian ought to be; if any man fixes his eye on the pattern of self-sacrifice, of purity, of truth, of tenderness, and measures his own distance from that standard, he might be ready to despair. But fear not, because you are far from being like the pattern set before you; fear not because your faults are painful to think of: continue the battle and fear not. If, indeed, you are content with yourself, and are making no endeavor to rise above the poor level at which you now stand, then there is reason to fear. But if you are fighting with all your might, fear not, however often you may have fallen, however deeply, however ungratefully, however inexcusably. This one thing we can give, and this is what He asks, hearts that shall never cease from this day forward, till we reach the grave, to strive to be more like Him; to come nearer to Him; to root out from within us the sin that keeps us from Him. To such a battle, brethren, I call you in His name.

FREDERICK TEMPLE

The Lord make you to increase and abound in love one toward another, and toward all men, even as we do toward you.
1 THESSALONIANS iii. 12

IF we love God, we know what loving is,
    For love is God's, He sent it to the earth,
      Half-human, half-divine, all glorious,—
    Half-human, half-divine, but wholly His;
    Not loving God, we know not love's true worth,
      We taste not the great gift He gave to us.
MAURICE FRANCIS EGAN

LET us see that whenever we have failed to be loving, we have also failed to be wise; that whenever we have been blind to our neighbors' interests, we have also been blind to our own; whenever we have hurt others, we have hurt ourselves still more. Let us, at this blessed Whitsuntide, ask forgiveness of God for all acts of malice and uncharitableness, blindness and hardness of heart; and pray for the spirit of true charity, which alone is true wisdom. And let us come to Holy Communion in charity with each other and with all; determined henceforth to feel for each other, and with each other; to put ourselves in our neighbors' places; to see with their eyes, and to feel with their hearts, so far as God shall give us that great grace; determined to make allowances for their mistakes and failings; to give and forgive, even as God gives and forgives, for ever; that so we may be indeed the children of our Father in heaven, whose name is Love.
CHARLES KINGSLEY

Be renewed in the spirit of your mind, and put on the new man, which after God is created in righteousness and true holiness.

EPHESIANS iv. 23, 24

BE constant, O happy soul, be constant, and of good courage; for, however intolerable thou art to thyself, yet thou wilt be protected, enriched, and beloved by that greatest Good, as if He had nothing else to do than to lead thee to perfection by the highest steps of love; and if thou dost not turn away, but perseverest constantly, know that thou offerest to God the most acceptable sacrifice. If, from the chaos of nothing, His omnipotence has produced so many wonders, what will He do in thy soul, created after His own image and likeness, if thou keepest constant, quiet, and resigned.

MIGUEL DE MOLINOS

Wouldst thou feel thy soul's rest in Christ? Thou must know His voice, hear it, learn daily of Him, become His disciple; take up, from *His* nature, what is contrary to *thy* nature. And then, as thy nature is worn out, and His nature comes up in thee, thou wilt find all easy; all that is of life easy, and transgression hard—unbelief hard: yea, thou wilt find it very hard and unnatural, when His nature is grown up in thee, either to distrust the Lord or hearken to His enemy.

ISAAC PENINGTON

He hath chosen us in Him before the foundation of the world, that we should be holy and without blame before Him in love.

EPHESIANS i. 4

O LOVE, who formedst me to wear
    The image of Thy Godhead here;
Who soughtest me with tender care
    Through all my wanderings wild and drear;
    O Love! I give myself to Thee,
    Thine ever, only Thine to be.

JOHANN SCHEFFLER

W E live not for ourselves, but for God; for some purpose of His; for some special end to be accomplished, which He has willed to be accomplished by oneself, and not by another; something which will be left undone, if we do it not, or not be done as it would have been done, if the one ordained to it had done it. We live gifted with certain forms of spiritual grace embodied in us, for some purpose of Divine Love to be fulfiled by us, some idea of the Divine Mind to be imaged forth in our creaturely state. To devote oneself to God is to concentrate the powers of one's being to their ordained end, and therefore to have the happiest and truest life—happiest, because happiness must be in the accordance of these powers with the law of their creation, and truest, because the attainment of the highest glory must be in the accomplishment of the end for which we were created.

T. T. CARTER

To them who by patient continuance in well-doing, seek for glory and honor and immortality, eternal life.

ROMANS ii. 7

Let us run with patience the race that is set before us.

HEBREWS xii. 1

THUS would I press on to the glory,
  A knight in the army of God,
Whose march will be onward and forward,
  Because of the foes on the road.
Before me the guerdon Thou givest,
  My glorious eternal reward,
And with me Thy peace and Thy wisdom,
  Because of the Cross of the Lord.

HENRY SUSO

IF He calls you to a kind of service which is according to His will but not according to your taste, you must not go to it with less, rather with more courage and energy than if your taste coincided with His will. The less of self and self-will there is in anything we do, the better. You must not amuse yourself with going from side to side, when duty calls you straight on; nor make difficulties, when the real thing is to get over them. Let your heart be full of courage, and then say, "I shall succeed. Not I, but the grace of God which is with me."

ST. FRANCIS DE SALES

Not slothful in business; fervent in spirit; serving the Lord.

ROMANS xii. 11

LET us begin from this moment to acknowledge Him in all our ways, and do everything, whatsoever we do, as service to Him and for His glory, depending upon Him alone for wisdom, and strength, and sweetness, and patience, and everything else that is necessary for the right accomplishing of all our living. It is not so much a change of acts that will be necessary, as a change of motive and of dependence. The house will be kept, or the children cared for, or the business transacted, perhaps, just the same as before as to the outward, but inwardly God will be acknowledged, and depended on, and served; and there will be all the difference between a life lived at ease in the glory of His Presence, and a life lived painfully and with effort apart from Him. There will result also from this bringing of God into our affairs a wonderful accession of divine wisdom in the conduct of them, and a far greater quickness and despatch in their accomplishment, a surprising increase in the fertility of resource, and an enlargement on every side that will amaze the hitherto cramped and cabined soul.

HANNAH WHITALL SMITH

When I sit in darkness, the Lord shall be a light unto me.

MICAH vii. 8

> WHEN doubts disturb my troubled breast,
>   And all is dark as night to me,
> Here, as on solid rock, I rest,—
>   That so it seemeth good to Thee.
>
> RAY PALMER

WHEN trouble, restless fears, anxious fretfulness, strive to overpower the soul, our safety is in saying, "My God, I believe in Thy perfect goodness and wisdom and mercy. What Thou doest I cannot now understand; but I shall one day see it all plainly. Meanwhile I accept Thy will, whatever it may be, unquestioning, without reserve." There would be no restless disturbance, no sense of utter discomfort and discomposure in our souls, if we were quite free from any—it may be almost unconscious—opposition to God's will. But we do struggle against it, we do resist; and so long as that resistance endures we cannot be at peace. Peace, and even joy, are quite compatible with a great deal of pain—even mental pain—but never with a condition of antagonism or resistance.

H. L. SIDNEY LEAR

Let him set his heart firmly upon this resolution: "I must bear it inevitably, and I will, by God's grace, do it nobly."

JEREMY TAYLOR

Cause me to know the way wherein I should walk;
for I lift up my soul unto Thee.   PSALMS cxliii. 8

I will guide thee with mine eye.   PSALMS xxxii. 8

TEACH me to do the thing that pleaseth Thee;
Thou art my God, in Thee I live and move;
Oh, let Thy loving Spirit lead me forth
Into the land of righteousness and love.
                              J. B. S. MONSELL

THE minds that are alive to every word from God,
give constant opportunity for His divine interference
with a suggestion that may alter the courses of their
lives; and, like the ships that turn when the steers-
man's hand but touches the helm, God can steer them
through the worst dangers by the faintest breath of
feeling, or the lightest touch of thought.
                              RICHARD H. HUTTON

It is no delusion, no dream of a hot brain, no error
of a too confiding soul, that has made the children
of God delight to trust in His Providential aid.
When God, in deed and in truth, is *present* and
dominant in the soul of a man, He can, and He will
give to that soul a real guidance. He will guide it,
with the guidance of an eye that seeth and foreseeth,
—that knoweth what is best for us and the world,
and leadeth us in that way wherein, for our sakes, and
the world's, it is best for us to go.

                              HENRY SEPTIMUS SUTTON

Serve the Lord with gladness. For the Lord is good; His mercy is everlasting; and His truth endureth to all generations.

PSALMS c. 2, 5

> TEACH me Thy love to know;
> That this new light which now I see,
> May both the work and workman show:
> Then by a sunbeam I will climb to Thee.
>
> GEORGE HERBERT

WHY should we not rejoice in the good things of God? If the day is pure and serene, we enjoy its gladness. Why should we not rejoice in the serene light of truth that shines from Heaven upon us? We find a joy in the presence and cheerful greeting of our friends. Why should we not look up to Heaven, whence so many pure and most loving faces look upon us with divine affection, and with most tender desires to cheer and help us? Having an almighty and most loving Father, in whom we live, and move, and have our being, let us rejoice in Him. Having a most loving Saviour, who has made Himself our brother, and feeds us with His life, we ought surely to rejoice in Him. Having the Holy Spirit of God with us, making us His temples, and pouring His love into our hearts, we ought certainly to answer His love, and rejoice in His overflowing goodness. "Rejoice in the Lord alway, and again I say, Rejoice."

WILLIAM BERNARD ULLATHORNE

Blessed is every one that feareth the Lord; that walketh in His ways . . . Happy shalt thou be, and it shall be well with thee.

PSALMS cxxviii. 1, 2

WE think it a gallant thing, to be fluttering up to heaven with our wings of knowledge and speculation; whereas the highest mystery of a divine life here, and of perfect happiness hereafter, consists in nothing but mere obedience to the Divine will. Happiness is nothing but that inward sweet delight, which will arise from the harmonious agreement between our wills and the will of God. There is nothing in the whole world able to do us good or hurt, but God, and our own will: neither riches nor poverty, nor disgrace nor honor, nor life nor death, nor angels nor devils; but willing, or not willing, as we ought.

RALPH CUDWORTH

The one misery of man is self-will, the one secret of blessedness is the conquest over our own wills. To yield them up to God is rest and peace. What disturbs us in this world is not "trouble," but our opposition to trouble. The true source of all that frets and irritates, and wears away our lives, is not in external things, but in the resistance of our wills to the will of God expressed by external things.

ALEXANDER MACLAREN

Now, O Lord, Thou art our Father; we are the clay, and Thou our potter; and we all are the work of Thy hand.

ISAIAH lxiv. 8

To be conformed to the image of His Son.

ROMANS viii. 29

THOU shalt do what Thou wilt with Thine own hand.
Thou form'st the spirit like the moulded clay;
For those who love Thee keep Thy just command,
And in Thine image grow as they obey.

JONES VERY

HE who hath appointed thee thy task, will proportion it to thy strength, and thy strength to the burden which He lays upon thee. He who maketh the seed grow thou knowest not how, and seest not, will, thou knowest not how, ripen the seed which He hath sown in thy heart, and leaven thee by the secret workings of His good Spirit. Thou mayest not see the change thyself, but He will gradually change thee, make thee another man. Only yield thyself to His moulding hand, as clay to the potter, having no wishes of thy own, but seeking in sincerity, however faint, to have His will fulfilled in thee, and He will teach thee what to pray for, and will give thee what He teacheth thee. He will retrace His own image on thee line by line, effacing by His grace and gracious discipline the marks and spots of sin which have defaced it.

EDWARD B. PUSEY

A new commandment I give unto you, That ye love one another; as I have loved you, that ye also love one another.

JOHN xiii. 34

ONE with our brethren here in love,
And one with saints that are at rest,
And one with angel hosts above,
And one with God for ever blest.

ISAAC WILLIAMS

ALL extreme sensitiveness, fastidiousness, suspicion, readiness to take offence, and tenacity of what we think our due, come from self-love, as does the unworthy secret gratification we sometimes feel when another is humbled or mortified; the cold indifference, the harshness of our criticism, the unfairness and hastiness of our judgments, our bitterness towards those we dislike, and many other faults which must more or less rise up before most men's conscience, when they question it sincerely as to how far they do indeed love their neighbors as Christ has loved them. He will root out all dislikes and aversions, all readiness to take offence, all resentments, all bitterness, from the heart which is given up to His guidance. He will infuse His own tender love for man into His servant's mind, and teach him to "love his brother as Christ has loved him."

JEAN NICOLAS GROU

Enjoying each other's good is heaven begun.

LUCY C. SMITH

Therefore are they before the throne of God, and serve Him day and night in His temple; and He that sitteth on the throne shall dwell among them.
REVELATION vii. 15

> So many worlds, so much to do,
>   So little done, such things to be,
>   How know I what had need of thee,
> For thou wert strong as thou wert true?
ALFRED TENNYSON

THEY who have gone before have not therefore passed into a condition of lethargy or vacancy. They may be nearer to us, as they are nearer to the perfect love. They may guide us towards a holier and ampler freedom, since they suffer no more the limitations of time. The veil is rent. There is with us the presence of the unseen host.

ELISHA MULFORD

The work of God hath not lost them, if we take it in its most capacious, comprehensive acceptation. God hath a will to be done not in earth only, but also in heaven; they are not dismissed from the King's business who are called from the camp to the Court, from being common soldiers to be Privy Councillors.

ABRAHAM CHEARE

We pray always for you, that our God would count you worthy of this calling, and fulfil all the good pleasure of His goodness, and the work of faith with power.

2 THESSALONIANS i. 11

THOU settest us each task divine,
We bless that helping hand of Thine,
  That strength by Thee bestowed.
Thou minglest in the glorious fight;
Thine own the cause! Thine own the might!
  We serve the Living God.

THOMAS H. GILL

EVERY hard effort generously faced, every sacrifice cheerfully submitted to, every word spoken under difficulties, raises those who speak or act or suffer to a higher level; endows them with a clearer sight of God; braces them with a will of more strength and freedom; warms them with a more generous and large and tender heart.

HENRY P. LIDDON

A man's best desires are always the index and measure of his possibilities; and the most difficult duty that a man is capable of doing is the duty that above all he should do.

CHARLES H. BRENT

Under the laws of Providence, we have duties which are perilous.

AUSTIN PHELPS

151

*Then shall thou call, and the Lord shall answer;
thou shalt cry, and He shall say, Here I am.*

ISAIAH lviii. 9

EVER quickly Thou dost hear
Thy children's feeble cry,
And dost keep them everywhere
Beneath Thy watchful eye;
And 'midst the worlds that lean on Thee
Thou hast faithful thoughts of me.

ANON

"HE will be very gracious unto thee at the voice
of thy cry." That has comforted me often, more than
any promise of answer; it includes answers, and a
great deal more besides; it tells us what He *is* towards us, and that is more than what He will *do*. And
the "cry" is not long, connected, thoughtful prayers,
a cry is just an *unworded dart upwards* of the heart,
and at *that* "voice" He will be very gracious. What a
smile there is in these words!

F. R. HAVERGAL

He that hath not tempted you hitherto above your
strength will continue so to the end. If, for a time,
He hide His face from you, yet He doth it but for a
moment, to make you the more heartily to cry to
Him; and surely He will hear you, not only when you
are in crying, but also whilst you are in thinking how
to cry. He is with you in trouble, and will indeed
deliver you.

JOHN BRADFORD

Hitherto have ye asked nothing in my name, ask, and ye shall receive, that your joy may be full.

JOHN xvi. 24

GOD'S "ask"
Meaneth all fulness and all grace,
Access in every time and place;
Yet we
To whom this mercy is so free,
This privilege of light to bask
In the full sunshine of His face,
Regard prayer even as a task.

ANNA E. HAMILTON

THERE is some power we have not yet discovered, some secret as yet unknown—but oh! what a marvellous power! what a blessed secret! that can make the Christian life a life of love, and trust, and bright serenity; something different from the duty-life, which, though real, does not satisfy; having all the activity and earnestness of the duty-life, but having with it the peace and joy which many and many a soul is craving.

WILLIAM R. HUNTINGTON

We do not value as we ought our inestimable privilege of being allowed to worship God. We do not prize our heavenly prerogative of being permitted to keep His commandments. We look at that as an obligation which is more properly a boon.

FREDERICK W. FABER

JUNE 2

That ye may be counted worthy of the Kingdom of God.

2 THESSALONIANS i. 5

FEAR not, for He hath sworn;
  Faithful and true His name;
The glorious hours are onward borne;
  'Tis lit, th'immortal flame;
It glows *around* thee; kneel, and strive, and win
Daily one living ray—'twill brighter glow within.

JOHN KEBLE

COUNT that day lost (though thou mayest have despatched much business therein) in which thou hast neither gained some victory over thine own evil inclinations and thy self-will, nor returned thanks to thy Lord for His mercies.

LORENZO SCUPOLI

Between dawn and dark there is time enough for the collisions of disinterestedness with selfishness in our dealings with our fellow-creatures, in the life of our own homes; time enough to meet or to evade the demands of homely faithfulness in our several work, time enough to confront the sturdy rebellion of passions and besetting sins against our spiritual nature, time enough to win or to lose heaven in.

HENRY WILDER FOOTE

It is no small matter to lose or to gain the Kingdom of God.

THOMAS À KEMPIS

All things are yours; whether Paul, or Apollos, or Cephas, or the world, or life, or death, or things present, or things to come; all are yours; and ye are Christ's; and Christ is God's.

1 CORINTHIANS iii. 21-23

FOR those who worship Thee there is no death,
For all they do is but with Thee to dwell;
Now while I take from Thee this passing breath,
It is but of Thy glorious name to tell.

JONES VERY

MARK those men whose life is hidden in God, so that of themselves they make no account. Thus can they delight themselves fully and freely in all that which God is doing, apart from the thought of themselves; and to them therefore it is true that heaven and earth are theirs, and all things are theirs, and fulfil their will, because the will of God is their will. And their cup overfloweth with joy even here below, because in all things they have a joy and delight that is steadfast and full. Whilst they walk with God, all is peace. For in Him sorrow is not sorrow, and pain is not pain, but all is peace and rest, all that God willeth, to them is sweet and pleasant. Nor is it only that to them the will of God is sweet. It is more than this. For to them He gives the fair sunshine of His comfort, and the blessed joy of heaven, even here below. So that they live already as it were in heaven.

HENRY SUSO

JUNE 4

*Blessed is the man that trusteth in the Lord, and
whose hope the Lord is.*

JEREMIAH xvii. 7

> THUS will I live and walk from day to day,
>   Contented, trustful, satisfied, and still;
> What life so shielded, or what life so free,
>   As that within the centre of Thy will!
>
> JANE WOODFALL

FOLLOW Christ in the denial of *all the wills of
self*, and then all is put away that separates you from
God; the heaven-born new creature will come to life
in you, which alone knows and enjoys the things of
God, and has his daily food of gladness in that manifold BLESSED, and BLESSED, which Christ preached on
the mount.

WILLIAM LAW

Divine tranquillity grows from the life of God in
the soul, which is the same as the life of pure love.
Why should a soul be otherwise than tranquil, which
seeks for nothing but what comes in the providence
of God; and which, forgetful of self, has nothing to
do but to love? It has an innate conviction, strong as
the everlasting foundations, that, if there is a God
above us, all is well, *all must be well.*

THOMAS C. UPHAM

And now I exhort you to be of good cheer.

ACTS xxvii. 22

I will be glad and rejoice in Thee; I will sing praise to Thy name, O Thou most High.

PSALMS ix. 2

IF you have a murmuring spirit, you cannot have true cheerfulness; it will generally show in your countenance and your voice. Some little fretfulness or restlessness of tone will betray it. Your cheerfulness is forced, it does not spring up freely and healthily out of your heart, which it can only do when that is truly at rest in God; when you are satisfied with His ways, and wishing no change in them. When this is truly your case, then your heart and mind are free, and you can rejoice in spirit.

PRISCILLA MAURICE

Let us seek the grace of a cheerful heart, an even temper, sweetness, gentleness, and brightness of mind, as walking in His light, and by His grace. Let us pray to Him to give us the spirit of ever-abundant, ever-springing love, which overpowers and sweeps away the vexations of life by its own richness and strength, and which, above all things, unites us to Him who is the fountain and the centre of all mercy, loving-kindness, and joy.

JOHN HENRY NEWMAN

I will run the way of Thy commandments, when Thou shalt enlarge my heart.

PSALMS cxix. 32

My hands also will I lift up unto Thy commandments, which I have loved.

PSALMS cxix. 48

LOVE is higher than duty. But the reason is that love in reality contains duty in itself. Love without a sense of duty is a mere delusion, from which we cannot too soon set ourselves free. Love is duty and something more.

FREDERICK TEMPLE

Think not anything little, wherein we may fulfil His commandments. It is in the midst of common and ordinary duties that our life is placed; common occupations make up our lives. By faith and love we obey; but by obedience are the faith and love, which God gives us, strengthened. Then shall we indeed love our Lord, when we seek to please Him in all things, speak or are silent, sleep or wake, labor or rest, do or suffer, with a single eye to His service. God give us grace so to love Him, that we may in all things see Him; in all, obey; and, obeying, see Him more clearly and love Him less unworthily; and so, in that blissful harmony of obedience and of love, be prepared to see Him "face to face."

EDWARD B. PUSEY

Strengthened with might by His Spirit in the inner man; that Christ may dwell in your hearts by faith.

EPHESIANS iii. 16, 17

MAY we not only be delivered from the outward act or word that grieves Thee, but may the very springs of our nature be purified!

F. B. MEYER

Take the last transient swell of petty impatience, or of unkind criticism; things which to the unawakened conscience look so small, to the awakened conscience so large. There is not one that need have taken place. Had I been walking that moment with God, abiding that moment in Christ, drawing that moment on the sanctifying Spirit's power, I should not have lost temper, I should not have thought unkindly;—not only should I not have *looked* impatience, or indulged in needless severity of *words*. The occasion for the very feeling would have been as if it were not, because neutralized in Jesus Christ. And if that might have been true for the last five minutes, why should it not be true for the next five, for the present minute? "I can do all things," I have resources for all circumstances, "in Him that strengtheneth me."

HANDLEY C. G. MOULE

JUNE 8

Put on therefore, a heart of compassion, kindness, humility, meekness, longsuffering; forbearing one another, and forgiving each other, if any man have a complaint against any; even as the Lord forgave you, so also do ye.

COLOSSIANS iii. 12, 13 (R. V.)

> THE discord is within, which jars
>   So sadly in life's song;
> 'Tis we, not they who are in fault,
>   When others seem so wrong.
>
> FREDERICK WM. FABER

SELF-PREOCCUPATION, self-broodings, self-interest, self-love,—these are the reasons why you go jarring against your fellows. Turn your eyes off yourself; look up, and out! There are men, your brothers, and women, your sisters; they have needs that you can aid. Listen for their confidences; keep your heart wide open to their calls, and your hands alert for their service. Learn to give, and not to take; to drown your own hungry wants in the happiness of lending yourself to fulfil the interests of those nearest or dearest. Look up and out, from this narrow, cabined self of yours, and you will jar no longer; you will fret no more, you will provoke no more; but you will, to your own glad surprise, find the secret of "the meekness and the gentleness of Jesus"; and the fruits of the Spirit will all bud and blossom from out of your life.

HENRY SCOTT HOLLAND

The Lord bless thee, and keep thee; the Lord make His face shine upon thee, and be gracious unto thee; the Lord lift up His countenance upon thee, and give thee peace.

NUMBERS vi. 24—26

The eternal God is thy refuge, and underneath are the everlasting arms.

DEUTERONOMY xxxiii. 27

THOU wilt in time experience that thou dost belong not only to this life, but also art capable of enjoying and beholding God and eternal things, to thy perfect contentment and rest. Thou wilt then fix thine eyes, like a little innocent child, upon the face of God, steadfastly and joyfully; and He in return, like a faithful and loving mother, will keep His eyes upon thee, by which thou wilt be made holy through and through, and transformed into the same image from glory to glory. All thy delight, joy, and bliss will be in God, and God, in return, will have His joy and good pleasure in thee. He will rest and dwell in thee, as in His serene throne of peace; and thy spirit, that had so long gone astray, like a friendless child in a foreign land, will again sweetly repose in its true rest and home, in undisturbed peace. And thus thou wilt become a clear heaven of the everblessed God, in which He will dwell, and which He will fill with His divine light and love, and in which He will be glorified in time and in eternity.

GERHARD TERSTEEGEN

161

Now the God of hope fill you with all joy and peace in believing, that ye may abound in hope, through the power of the Holy Ghost.

ROMANS XV. 13

DO, I entreat you, drive away all these anxious thoughts which hinder your soul, and try to serve God cheerfully. Be resolute in overcoming self, and in bearing with your mental troubles whatever they be, leaving all to God, and doing whatever you know to be His will, quickly and heartily; be gentle, patient, humble, and courteous to all, but especially be gentle and patient with yourself. I think that many of your troubles arise from an exaggerated anxiety, a secret impatience with your own faults; and this restlessness, when once it has got possession of your mind, is the cause of numberless trifling faults, which worry you, and go on adding to your burden until it becomes unbearable. I would have you honest in checking and correcting yourself, but at the same time patient under the consciousness of your frailty. Remember that Jesus our Lord loves to dwell within a quiet heart, and to come to those who are at peace with themselves; restlessness and anxiety hinder our seeing Him, even when He is beside us and speaking to us.

PÈRE HYACINTHE BESSON

Though I walk in the midst of trouble, Thou wilt revive me.

PSALMS CXXXViii. 7

IT is very helpful to make a habit of offering, morning by morning, the troubles of the day just beginning to our dear Lord, accepting His will in all things, expecially in all little personal trials and vexations. Some persons have found great benefit from making, when first they wake, the act taught to Madame de Chantal by St. Francis de Sales, accepting "all things tolerable and intolerable" for love of Christ; then at midday, a moment's inward search to see whether there has been any voluntary slackening of submission, any deliberate opposition to God's will, any hesitation in resisting the distaste or fretfulness, the impatience or discouragement we are tempted to feel when things go contrary to our own will and likings, making a fresh resolution to go on heartily; and, at night, a quick review of the day's failures for which to ask pardon, and strength to go on better anew. Some such habit as this is a great check to that terrible hindrance of the spiritual life which, terrible though it be, is so apt to steal upon many good and earnest souls,—a complaining, grumbling, self-pitying spirit.

H. L. SIDNEY LEAR

That Christ may dwell in your hearts by faith.

EPHESIANS iii. 17

Christ in you, the hope of glory.

COLOSSIANS i. 27

ENTER my opening heart;
Fill in with love and peace and light from heaven;
Give me Thyself—for all in Thee is given;
Come—never to depart.

THOMAS WILLIAM WEBB

WHEREVER thou goest, whatever thou dost at home, or abroad, in the field, or at church, do all in a desire of union with Christ, in imitation of His tempers and inclinations, and look upon all as nothing, but that which exercises, and increases the spirit and life of Christ in thy soul. From morning to night keep Jesus in thy heart, long for nothing, desire nothing, hope for nothing but to have all that is within thee changed into the spirit and temper of the holy Jesus. This new birth in Christ, thus firmly believed and continually desired, will do everything that thou wantest to have done in thee, it will dry up all the springs of vice, stop all the workings of evil in thy nature, it will bring all that is good into thee, it will open all the gospel within thee, and thou wilt know what it is to be taught of God.

WILLIAM LAW

The Lord God is a sun and shield: the Lord will give grace and glory; no good thing will He withhold from them that walk uprightly.

PSALMS lxxxiv. 11

> JUST to trust Him, this is all!
> Then the day will surely be
> Peaceful, whatsoe'er befall,
> Bright and blesséd, calm and free.
> **FRANCES R. HAVERGAL**

WHAT we should do is really, very often, to be still. And if we want something to make us more active and energetic, watchful and holy, I know but one thought, that is *faith,*—faith producing love. More trust and confidence and joy in God would be the secret—the only true or successful secret—of more goodness. And this should come quietly and calmly, not in great effort; this kingdom of God has come not with observation. Rest and quiet growth are what you want.

JAMES HINTON

Open wide every avenue of your being to receive the blessed influences your Divine Husbandman may bring to bear upon you. Bask in the sunshine of His love. Drink in of the waters of His goodness. Keep your face upturned to Him. You need make no efforts to grow. But let your efforts instead be all concentrated on this, that you abide in the Vine.

HANNAH WHITALL SMITH

JUNE 14

This day is salvation come to this house.

LUKE xix. 9

From this day will I bless you.

HAGGAI ii. 19

> EVERY day is a fresh beginning;
> Listen, my soul, to the glad refrain,
> And spite of old sorrow and older sinning,
> And puzzles forecasted and possible pain,
> Take heart with the day, and begin again.
> SUSAN COOLIDGE

EVERY temptation to evil temper which can assail us to-day will be an opportunity to decide the question whether we shall gain the calmness and the rest of Christ, or whether we shall be tossed by the restlessness and agitation of the world. Nay, the very vicissitudes of the seasons, day and night, heat and cold, affecting us variably, and producing exhilaration or depression, are so contrived as to conduce towards the being which we become, and decide whether we shall be master of ourselves, or whether we shall be swept at the mercy of accident and circumstance, miserably susceptible of merely outward influences. F. W. ROBERTSON

Why wilt thou defer thy good purpose from day to day? Arise, and begin in this very instant, and say, "Now is the time to be doing; now is the time to be striving; now is the fit time to amend myself." Unless thou dost earnestly force thyself, thou shalt never get the victory over sin. THOMAS À KEMPIS

Lying lips are abomination to the Lord, but they that deal truly are His delight.

PROVERBS xii. 22

Wherefore, putting away lying, speak every man truth with his neighbor; for we are members one of another.

EPHESIANS iv. 25

IT seems to me, that the shortest way to check the darker forms of deceit is to set watch more scrupulous against those which have mingled, unregarded and unchastised, with the current of our life. Do not let us lie at all. Do not think of one falsity as harmless, and another as slight, and another as unintended. Cast them all aside; they may be light and accidental; but they are an ugly soot from the smoke of the pit, for all that; and it is better that our hearts should be swept clean of them, without over care as to which is largest or blackest. Speaking truth is like writing fair, and comes only by practice; it is less a matter of will than of habit, and I doubt if any occasion can be trivial which permits the practice and formation of such a habit.

JOHN RUSKIN

If you tell the truth, you have infinite power *supporting you;* but if not, you have infinite power against you.

CHARLES GEORGE GORDON

Thy statutes have been my songs in the house of my pilgrimage.

PSALMS cxix. 54

My God shall supply all your need according to His riches in glory by Christ Jesus.

PHILIPPIANS iv. 19

How must the pilgrim's load be borne?
With staggering limbs and look forlorn?
His Guide chose all that load within;
There's need of everything but sin.

So, trusting Him whose love He knows,
Singing along the road he goes;
And nightly of his burden makes
A pillow, till the morning breaks.

LUCY LARCOM

THEY live contented with what they have, whether it be little or much, because they know that they receive as much as is profitable for them; little, if little be profitable, and much, if much be profitable for them, but the Lord only can, who has an eternal end in view in all things which He provides.

EMANUEL SWEDENBORG

I hope you will learn, what I am always hoping to learn, to rejoice in God continually, knowing that He is really ordering all your circumstances to the one end of making you a partaker of His own goodness, and bringing you within His own sympathy.

THOMAS ERSKINE

None of them that trust in Him shall be desolate.

PSALMS xxxiv. 22

That ye sorrow not, even as others who have no hope.

1 THESSALONIANS iv. 13

Are the consolations of God too small for thee?

JOB xv. 11 (R. V.)

> WHAT shall make trouble? Not the holy thought
>   Of the departed; that will be a part
> Of those undying things His peace hath wrought
>   Into a world of beauty in the heart.
>
> SARAH J. WILLIAMS

SHE spoke of those who had walked with her long ago in her garden, and for whose sake, now that they had all gone into the world of light, every flower was doubly dear. Would it be a true proof of loyalty to them if she lived gloomily or despondently because they were away? She spoke of the duty of being ready to welcome happiness as well as to endure pain, and of the strength that endurance wins by being grateful for small daily joys, like the evening light, and the smell of roses, and the singing of birds. She spoke of the faith that rests on the Unseen Wisdom and Love like a child on its mother's breast, and the melting away of doubts in the warmth of an effort to do some good in the world.

HENRY VAN DYKE

That they might be called trees of righteousness, the planting of the Lord, that He might be glorified. ISAIAH lxi. 3

For so an entrance shall be ministered unto you abundantly into the everlasting kingdom of our Lord and Saviour Jesus Christ. 2 PETER i. 11

Hast thou a sense of the way to the Father? Then be careful that thy spirit daily bow before Him, that He would continue His mercy to thee; making thy way more and more clear before thee every day;— yea, and bearing thee up in all the exercises and trials which may befall thee, in every kind; that, by His secret working in thy spirit, and helping thee with a little help from time to time, thou mayest still be advancing nearer and nearer towards the kingdom; until thou find the Lord God administer an entrance unto thee thereinto, and give thee an inheritance of life, joy, righteousness, and peace therein; which is strength unto the soul against sin and death.

ISAAC PENINGTON

Probably the greatest result of the life of prayer is an unconscious but steady growth into the knowledge of the mind of God and into conformity with His will; for after all prayer is not so much the means whereby God's will is bent to man's desires, as it is that whereby man's will is bent to God's desires.

CHARLES H. BRENT

That which I see not teach Thou me: if I have done iniquity, I will do it no more.

JOB xxxiv. 32

He will teach us of His ways, and we will walk in His paths.

ISAIAH ii. 3

YES, take my heart, and in it rule;
    Direct it as it pleaseth Thee;
I will be silent in Thy school,
    And learn whate'er Thou teachest me.

GERHARD TERSTEEGEN

PEOPLE cannot become perfect by dint of hearing or reading about perfection. The chief thing is not to listen to yourself, but silently to listen to God. Talk little and do much, without caring to be seen. God will teach you more than all the most experienced persons or the most spiritual books can do. You already know a great deal more than you practise. You do not need the acquirement of fresh knowledge half so much as to put in practice that which you already possess.

FRANÇOIS DE LA MOTHE FÉNELON

To speak with the tongues of men or angels on religious matters, is a much less thing than to know how to stay the mind upon God, and abide with Him in the closet of our hearts, observing, loving, adoring, and obeying His holy power within us.

WILLIAM LAW

Be kindly affectioned one to another with brotherly love.

ROMANS xii. 10

Love as brethren, be pitiful, be courteous.

1 PETER iii. 8

LET your religion make you more considerate, more loving and attractive, more able to think of and enter into the pleasure and interests of others.

ARTHUR C. A. HALL

Love one another in spite of your differences, in spite of your faults. Love one another, and make the best of one another, as He loved us, who, for the sake of saving what was good in the human soul, forgot, forgave, put out of sight what was bad—who saw and loved what was good even in the publican Zaccheus, even in the penitent Magdalen, even in the expiring malefactor, even in the heretical Samaritan, even in the Pharisee Nicodemus, even in the heathen soldier, even in the outcast Canaanite. It is very easy to fix our attention only on the weak points of those around us, to magnify them, to irritate them, to aggravate them; and, by so doing, we can make the burden of life unendurable, and can destroy our own and others' happiness and usefulness wherever we go. But this was not the love wherewith Christ loved us; this is not the new love wherewith we are to love one another.

ARTHUR P. STANLEY

*That which is altogether just shalt thou follow,
that thou mayest live.*

DEUTERONOMY xvi. 20

*This day the Lord thy God hath commanded thee
to do these statutes and judgments: thou shalt
therefore keep and do them with all thine heart,
and with all thy soul.*

DEUTERONOMY xxvi. 16

NEVER pass by or palter with the clear voice of
conscience, with the plain command of duty; never
let it be doubtful to your own soul whether you belong to the right side or wrong, whether you are a
true soldier or a false traitor. Never deliberate about
what is clearly wrong, and try to persuade yourself
that it is not.

FREDERICK TEMPLE

The first resolve of one who gives himself wholly
to God must be never to give way deliberately to any
fault whatever; never to act in defiance of conscience,
never to refuse anything God requires, never to say
of anything, It is too small for God to heed. Such a
resolution as this is an essential foundation in the
spiritual life. I do not mean but that in spite of it we
shall fall into inadvertencies, infirmities, errors; but
we shall rise up and go on anew from such faults—
because they are involuntary, the will has not con-
sented to them.

JEAN NICOLAS GROU

Be not therefore anxious for the morrow.

MATTHEW vi. 34 (R. V.)

I will not fail thee, nor forsake thee; be strong and of a good courage.

JOSHUA i. 5, 6

I have laid help upon one that is mighty.

PSALMS lxxxix. 19

THOU hast Thy help upon the mighty laid;
In Him I trust, nor know to want or fear,
But ever onward walk, secure from sin,
For He has conquered every foe within.

JONES VERY

WHY should we, then, burden ourselves with superfluous cares, and fatigue and weary ourselves in the multiplicity of our ways? Let us rest in peace. God Himself inviteth us to cast our cares, our anxieties upon Him.

MADAME GUYON

If we may take one test or sign by which to judge of advance in the spiritual life, it would be this,—whether more and more calmness is being maintained in the midst of all the disturbances and troubles which are wont to come, which may ever be looked for in some form or other,—whether there be peacefulness of mind, and order of thought in the midst of all that once too much distracted and agitated the soul.

T. T. CARTER

Behold the fowls of the air . . . consider the lilies of the field.

MATTHEW vi. 26, 28

I WAS in the act of kneeling down before the Lord my God, when a little bird came and perched near my window, and thus preached to me: "O thou grave man, look on me, and learn something, if not the deepest lesson, then a true one. Thy God made me, and the like of me; and, if thou canst conceive it, loves me and cares for me. *Thou* studiest Him in great problems, which oppress and confound thee: thou losest sight of one half of His ways. Learn to see thy God not in great mysteries only, but in me also. His burden on me is light, His yoke on me is easy; but thou makest burdens and yokes for thyself which are very grievous to be borne. Things deep as Hell and high as Heaven thou considerest overmuch; but thou dost not 'consider the lilies' sufficiently. If *thou* couldst be as a lily before God, for at least one hour in the twenty-four, it would do thee good: I mean, if thou couldst cease to will and to think, and *be* only. Consider, the lily is as really from God as thou art, and is a figure of something *in Him,*—the like of which should also be in thee. Thou longest to grow, but the lily grows without longing; yes, without even thinking or willing, *grows* and *is* beautiful both to God and man."

JOHN PULSFORD

In God I will praise His word, in God I have put my trust; I will not fear what flesh can do unto me.

PSALMS lvi. 4

D O not fear circumstances. They cannot hurt us, if we hold fast by God and use them as the voices and ministries of His will. Trust Him about every one and everything, for all times and all needs, earth and heaven, friends and children, the conquest of sin, the growth of holiness, the cross that chafes, the grace that stirs.

ANTHONY W. THOROLD

I find that it is not the circumstances in which we are placed, but the spirit in which we meet them, that constitutes our comfort; and that this may be undisturbed, if we seek for and cherish a feeling of quiet submission, whatever may be the privations allotted us.

ELIZABETH T. KING

Wheresoever God may lead you, there you will find Himself, in the most harassing business, as in the most tranquil prayer.

FRANÇOIS DE LA MOTHE FÉNELON

Teach me Thy way, O Lord; I will walk in Thy truth; unite my heart to fear Thy name.

PSALMS lxxxvi. 11

IF thou but suffer God to guide thee,
And hope in Him through all thy ways,
He'll give thee strength, whate'er betide thee,
And bear thee through the evil days;
Who trusts in God's unchanging love,
Builds on the rock that nought can move.

GEORG NEUMARK

IF we seek, indeed, that all our ways may be His ways, if we resolve and pray that we will keep to the path of obedience, of trust, of duty; then we know that His angels are in charge of us, and that they can bear us nowhere beyond our Father's eye, His hand, His care. Then we know that all worlds are His, all souls are His; we can trust to Him those He has taken from us, and know that when He has called them to pass out of our sight, He is with them still, to keep them in all their ways, even in that hidden path over which the dark shadow lies, until the day break and the shadows flee away.

JOHN ELLERTON

In the multitude of my thoughts within me, Thy comforts delight my soul.

PSALMS xciv. 19

Oh, listen then, Most Pitiful!
To Thy poor creature's heart;
It blesses Thee that Thou art God,
That Thou art what Thou art!

FREDERICK W. FABER

WHAT the particular thoughts or temptations are that disquiet you, I know not; but, whatsoever they are, look above them, and labor to fix your eye on that infinite goodness, which never faileth them that, by faith, do absolutely rely and rest upon it; and patiently wait upon Him, who hath pronounced them all, without exception, blessed that do so.

ROBERT LEIGHTON

Thoughts that disturb and trouble us seldom come from God. It is generally best to put them away, and throw ourself, with increased trust in Him and mistrust of self, at His feet. And never forget, amid whatever may befall you,—dryness, coldness, desolation, and disappointment, consciousness of many faults, and of great weakness, and want of faith,—that where love is, there God is sure to be. He never yet has suffered any soul to fall wholly from Him which, amid all its frailties and falls, clings to Him in love.

H. L. SIDNEY LEAR

On whatsoever errand I shall send thee thou shalt go; and whatsoever I shall command thee thou shalt speak.

JEREMIAH i. 7 (R. V. MARGIN)

THERE is no change of time and place with Thee;
  Where'er I go, 't is still with me the same;
Within Thy presence I rejoice to be,
  And always hallow Thy most holy name.

JONES VERY

BE assured of this, you do not know God in truth, and have no true peace, if you are depending upon times and places. Remember that whatever God gives you to do, from moment to moment, that is the very best thing you could possibly be doing, and you little know where and when the Lord will meet you. He who does not seek and find God everywhere, and in everything, finds Him nowhere and in nothing. And he who is not at the Lord's service in everything, is at His service in nothing.

JOHN TAULER

God must be sought and seen in His providences; it is not our actions in themselves considered which please Him, but the spirit in which they are done, more especially the constant ready obedience to every discovery of His will, even in the minutest things, and with such a suppleness and flexibility of mind as not to adhere to anything, but to turn and move in any direction where He shall call.

MADAME GUYON

Thou wilt show me the path of life; in Thy presence is fulness of joy; at Thy right hand there are pleasures for evermore.

PSALMS xvi. 11

LORD, it is not life to live,
  If Thy presence Thou deny;
Lord, if Thou Thy presence give,
  'T is no longer death to die.
Source and giver of repose,
Singly from Thy smile it flows;
Peace and happiness are Thine;
Mine they are, if Thou art mine.

A. M. TOPLADY

WE live from day to day, as it were, by chance; and forget that human life itself is as much an Art, governed by its own rules and precepts of perfection, as the most complicated profession by which that life is maintained or adorned.

WM. ARCHER BUTLER

The art of life consists in taking each event which befalls us with a contented mind, confident of good. This makes us grow younger as we grow older, for youth and joy come from the soul to the body more than from the body to the soul. With this method and art and temper of life, we live, though we may be dying. We rejoice always, though in the midst of sorrows; and possess all things, though destitute of everything.

JAMES FREEMAN CLARKE

Let not your hearts faint, fear not, and do not tremble, neither be ye terrified because of them.

DEUTERONOMY XX. 3

Son of the living God! Oh, call us
　Once and again to follow Thee,
And give us strength, whate'er befall us,
　Thy true disciples still to be.

And if our coward hearts deny Thee,
　In inmost thought, or deed, or word,
Let not our hardness still defy Thee,
　But with a look subdue us, Lord.

HENRY A. MARTIN

HALF our difficulty in doing anything worthy of our high calling, is the shrinking anticipation of its possible after-consequences. But if Peter had tarried, and cast up all that was to come, the poverty, and wandering, and solitude, and lonely old age, the outcast life, and chance of a fearful death, it may be he would have been neither an Apostle nor a Christian.

HENRY EDWARD MANNING

Some men will follow Christ on certain conditions —if He will not lead them through rough roads—if He will not enjoin them any painful tasks—if the sun and wind do not annoy them—if He will remit a part of His plan and order. But the true Christian, who has the spirit of Jesus, will say, as Ruth said to Naomi, "Whither thou goest I will go," whatever difficulties and dangers may be in the way.

RICHARD CECIL

We know that we have passed from death unto life, because we love the brethren. He that loveth not his brother abideth in death.

1 JOHN iii. 14

For who has aught to love and loves aright,
  Will never in the darkest strait despair,
For out of love exhales a living light,
  The light of love, that spends itself in prayer.
HARTLEY COLERIDGE

LOVE is life, and lovelessness is death. As the grace of God changes a man's heart and cleanses and sanctifies him, this is the great evidence of the change, this is the great difference which it makes; that he begins to grow in love, to lay aside self-seeking, and to live for others—and so he may know that he has passed from death unto life. He may know it even here and now—yes, that great discovery of love, that learning to live for others and finding the grace and gentleness that God is keeping up all over the world— even now it is the way from death to life. Even now it changes homes, it lightens every burden, it brings peace and gladness into the hardest days; it alters even the tone of a man's voice and the very look of his face. But all this, blessed and surpassing as it is, far above all else in the world, still is but the beginning. For that life into which we pass, as God's dear grace of love comes in us and about us, is the very life of heaven.

FRANCIS PAGET

For Thou, Lord, hast made me glad through Thy work: I will triumph in the works of Thy hands.
PSALMS xcii. 4

CONSIDER it
(This outer world we tread on) as a harp,—
A gracious instrument on whose fair strings
We learn those airs we shall be set to play
When mortal hours are ended.

JEAN INGELOW

EVERY year has been to me a softening of the impressible nature, and a clearing of the eye in all the fields of divine goodness, quite irrespective of the hard, hot, choking work of the external world and its attacks. I feel more and more how all right spirit life is a gladness and a glory increasing; how divine goodness is speaking in all tones that reach the heart with joy or sorrow, awe or ecstasy, everywhere and in all things, if we can but hear it; how completely the spirit within can be in communion with light, independent of external circumstances; and yet how external circumstances and creation are the medium through which God speaks. And if it is indeed a speech of God, an ever present incarnation of the divine mind, then the power of reading the divine mind can only exist for those who are in accordance with it.

EDWARD THRING

In this was manifested the love of God toward us, because that God sent His only begotten Son into the world, that we might live through Him.

1 JOHN iv. 9

> THY love to me, O God,
> Not mine, O Lord, to Thee,
> Can rid me of this dark unrest,
> And set my spirit free.
>
> HORATIUS BONAR

THE spirit of prayer is a pressing forth of the soul out of this earthly life, it is a stretching with all its desire after the life of God, it is a leaving, as far as it can, all its own spirit, to receive a spirit from above, to be one life, one love, one spirit with Christ in God. For the love which God bears to the soul, His eternal, never-ceasing desire to enter into it, and to dwell in it, stays no longer than till the door of the heart opens for Him. For nothing does, or can keep God out of the soul, or hinder His holy union with it, but the desire of the heart turned from Him.

WILLIAM LAW

Holiness is the beauty of the Lord God or hosts. Thou canst not separate the one from the other. To have it, thou must have Him. Nor will it be hard to obtain either; for He longs to enter into thy being. Thy longing is the faint response of thy heart to His call.

F. B. MEYER

Continue in prayer, and watch in the same.
COLOSSIANS iv. 2

> BUT if distractions manifold prevail,
> And if in this we must confess we fail,
> Grant us to keep at least a prompt desire,
> Continual readiness for prayer and praise,
> An altar heaped and waiting to take fire
> With the least spark, and leap into a blaze.
> RICHARD CHENEVIX TRENCH

WHEN the set time comes round for prayer, it may be, and often is, the case that the mind is depressed, and finds it a hard struggle to raise itself up to communion with God. Your purpose is to hold communion with the Infinite Wisdom and Infinite Love; can you do this, or even attempt this, without coming away from the exercise brighter, calmer, happier, stronger against evil? Make a vigorous effort to throw your whole soul into some very short petition, and the spirit of inertness and heaviness shall be exorcised. But if not, and thy mind be dry to the end, do not disquiet thyself. If only thou makest a sincere effort to draw near to God, all shall be well. He sees that thou hast a will to pray, and accounts the will for the deed.

EDWARD MEYRICK GOULBURN

Pray hardest when it is hardest to pray.
CHARLES H. BRENT

JULY 4

*If any man be in Christ, he is a new creature;
old things are passed away; behold, all things are
become new.*

2 CORINTHIANS v. 17

HIS perfect peace has swept from sight
The narrow bounds of time and space,
And, looking up with still delight,
We catch the glory of His face.

AUGUSTA LARNED

IN every moment of our days, when once our hearts
are yielded to His service, God is working in us and
through us. Hitherto, perhaps, our little world has
only been large enough to hold self and the present.
But, gradually, through tender leadings and unfold-
ings, and, it may be, through pain and suffering, we
come to learn life's lesson,—that it is God's world, not
ours; that our existence is not finished and rounded
off here, but forms part of one vast scheme to which
mind and heart and spirit expand and grow, while
all the horizon round them grows and expands too,
until it touches the shore of the illimitable future, and
we become conscious that earth and heaven are not
so far separated but that the first is but the vestibule
of the second,—imperfect, cloudy, full of broken fragments, but still part of the same Temple of God as
that to which we shall pass in by and by.

H. BOWMAN

All things are possible to him that believeth.

MARK ix. 23

My grace is sufficient for thee; for my strength is made perfect in weakness.

2 CORINTHIANS xii. 9

IT is possible, I dare to say, for those who will indeed draw on their Lord's power for deliverance and victory, to live a life in which His promises are taken as they stand, and found to be true. It is possible to cast *every* care on Him, daily, and to be at peace amidst the pressure. It is possible to see the will of God in everything, and to find it, as one has said, no longer a sigh, but a song. It is possible, in the world of inner act and motion, to put away, to get put away, *all* bitterness, and wrath, and anger, and evil speaking, daily and hourly. It is possible, by unreserved resort to divine power, under divine conditions, to become strongest, through and through, at our weakest point; to find the thing which yesterday upset all our obligations to patience, or to purity, or to humility, an occasion to-day, through Him who loveth us, and worketh in us, for a joyful consent to His will, and a delightful sense of His presence and sin-annulling power. These are things divinely possible.

HANDLEY C. G. MOULE

JULY 6

But we all, with open face, beholding as in a glass the glory of the Lord, are changed into the same image from glory to glory.

2 CORINTHIANS iii. 18

THY life in me be shown!
Lord! I would henceforth seek
To think and speak
Thy thoughts, Thy words alone;
No more my own

FRANCES R. HAVERGAL

NOTHING short of the Life of the Eternal Son of God—the Holiness, the Purity of God, is the standard at which we are to aim; *that* is to be reproduced in our circumstances; the Divine Perfections are to be translated, reproduced in *our* life, *our* home, *our* trials, *our* difficulties, *our* age of the world. Let us ask ourselves, What is the special likeness of Christ that He would reproduce in *me*? What are the features of His Life that He calls *me* to imitate? What pattern would He set before me in my work, my circumstances, my difficulties? What are the inspirations of grace that He would urge me to cultivate and cherish?

ARTHUR C. A. HALL

The Christian life must be in its own degree something like the Master's own life, luminous with His hope, and surrounded by a bracing atmosphere which uplifts all who even touch its outer fringe.

HUGH BLACK

And, whatsoever ye do, do it heartily, as to the Lord, and not unto men.

COLOSSIANS iii. 23

IF you love Him as I want you to do, you will offer Him the whole use of your day, as you open your eyes to the light of each morning, to be spent in active service or silent suffering, according to His good pleasure. You will not select the most agreeable task, but *His* task, whatever it may be; you will not disdain humble service, or be ambitious for distinguished service; you will lie, like a straw, on the current of His will, to be swept away and be forgotten, if it pleases Him, or to be caught up by His mighty hand and transformed thereby into a thunderbolt.

ELIZABETH PRENTISS

Let us pray Him, therefore, to shed abroad in us the mind that was in Christ; that we may offer up ourselves to be disposed of as He sees best, whether for joy or sorrow; to be slighted, or esteemed; to have many friends, or to dwell in a lonely home; to be passed by, or called to serve Him and His kingdom in our own land, or among people of a strange tongue; to be, to go, to do, to suffer even as He wills, even as He ordains, even as Christ endured, "who, through the Eternal Spirit, offered Himself without spot to God."

HENRY EDWARD MANNING

JULY 8

Behold, I will reveal unto them the abundance of peace and truth.

JEREMIAH xxxiii. 6

Glory, honor, and peace, to every man that worketh good.

ROMANS ii. 10

TRUE peace is when the soul revolves around its centre, Almighty God, craving for nothing but what God continually supplies, its passions subdued to itself, itself lovingly loyal to God, in harmony with its God and His laws. God made the soul for Himself, to have its bliss in His infinite, unchanging, exhaustless love. The soul then "must needs be restless, until it repose in Him." Everything, whether it belongs to the keenest intellect, or the lowest senses, is an idol if the soul rests in it, apart from God. The soul's craving for peace is its natural yearning for its End, its Maker and its God. Since the soul is large enough to contain the infinite God, nothing less than Himself can satisfy or fill it.

E. B. PUSEY

With those who have made ready to receive Him in peaceful trust, He will come and dwell in love and joy; and great is their rest and blessedness.

ABBÉ GUILLORÉ

*And we have known and believed the love that
God hath to us. God is love; and he that dwelleth
in love, dwelleth in God, and God in him.*

1 JOHN iv. 16

As flame streams upward, so my longing thought
    Flies up with Thee,
Thou God and Saviour, who hast truly wrought
Life out of death, and to us, loving, brought
A fresh, new world; and in Thy sweet chains caught,
    And made us free!

MAURICE FRANCIS EGAN

W HAT a blessed and glorious thing human existence would be, if we fully realized that the infinitely
wise and infinitely powerful God loves each one of us,
with an intensity infinitely beyond what the most
fervid human spirit ever felt towards another, and
with a concentration as if He had none else to think
of! And this love has brought us into being, just that
we might be taught to enter into *full sympathy* with
Him, receiving His,—giving our own—thus entering
into the joy of our Lord. This is the hope—the sure
and certain hope—set before us,—sure and certain,—
for "the mountains shall depart, and the hills be removed; but my kindness shall not depart from thee,
neither shall the covenant of my peace be removed,
saith the Lord that hath mercy on thee."

THOMAS ERSKINE

Most gladly, therefore, will I rather glory in my infirmities, that the power of Christ may rest upon me.

2 CORINTHIANS xii. 9

The Lord stood with me, and strengthened me.

2 TIMOTHY iv. 17

> To His own the Saviour giveth
>   Daily strength;
> To each troubled soul that liveth,
>   Peace at length.

KARL RUDOLPH HAGENBACH

REMEMBER that your work comes only moment by moment, and as surely as God calls you to work, He gives the strength to do it. Do not think in the morning, "How shall I go through this day? I have such-and-such work to do, and persons to see, and I have not strength for it." No, you have not, for you do not need it. Each moment, as you need it, the strength will come, only do not look forward an hour; circumstances may be very different from what you expect. At any rate you will be borne through each needful and right thing "on eagles' wings." Do not worry yourself with misgivings; take each thing quietly.

PRISCILLA MAURICE

God does not demand impossibilities.

ST. AUGUSTINE

Do all things without murmurings and disputings.
PHILIPPIANS ii. 14

He that hath no rule over his own spirit is like a city that is broken down, and without walls.
PROVERBS xxv. 28

BEHOLD, the paths of life are ours,—we see
Our blest inheritance where'er we tread;
Sorrow and danger our security,
And disappointment lifting up our head.
ANNA L. WARING

ONE valuable way of practising self-control is in checking grumbling, and an unnecessary display of vexation at petty inconveniences. A workman has fulfilled his task imperfectly, some order is wrongly executed, some one keeps you waiting unreasonably; people are careless or forgetful, or do what they have in hand badly. Try not to be disturbed; be just, and show the persons to blame where they are wrong, even (if it be needful) make them do the thing over again properly; but refrain from diffuse or vehement expressions of displeasure. A naturally quick, impetuous person will find that to cultivate a calm external habit is a great help towards gaining the inward even spirit he needs.

H. L. SIDNEY LEAR

A repining life is a lingering death.
BENJAMIN WHICHCOTE

Withhold not good from them to whom it is due when it is in the power of thine hand to do it. Say not unto thy neighbor, Go, and come again, and tomorrow I will give; when thou hast it by thee.
PROVERBS iii. 27, 28

Do not only take occasions of doing good when they are thrust upon you; but study how to do all the good you can, as those "that are zealous of good works." Zeal of good works will make you plot and contrive for them; consult and ask advice for them; it will make you glad when you meet with a hopeful opportunity; it will make you do it largely, and not sparingly, and by the halves; it will make you do it speedily, without unwilling backwardness and delay; it will make you do it constantly to your lives' end. It will make you labor in it as your trade, and not consent that others do good at your charge. It will make you glad, when good is done, and not to grudge at what it cost you. In a word, it will make your neighbors to be to you as yourselves, and the pleasing of God to be above yourselves, and therefore to be as glad to do good as to receive it.

RICHARD BAXTER

*The steps of a good man are ordered by the Lord,
and He delighteth in his way.*

PSALMS xxxvii. 23

So her life was full of sunshine, for in toiling for the Lord
She had found the hidden sweetness that in common things
    lies stored;
He has strewn the earth with flowers, and each eye their
    brightness sees;
But He filled their cups with honey for His humble working
    bees.

FRANCESCA ALEXANDER

THE occupations of every day seem often trifling, we may do them without thinking as ordinary things, yet they are the scenes of our appointed lot— appointed by God for you and me. The ordering, the application of these ordinary occupations, is the appointing of the Divine purpose; it is for ourselves to carry them out. And secretly our character forms according as we handle them. Give thy heart to God Eternal, since thou art thyself eternal. Join thy heart to what He has given thee to do. Join thy heart to His teaching, and thou becomest of a will like to His own will. Nothing comes by pure accident, not even the interruptions in our busy day. And such as follow on to know God's will see in all events what may lead to good, and so trust grows into a habit, as habit grows by perpetual use, till every circumstance may be seen to be but a fresh manifestation of the will of God working itself out in us.

T. T. CARTER

Are not five sparrows sold for two farthings, and not one of them is forgotten before God?

LUKE xii. 6

Fear ye not, therefore, ye are of more value than many sparrows.

MATTHEW x. 31

The trees of the Lord are full of sap; the cedars of Lebanon which He hath planted; where the birds make their nests; as for the stork, the fir trees are her house.

PSALMS civ. 16, 17

IT was a beautiful sight to see the herons come home, rising into the golden sunlight above the hills I could not tell from whence, and sailing on the glorious arches of their wings, on and on—always alone, and each as he came down with outstretched neck and pendent legs ready to settle, taking one last sweep down, then up, on to the summit of the tall Scotch fir, to take a survey of the realm, and, as another approached, plunging into the thick heads of lower trees with a loud good-night to his neighbors, and to all the fair land and water round about him, and a Deo Gratias for all his day's happiness, pleasant unto the ear of his dear God, if not consciously addressed to Him.

MY HEAVENLY FATHER CARETH FOR THEM, I AM OF MORE VALUE THAN MANY HERONS.

EDWARD WHITE BENSON

In Thy presence is fulness of joy.

PSALMS xvi. 11

My presence shall go with thee, and I will give thee rest.

EXODUS xxxiii. 14

> O REST of rests! O peace serene, eternal!
> Thou ever livest, and Thou changest never;
> And in the secret of Thy presence dwelleth
> Fulness of joy, for ever and for ever.
>
> HARRIET BEECHER STOWE

I HAVE no home, until I am in the realized presence of God. This holy presence is my inward home, and, until I experience it, I am a homeless wanderer, a straying sheep in a waste howling wilderness.

ANONYMOUS, 1841

Heaven consists in nothing else than walking, abiding, resting in the Divine Presence. There are souls who enter into this heaven before leaving the body. If thou believest that thy God, found, felt, and rested in, is heaven, why not, under the gracious help which He vouchsafes to thee in His Son, *begin at once to discipline and qualify thy soul for this heaven?* If this be thy chief good, why turn away from it, as though it were a thing not to be desired? If it be the very end of thy being, the only right, good, and blessed end, why postpone thy qualification for it, as though it were a bitter necessity? Suffer thy soul, so noble in its origin, to be withdrawn from dust, noise, multitudes, vain treasures, and vain pleasures, to find its sweetness and fulness in God.

JOHN PULSFORD

Art Thou not from everlasting, O Lord my God, mine Holy One? we shall not die.

HABAKKUK i. 12

My meditation of Him shall be sweet; I will be glad in the Lord.

PSALMS civ. 34

THE more our ideas about God are multiplied, the more various our thoughts, and images, and recollections of things which have to do with Him, of course the more our minds and hearts are engrossed with Him, and so it becomes easier to live all day in His sensible presence. And is not the practice of the presence of God one half of holiness? And so, weary with work or foiled with disappointment, when the dark night is closing in, bringing with it to our sick spirits a sense of imprisonment, and when the dismal rain curtains us round, and we fret to be at liberty and at large, there is the very freedom of a sovereign to a soul traversing this boundless empire of God and Jesus, angels, saints, men, and the blameless creatures, and rejoicing in that never-ceasing sacrifice of praise which is rising up from every nook and corner of creation to the dear Majesty of our most loving God and Father!

FREDERICK WM. FABER

Delight in the happiness of God.

LORENZO SCUPOLL

Trust ye in the Lord for ever: for in the Lord Jehovah is everlasting strength.

ISAIAH xxvi. 4

COME, children, let us go!
  Our Father is our guide;
And when the way grows steep and dark,
  He journeys at our side.
    Our spirits He would cheer,
  The sunshine of His love
Revives and helps us as we rove,
  Ah, blest our lot e'en here!

GERHARD TERSTEEGEN

WE are living out these lives of ours too much apart from God. We toil on dismally, as if the making or the marring of our destinies rested wholly with ourselves. It is not so. We are not the lonely, orphaned creatures we let ourselves suppose ourselves to be. The earth, rolling on its way through space, does not go unattended. The Maker and Controller of it is with it, and around it, and upon it. He is with us here and now. He knows us infinitely more thoroughly than we know ourselves. He loves us better than we have ever dared to believe could be possible.

WILLIAM R. HUNTINGTON

Some of us believe that God is all mighty, and may do all; and that He is all wisdom, and can do all; but that He is all love, and will do all, there we fail.

MOTHER JULIANA

For to-day the Lord will appear unto you.

LEVITICUS ix. 4

Behold, now is the accepted time; behold, now is the day of salvation.

2 CORINTHIANS vi. 2

DO not let your growth in holiness depend upon surrounding circumstances, but rather constrain those circumstances to minister to your growth. Beware of looking onward, or out of the present in any way, for the sanctification of your life. The only thing you can really control is the present—the actual moment that is passing by. Sanctify *that* from hour to hour, and you sanctify your whole life; but brood over the past, or project yourself into the future, and you will lose all. The little act of obedience, love, self-restraint, meekness, patience, devotion, offered to you actually, is all you can do now, and if you neglect that to fret about something else at a distance, you lose your real opportunity of serving God. A moment's silence, when some irritating words are said by another, may stem a very small thing; yet at that moment it is your one duty, your one way of serving and pleasing God, and if you break it, you have lost your opportunity.

H. L. SIDNEY LEAR

By love serve one another. For all the law is fulfilled in one word, even in this; Thou shalt love thy neighbor as thyself.

GALATIANS v. 13, 14

A MAN who habitually pleases himself will become continually more selfish and sordid, even among the most noble and beautiful conditions which nature, history, or art can furnish; and, on the other hand, any one who will try each day to live for the sake of others, will grow more and more gracious in thought and bearing, however dull and even squalid may be the outward circumstances of his soul's probation.

FRANCIS PAGET

It is the habit of making sacrifices in small things that enables us for making them in great, *when it is asked of us.* Temper, love of preeminence, bodily indulgence, the quick retort, the sharp irony,—in checking these let us find our cross and carry it. Or, when the moment comes for some really great service, the heart will be petrified for it, and the blinded eyes will not see the occasion of love.

ANTHONY W. THOROLD

Do Thou unto us whatsoever seemeth good unto Thee.

JUDGES X. 15

> DEAR Lord, whose mercy veileth all
> That may our coming days befall,
> Still hide from us the things to be,
> But rest our troubled hearts in Thee.
> HARRIET MCEWEN KIMBALL

PEACE of heart lies in perfect resignation to the will of God. What you need is true simplicity, a certain calmness of spirit which comes from entire surrender to all that God wills, patience and toleration for your neighbor's faults, and a certain candor and childlike docility in acknowledging your own faults. The trouble you feel about so many things comes from your not accepting everything which may happen to you, with sufficient resignation to God. Put all things, then, in His hands, and offer them beforehand to Him in your heart, as a sacrifice. From the moment when you cease to want things to be according to your own judgment, and accept unconditionally whatever He sends, you will be free from all your uneasy retrospects and anxieties about your own concerns.

FRANCOIS DE LA MOTHE FÉNELON

The Lord do that which seemeth Him good.

2 SAMUEL x. 12

> THE best will is our Father's will,
> And we may rest there calm and still;
> Oh! make it hour by hour thine own,
> And wish for nought but that alone
> Which pleases God.
>
> PAUL GERHARDT

"THY will be done." For instance, when you wish, and by every means endeavor, to be well, and yet remain ill,—then say, "Thy will be done." When you undertake something, and your undertaking does not succeed, say, "Thy will be done." When you do good to others, and they repay you with evil, say, "Thy will be done." Or when you would like to sleep, and are overtaken by sleeplessness, say, "Thy will be done." In general, do not become irritated when anything is not done in accordance with your will, but learn to submit in everything to the Will of the Heavenly Father.

FATHER JOHN

Try to make an instantaneous act of conformity to God's Will, at everything which vexes you.

EDWARD B. PUSEY

Behold, the heaven and the heaven of heavens is the Lord's thy God, the earth also with all that therein is.

DEUTERONOMY x. 14

FATHER, there is no change to live with Thee,
Save that in Christ I grow from day to day;
In each new word I hear, each thing I see,
I but rejoicing hasten on my way.

JONES VERY

THE immediate result of the coming of these good tidings of great joy to me was no outward change in anything, but an inward change of everything, making everything translucent with the light within and beyond. The sum of it all was always that the universe is full of God, and God is love. We are His, and all things are His; therefore in Him all things are ours. In the home, in society, in nature, our beloved moors and woods, and rivers and glens and seas, there was the touch, the breath of God's living, real presence.

ELIZABETH RUNDLE CHARLES

He is so infinitely blessed, that every perception of His blissful presence imparts a vital gladness to the heart. Every degree of approach to Him is, in the same proportion, a degree of happiness. And I often think that were He always present to our mind, as we are present to Him, there would be no pain, nor sense of misery.

SUSANNA WESLEY

I will bring the blind by a way that they knew not; I will lead them in paths that they have not known: I will make darkness light before them, and crooked things straight. These things will I do unto them, and not forsake them.

ISAIAH xlii. 16

WHEN over dizzy heights we go,
One soft hand blinds our eyes,
The other leads us, safe and slow,
O Love of God most wise!

ELIZA SCUDDER

THE simple thought of a life which is to be the unfolding of a Divine plan is too beautiful, too captivating, to suffer one indifferent or heedless moment. Living in this manner, every turn of your experience will be a discovery to you of God, every change a token of His fatherly counsel. Whatever obscurity, darkness, trial, suffering, falls upon you; your defeats, losses, injuries; your outward state, employment, relations; what seems hard, unaccountable, severe, or, as nature might say, vexatious—all these you will see are parts or constitutive elements in God's beautiful and good plan for you, and, as such, are to be accepted with a smile. Take your burdens, and troubles, and losses, and wrongs, if come they must and will, as your opportunities, knowing that God has girded you for greater things than these.

HORACE BUSHNELL

Seek the Lord, and His strength: seek His face evermore.

PSALMS CV. 4

> O JESUS CHRIST, grow Thou in me,
>   And all things else recede;
> My heart be daily nearer Thee,
>   From sin be daily freed.
>
> Make this poor self grow less and less,
>   Be Thou my life and aim;
> Oh, make me daily, through Thy grace,
>   More worthy of Thy name.

J. C. LAVATER

As, on rising, we should hear Him saying to us, "Take this yoke upon thee, my child, to-day," "Bear this burden for me and with me to-day," so, before retiring to rest, and collecting our mind for our evening prayer, it were well to put these questions to our conscience, "Have I, in a single instance this day, denied myself either in temper or appetite, and so submitted myself to the Saviour's yoke?" And again, "Have I, in a single instance, shown sympathy or considerateness for others, borne with their faults or infirmities of character, given time or taken trouble to help them, or be of use to them?" If so, I have gained ground; I have made an advance in the mind of Christ to-day, if it be only a single step. Let me thank God, and take courage. A single step is so much clear gain.

EDWARD MEYRICK GOULBURN

But God, who is rich in mercy, for His great love wherewith He loved us, even when we were dead in sins, hath quickened us together with Christ.

EPHESIANS ii. 4, 5

LORD, to Thy call of me I bow,
Obey like Abraham;
Thou lov'st me because Thou art Thou,
And I am what I am.

Doubt whispers, *"thou art such a blot
He cannot love poor thee."*
If what I am He loveth not,
He loves what I shall be.

GEORGE MACDONALD

WE may hate ourselves when we come to realize failings we have not recognized before, and feel that there are probably others which we do not yet see as clearly as other people see them, but this kind of impatience for our perfection is not felt by those who love us, I am sure. It is one's greatest comfort to believe that it is not even felt by God. Just as a mother would not love her child the better for its being turned into a model of perfection at once, but does love it the more dearly every time it tries to be good, so I do hope and believe our Great Father does not wait for us to be good and wise to love us, but loves us, and loves to help us in the very thick of our struggles with folly and sin.

JULIANA H. EWING

And He said to them all, If any man will come after me, let him deny himself, and take up his cross daily, and follow me.

LUKE ix. 23

WE pray Thee, grant us strength to take
Our daily cross, whate'er it be,
And gladly for Thine own dear sake
In paths of pain to follow Thee.

W. W. HOW

THE more you accept daily crosses as daily bread, in peace and simplicity, the less they will injure your frail, delicate health; but forebodings and frettings would soon kill you.

FRANÇOIS DE LA MOTHE FÉNELON

We speak of the crosses of daily life, and forget that our very language is a witness against us, how meekly we ought to bear them, in the blessed steps of our holy Lord; how in "every cross and care," we ought not to acquiesce simply, but to take them cheerfully,—not cheerfully only but joyfully; yea, if they should even deserve the name of "tribulation," to "joy in tribulation" also, as seeing in them our Father's hand, our Saviour's cross.

E. B. PUSEY

Take kindly and heartsomely with His cross, who never yet slew a child with the cross.

SAMUEL RUTHERFORD

Blessed are all they that wait for Him.

ISAIAH xxx. 18

I WILL trust again His love, His power,
  Though I cannot feel His hand to-day;
To His help anew I will betake me,
  Though His countenance seems turned away!
Though without one smile, one gracious token,
  Through the flames and floods my path must go,
When the fires subside, the waves pass over,
  My Deliverer I again shall know.

JOACHIM LANGE

IN the night of distress, feel after somewhat which may quiet and stay thy heart till the next springing of the day. The sun will arise, which will scatter the clouds. And in the day of His power thou wilt find strength to walk with Him; yea, in the day of thy weakness His grace will be sufficient for thee.

ISAAC PENINGTON

My times are in Thy hand, O Lord! And, surely, that is the best. Were I to choose, they should be in no other hands, neither mine own, nor any others. When He withholds mercies or comforts for a season, it is but till the due season. Therefore it is our wisdom and our peace to resign all things into His hands, to have no will nor desires, but only this, that we may still *wait for Him*. Never was any one who *waited for Him* miserable with disappointment.

ROBERT LEIGHTON

*Thou openest Thine hand, and satisfiest the desire
of every living thing.*

PSALMS cxlv. 16

> THERE's not a craving in the mind
>   Thou dost not meet and still;
> There's not a wish the heart can have
>   Which Thou dost not fulfil.
>
> FREDERICK W. FABER

YOU will see the truth about the eternal life soon;
I don't think it is possible to live up to the highest
point of duty *and of happiness* without this. I know
one can go on doing one's duty thoroughly under
clouds of doubt, and even in complete unbelief; there
are many who do, and they are dear to God, but the
duty is done sadly, without the spring of life and joy
that we are meant to have. That fountain of life and
strength is hid in God. Christ showed us the way to it,
and we get it into our souls when we utterly trust
Him and give up our hearts, and our lives, and our
aspirations to Him as to a faithful Creator, who will
not leave unsatisfied any of the longings of the souls
He has made; who will not let love die, or disappoint
finally the cravings for joy, for perfection, for light
and knowledge that He has implanted, and that are
parts of Himself, immortal as He is.

ANNIE KEARY

*I have made the earth, and created man upon it;
I, even my hands, have stretched out the heavens,
and all their host have I commanded. I have
raised him up in righteousness, and I will direct
all his ways.*

ISAIAH xlv. 12, 13

HE who suns and worlds upholdeth
Lends us His upholding hand;
He the ages who unfoldeth
Doth our times and ways command.
God is for us;
In His strength and stay we stand.

THOMAS H. GILL

YOU have trusted Him in a few things, and He has
not failed you. Trust Him now for everything, and see
if He does not do for you exceeding abundantly above
all that you could ever have asked or thought, not
according to your power or capacity, but according
to His own mighty power, that will work in you all
the good pleasure of His most blessed will. You find
no difficulty in trusting the Lord with the management of the universe and all the outward creation,
and can your case be any more complex or difficult
than these, that you need to be anxious or troubled
about His management of it?

HANNAH WHITALL SMITH

JULY 30

Who hath delivered us from the power of darkness, and hath translated us into the kingdom of His dear Son.

COLOSSIANS i. 13

IT is right that we should have an aim of our own, determined by our individuality and our surroundings; but this may readily degenerate into exclusive narrowness, unless it has for a background the great thought that there is a Kingdom of God within us, around us, and above us, in which we, with all our powers and aims, are called to be conscious workers. Toward the forwarding of this silent, ever-advancing Kingdom, our little work, whatever it be, if good and true, may contribute something. And this thought lends to any calling, however lowly, a consecration which is wanting even to the loftiest self-chosen ideals. But even if our aim should be frustrated and our work come to naught, yet the failure of our most cherished plans may be more than compensated. In the thought that we are members of this Kingdom, already begun, here and now, yet reaching forward through all time, we shall have a reserve of consolation better than any which success without this could give.

JOHN CAMPBELL SHAIRP

He that doeth the will of God abideth for ever.

1 JOHN ii. 17

I am Thine, save me.

PSALMS cxix 94

TAKE, O Lord, and receive all my liberty, my memory, my understanding, and my will, all that I have and possess. Thou hast given it to me; to Thee, O Lord, I restore it; all is Thine, dispose of it according to Thy will. Give me Thy love and Thy grace, for this is enough for me.

IGNATIUS LOYOLA

Are we willing to give ourselves entirely to God; to let Him do with us whatever He pleases; to follow anywhere at His bidding; to renounce anything at His call; asking only, in return, that He will give us Himself, with all His infinite love, to be ours from this time forever? If we are thus willing, let us kneel down this moment and tell Him so. Alone with God, let us give Him ourselves, all we have and are and shall be, to be unreservedly His.

WILLIAM R. HUNTINGTON

There is no stay so strong as an unreserved abandonment of self into God's hand

H. L. SIDNEY LEAR

AUGUST 1

I have sinned; for I have transgressed the commandment of the Lord; because I feared the people, and obeyed their voice.　　　1 SAMUEL xv. 24

Hearken unto me, ye that know righteousness, the people in whose heart is my law; fear ye not the reproach of men.　　　ISAIAH li. 7

Thou shalt not follow a multitude to do evil.
　　　EXODUS xxiii. 2

ALL timidity, irresolution, fear of ridicule, weakness of purpose, such as the Apostles showed when they deserted Christ, and Peter especially when he denied Him, are to be numbered among the tempers of mind which are childish as well as sinful; which we must learn to despise.

JOHN HENRY NEWMAN

You, who have yielded so readily to your friend's persuasion, and have joined him in doing wrong, you know not how many times a very little resistance would have saved both him and yourself; you know not how many times he was hesitating already, and would have drawn back altogether if you had but given him an opening to do so; you know not how often, at the very time he was arguing with you, he was in reality arguing against his own conscience, and might have been turned back with ease if you had not given way.

FREDERICK TEMPLE

Ye shall walk after the Lord your God, and fear Him, and keep His commandments, and obey His voice, and ye shall serve Him, and cleave unto Him.

DEUTERONOMY xiii. 4

GOD visits a soul when He brings before it a new vision of truth or duty, a new range of opportunities, a new endowment of force as well as insight, at some time to which all that precedes has led up, and from which all that follows depends in its solemn history. No Divine visitation leaves us where it found us; it always leaves us better or worse; if not better, then certainly worse.

HENRY PARRY LIDDON

The issues are with God, and His servants know not the word disappointment, for they are incapable of reading His designs. Only this they know, that the slightest hesitation in obeying what they believe to be a divine impulse, produces a suffering more intense than any consequences which may accrue to them from the world.

LAURENCE OLIPHANT

Never shrink from deep devotion, because you fear its trials or its sacrifices. Paul, in martyrdom, was unspeakably happier than God's half-hearted servants.

WILLIAM R. HUNTINGTON

AUGUST 3

Oh, that thou hadst hearkened to My commandments! then had thy peace been as a river, and thy righteousness as the waves of the sea.

ISAIAH xlviii. 18

IT is so easy to become more thick-skinned in conscience, more tolerant of evil, more hopeless of good, more careful of one's own comfort and one's own property, more self-satisfied in leaving high aims and great deeds to enthusiasts, and then to believe that one is growing older and wiser. And yet those high examples, those good works, those great triumphs over evil, which single hands effect sometimes, we are all grateful for, when they are done, whatever we may have said of the doing. But we speak of saints and enthusiasts for good, as if some special gifts were made to them in middle age which are withheld from other men. Is it not rather that some few souls keep alive the lamp of zeal and high desire which God lights for most of us while life is young?

JULIANA HORATIA EWING

To live with a high ideal is a successful life. It is not what one does, but what one tries to do, that makes the soul strong and fit for a noble career.

E. P. TENNEY

In His love and in His pity He redeemed them.

ISAIAH lxiii. 9

Like as a father pitieth his children, so the Lord pitieth them that fear Him.

PSALMS ciii. 13

GOD only knows the love of God:
Oh, that it now were shed abroad
In this poor stony heart;
For love I sigh, for love I pine;
This only portion, Lord, be mine,
Be mine this better part.
CHARLES WESLEY

DON'T measure God's mind by your own. It would be a poor love that depended not on itself, but on the feelings of the person loved. A crying baby turns away from its mother's breast, but she does not put it away till it stops crying. She holds it closer. For my part, in the worst mood I am ever in, when I don't feel I love God at all, I just look up to His love. I say to Him, "Look at me. See what state I am in. Help me!" Ah! you would wonder how that makes peace. And the love comes of itself; sometimes so strong, it nearly breaks my heart.

GEORGE MACDONALD

He does not love us because we art so lovely, but because He always loves what He pities.

ELIZABETH PRENTISS

217

That the name of our Lord Jesus Christ may be glorified in you, and ye in Him, according to the grace of our God and the Lord Jesus Christ.

2 THESSALONIANS i. 12

Put ye on the Lord Jesus Christ.

ROMANS xiii. 14

SEND down Thy likeness from above,
 And let this my adorning be:
Clothe me with wisdom, patience, love,
 With lowliness and purity.

JOACHIM LANGE

EVIDENTLY, in order to be a manifestation of Christ we must be in some way like Him. He is a Christian who follows Christ, who measures all things by the standard of His approbation, who would not willingly say a word which he would not like to have Christ hear, nor do an act which he would not like to have Christ see. He is a Christian who tries to be the kind of neighbor Christ would be, and the kind of citizen Christ would be, and who asks himself in all the alternatives of his business life, and his social life, and his personal life, what would the Master do in this case? The best Christian is he who most reminds the people with whom he lives of the Lord Jesus Christ. He who never reminds anybody of the Lord Jesus Christ is not a Christian at all.

GEORGE HODGES

And was transfigured before them: and His face did shine as the sun, and His raiment was white as the light.

MATTHEW xvii. 2

Master, it is good for us to be here.

MARK lx. 5

> MASTER, it is good to be
> Entranced, enwrapt, alone with Thee;
> Watching the glistering raiment glow,
> Whiter than Hermon's whitest snow;
> The human lineaments that shine
> Irradiant with a light Divine:
> Till we too change from grace to grace,
> Gazing on that transfigured face.
>
> A. P. STANLEY

THE Transfiguration has lived on through ages, and has shed its light upon all ages. It has brought the past into union with the present. "The decease which He should accomplish at Jerusalem" has been owned as the bond of fellowship between those who walk the earth and suffer in it, and those who are departed from it. In the light of that "countenance which was altered, of that raiment which was white and glistering," all human countenances have acquired a brightness, all common things have been transfigured. A glimpse of the Divine beauty has broken through the darkness, and has cheered the humblest pilgrims.

FREDERIC DENISON MAURICE

With Thee is the fountain of life; in Thy light shall we see light.

PSALMS XXXVI. 9

How beautiful our lives may be; how bright
In privilege; how fruitful of delight!
And lo! all round us His bright servants stand;
Events, His duteous ministers and wise,
With frowning brows, perhaps, for their disguise,
But with such wells of love in their deep eyes,
And such strong rescue hidden in their hands!

HENRY SEPTIMUS SUTTON

WE see always what we are looking for, and if our mind has become trained to look for trouble and difficulty and all dark and dreary things, we find just what we seek. On the other hand, it is quite as easy to form the habit of looking always for beauty, for good, for happiness, for gladness, and here, too, we shall find precisely what we seek.

J. R. MILLER

I never knew her [Mrs. Ewing] fail to find happiness wherever she was placed, and good in whomever she came across. Whatever her circumstances might be, they always yielded to her causes for thankfulness, and work to be done with a ready and hopeful heart.

HORATIA K. F. EDEN

Whoso trusteth in the Lord, happy is he.

PROVERBS xvi. 20

THIS world of ours is a happy world, so that God is our end, so that we can say to Him, "Thou art my God." Then everything takes new hues of joy and love. Our daily comforts have a soul in them, for they abound in thanksgiving; our daily infirmities or crosses have a special joy in them, because they are so tenderly fitted to us by the medicinal hand of our God; the commonest acts of life are full of deep interest, because their end is God; daily duties are daily joys, because they are something which God gives us to offer unto Him, to do to our very best, in acknowledgment of His love. It is His earth we walk on; His air, we breathe; His sun, the emblem of His all-penetrating love, which gladdens us. Eternity! Yes, that too is present to us, and is part of our joy on earth. God has given us faith to make our future home as certain to us, as this our spot of earth; and hope, to aspire strongly to it; and love, as a foretaste of the all-surrounding, ever-unfolding, Almighty love of our own God.

E. B. PUSEY

AUGUST 9

Rejoice the soul of Thy servant; for unto Thee,
O Lord, do I lift up my soul.

PSALMS lxxxvi. 4

> AH, dearest Lord! to feel that Thou art near,
> Brings deepest peace, and hushes every fear;
> To see Thy smile, to hear Thy gracious voice,
> Makes soul and body inwardly rejoice
> With praise and thanks!
>
> CHRISTIAN GREGOR

PRAYER is a habit; and the more we pray the better we shall pray. Sometimes to go to be alone with God and Christ in the fellowship of the Spirit, just for the joy and blessedness of it; to open, with reverent yet eager hands, the door into the presence chamber of the great King, and then to fall down before Him, it may be, in silent adoration; our very attitude an act of homage, our merely being there, through the motive that prompts it, being the testimony of our soul's love; to have our set day-hours of close communion, with which no other friends shall interfere, and which no other occupations may interrupt; to which we learn to look forward with a living gladness; on which we look back with satisfaction and peace; this indeed is prayer.

ANTHONY W. THOROLD

Make me to go in the path of Thy commandments, for therein do I delight.

PSALMS cxix. 35

Peace I leave with you, my peace I give unto you: not as the world giveth, give I unto you. Let not your heart be troubled, neither let it be afraid.

JOHN xiv. 27

> THEN may Thy glorious, perfect will
> Be evermore fulfilled in me,
> And make my life an answering chord
> Of glad, responsive harmony.
>
> JEAN SOPHIA PIGOTT

CHRIST is the embodied harmony of God, and he that receives Him settles into harmony with Him. "My peace I give unto you," are the Saviour's words; and this peace of Christ is the equanimity, dignity, firmness, serenity, which made His outwardly-afflicted life appear to flow in a calmness so sublime. The soul is such a nature that, no sooner is it set in peace with itself, than it becomes an instrument in tune, a living instrument, discoursing heavenly music in its thoughts, and chanting melodies of bliss, even in its dreams. We may even say, that when a soul is in this harmony, no fires of calamity, no pains of outward torment can for one moment break the sovereign spell of its joy. It will turn the fires to freshening gales, and the pains to sweet instigations of love and blessing.

HORACE BUSHNELL

Thou hast given a banner to them that fear Thee,
that it may be displayed because of the truth.

PSALMS lx. 4

My cloud of battle-dust may dim,
His veil of splendor curtain Him;
And, in the midnight of my fear,
I may not feel Him standing near:
But, as I lift mine eyes above,
His banner over me is love.

GERALD MASSEY

M Y son, thou art never secure in this life, but, as
long as thou livest, thou shalt always need spiritual
armor.

Thou oughtest manfully to go through all, and to
use a strong hand against whatsoever withstandeth
thee.

For to him that overcometh is manna given, and
for the indolent there remaineth much misery.

Dispose not thyself for much rest, but for great
patience.

Wait for the Lord, behave thyself manfully, and be
of good courage; do not distrust Him, do not leave
thy place, but steadily expose both body and soul for
the glory of God.

THOMAS À KEMPIS

*Our heart shall rejoice in Him, because we have
trusted in His holy name.*

PSALMS xxxiii. 21

ON our way rejoicing as we homeward move,
Hearken to our praises, O Thou God of love!
Is there grief or sadness? Thine it cannot be!
Is our sky beclouded? Clouds are not from Thee!
On our way rejoicing as we homeward move,
Hearken to our praises, O Thou God of love!

J. B. S. MONSELL

MY position has come to this, Am I living near
my Saviour; then I am as happy as the day is long,
and as light-hearted as a child. It may be that I have
plenty of annoyances, but they don't trouble me when
His presence is with me. Am I downcast and worried:
then I am away from God.

JOHN KENNETH MACKENZIE

We may sing beforehand, even in our winter storm,
in the expectation of a summer sun at the turn of the
year; no created powers can mar our Lord Jesus' music, nor spill our song of joy. Let us then be glad and
rejoice in the salvation of our Lord; for faith had
never yet cause to have wet cheeks, and hanging-down
brows, or to droop or die.

SAMUEL RUTHERFORD

AUGUST 13

I will delight myself in Thy statutes: I will not forget Thy word.

PSALMS cxix. 16

Which also sat at Jesus' feet, and heard His word.

LUKE x. 39

Lo! at Thy feet I wait Thy will,
Let that alone my being fill,
All earthly passions calm and still.

C. S.

WHATEVER happens let us not be too busy to sit at Jesus' feet. We shall not really lose time by enjoying this; nay, we shall redem the time; for there is usually much more time and strength forfeited by friction than by toil, and we shall gain in blessedness and enjoyment of our work, and gain in the quality of our work; and, above all, we shall gain in that we shall give Him pleasure where otherwise we might only grieve Him. And this is indeed the crown of all our endeavors. He who pleases Him does not live in vain.

WM. HAY M. H. AITKEN

A low standard of prayer means a low standard of character and a low standard of service. Those alone labor effectively among men who impetuously fling themselves upward towards God.

CHARLES H. BRENT

*There is a spirit in man; and the inspiration of
the Almighty giveth them understanding.*

JOB xxxii. 8

*If ye then, being evil, know how to give good gifts
unto your children; how much more shall your
heavenly Father give the Holy Spirit to them that
ask Him?*

LUKE xi. 13

Is it supposable that God has permitted personal
intercourse between man and man to be such a potent
instrument in the building up of character, and yet
has made all intercourse with Himself impossible? If
the spirit of man can, through the power of influence
and sympathy, bless and uplift the spirit of his fellow-
man, much more, a thousand-fold more, shall God
who, be it remembered, is a Spirit also, aid by intercourse and influence the creature spirit whom He permits to call himself His child.

WILLIAM REED HUNTINGTON

In the fellowship which is established in prayer between man and God we are brought into personal
union with Him in whom all things have their being.
In this lies the possibility of boundless power; for
when the connection is once formed, who can lay
down the limits of what man can do in virtue of the
communion of his spirit with the Infinite Spirit?

BROOKE FOSS WESTCOTT

AUGUST 15

The children of Ephraim, being armed and carrying bows, turned back in the day of battle.

PSALMS lxxviii. 9

Be thou strong, and very courageous.

JOSHUA i. 7

Go forward, Christian soldier,
　Beneath His banner true!
The Lord Himself, thy Leader,
　Shall all thy foes subdue.
His love foretells thy trials;
　He knows thine hourly need;
He can with bread of heaven
　Thy fainting spirit feed.

LAWRENCE TUTTIETT

WHILE there is left in you a trace of ill-temper, or of vanity, of pride, or of selfishness; while there is left in you a single sin, or germ of sin, you must not rest from the battle. God does not require from you to be sinless when you come before Him, but He does require you to be unceasing in your perseverance. He does not require that you shall never have fallen; but He does require unwearied efforts. He does not require you to win, but He does require you to fight.

FREDERICK TEMPLE

Still fight resolutely on, knowing that, in this spiritual combat, none is overcome but he who ceases to struggle and to trust in God.

LORENZO SCUPOLI

228

*When I cry unto Thee, then shall mine enemies
turn back: this I know; for God is for me.*

PSALMS lvi. 9

SOUL! wouldst thou from the battle shrink,
  And flee before the foe?
Dost thou beneath the burden sink,
  And in the dust lie low?
Oh! waste not there vain tears and sighs:
  The trumpet soundeth clear;
O'ercome, and to My glory rise!
  O'ercome, and triumph here!

THOMAS H. GILL

BE not discouraged because of your soul's enemies.
Are ye troubled with thoughts, fears, doubts, imaginations, reasonings? yea, do ye see, yet, much in you unsubdued to the power of life? Oh! do not fear it; do not look at it, so as to be discouraged by it; but look to Him! look up to the power which is over all their strength; wait for the descendings of the power upon you; abide in faith of the Lord's help, and wait in patience till the Lord arise; and see if His arm do not scatter what yours could not. So, be still before Him, and, in stillness, believe in His name; yea, enter not into the hurryings of the enemy, though they fill the soul; for, there is yet somewhat to which they cannot enter, from whence patience, faith, and hope, will spring up in you, even in the midst of all they can do.

ISAAC PENINGTON

Always bearing about in the body the dying of the Lord Jesus, that the life also of Jesus might be made manifest in our body.

2 CORINTHIANS iv. 10

BUT we as in a glass espy
　The glory of His countenance,
Not in a whirlwind hurrying by
　The too presumptuous glance,
But with mild radiance every hour,
　From our dear Saviour's face benign
Bent on us with transforming power
　Till we, too, faintly shine.

JOHN KEBLE

IF we be faithful and humble, God will increase our faith by enabling us to obey more faithfully, and will strengthen our sight by enabling us to do what we now see. As in our daily walk we come nearer towards heaven, He will open to us more of heaven. And so the veil which sin laid upon our sight being taken away, "we all, with open face, beholding, as in a glass, the glory of the Lord," studying His countenance, watching His looks, seeking to have His gracious and compassionate look cast upon us in the midst of our frailties and infirmities, may catch some faint reflections of its brightness, and be changed into the image whereon we gaze, which we love, which, in our weakness, we would long to copy and transfuse into ourselves; we too may be "changed into the same image, from glory to glory, as by the Spirit of the Lord."

EDWARD B. PUSEY

Thou makest the outgoings of the morning and evening to rejoice. Thou crownest the year with Thy goodness.

PSALMS lxv. 8, 11

He loveth righteousness and justice: the earth is full of the lovingkindness of the Lord.

PSALMS xxxiii. 5 (R. V.)

I SING because Thy works are fair,
Thy glory makes me glad,
The garments bright of praise I wear,
For Thou art brightly clad.

Full triumph doth my soul possess,
Because Thy ways are right;
The glory of Thy righteousness
Maketh my dear delight.

THOMAS H. GILL

THE fulness of joy is to behold God in all; for by the same blessed might, wisdom, and love, that He made all things, to the same end our good Lord leadeth it continually, and there to Himself shall bring it, and, when it is time, we shall see it.

MOTHER JULIANA

God gives us richly all things to enjoy, while He Himself is His own best gift, and to be enjoyed not in a way of duty, but in the simple, natural realizing aright of what we possess in Him.

JOHN MCLEOD CAMPBELL

It is required in stewards that a man be found faithful.

1 CORINTHIANS iv. 2

Too many people are not faithful in little things. They are not to be absolutely depended upon. They do not always keep their promises. They break engagements. They fail to pay their debts promptly. They come behind time to appointments. They are neglectful and careless in little things. In general they are good people, but their life is honeycombed with small failures. One who can be positively depended upon, who is faithful in the least things as well as in the greatest, whose life and character are true through and through, gives out a light in this world which honors Christ and blesses others.

J. R. MILLER

Duties retire evermore from the observation of those who slight them.

SARAH W. STEPHEN

Great thoughts go best with common duties. Whatever therefore may be your office regard it as a fragment in an immeasurable ministry of love.

BROOKE FOSS WESTCOTT

Brethren, I count not myself to have apprehended; but this one thing I do, forgetting those things which are behind, and reaching forth unto those things which are before, I press toward the mark.

PHILIPPIANS iii. 13, 14

TILL, as each moment wafts us higher,
By every gush of pure desire,
And high-breathed hopes of joys above,
By every sacred sigh we heave,
Whole years of folly we outlive,
In His unerring sight, who measures Life by Love.

JOHN KEBLE

WHAT we can *do* is a small thing; but we can will and aspire to great things. Thus, if a man cannot be great, he can yet be good in will; and what he, with his whole heart and mind, love and desire, wills to be, that without doubt he most truly is. It is little we can bring to pass; but our will and desire may be large. Nay, they may grow till they lose themselves in the infinite abyss of God. And if ye cannot be as entirely His as ye fain would be, be His as much as ye may attain unto; but, whatever ye are, be that truly and entirely; and what ye cannot be, that be contented not to be, in a sincere spirit of resignation, for God's sake and in Him. So shall you peradventure possess more of God in lacking than in having.

JOHN TAULER

*The God of Israel is He that giveth strength and
power unto His people. Blessed be God.*

PSALMS lxviii. 35

> I WILL meet distress and pain,
> I will greet e'en Death's dark reign,
> I will lay me in the grave
> With a heart still glad and brave;
>   Whom the Strongest doth defend,
>   Whom the Highest counts His friend,
>   Cannot perish in the end.
>
> **PAUL GERHARDT**

COULD we but live more entirely in the unseen
Presence, and trust to the unseen support,—and if
lonely, or disappointed, or depressed, turn more
quickly to God, fully confident of His all-embracing
care, believing in His perfect love, the tender sympathy with which He ever regards us, how different
life would be from what it ordinarily is! Yet we doubt
not that Divine support is assured to us, if we seek
to do what is pleasing in His sight. If the end we
desire comes not, yet there is rest in the assurance
that we have told Him all, and left it to Him to do
what He wills.

T. T. CARTER

How reasonable it is to trust ourselves to the keeping of infinite love, and infinite wisdom, and infinite
power!

THOMAS ERSKINE

Forasmuch then as Christ hath suffered for us in the flesh, arm yourselves likewise with the same mind.

1 PETER iv. 1

TAKE thy whole portion with thy Master's mind—
Toil, hindrance, hardness, with His virtue take—
And think how short a time thy heart may find
To labor or to suffer for His sake.

ANNA L. WARING

YOUR portion is to love, to be silent, to suffer, to sacrifice your inclinations, in order to fulfil the will of God, by moulding yourself to that of others. Happy indeed you are thus to bear a cross laid on you by God's own hands, in the order of His Providence. The discipline which we choose for ourselves does not destroy our self-love like that which God assigns us Himself each day. All we have to do is to give ourselves up to God day by day, without looking further. He carries us in His arms as a loving mother carries her child. In every need let us look with love and trust to our Heavenly Father.

FRANÇOIS DE LA MOTHE FÉNELON

The loving heart which seeks to offer all, even disappointments and vexations which touch the tenderest places, to God, will be more likely to grow in generosity of spirit than one who bears grudgingly what cannot be averted.

H. L. SIDNEY LEAR

According as His divine power hath given unto us all things that pertain unto life and godliness, through the knowledge of Him that hath called us to glory and virtue.

2 PETER i. 3

WE often try in vain to cut up our errors by the roots, to fight evil hand to hand on its own ground, where it has us at a disadvantage, whereas our most sure way to victory is by developing and fortifying the good that is in us. We have but a certain measure of strength and activity; as much of this as is added to the good is taken from the evil.

MADAME SWETCHINE

I think you will find that it is not by making resolutions in a difficulty that you will conquer a fault—tackling it, I mean,—but much more by opening a window to Almighty God, and letting Him speak to you. As long as we are young we set so much importance on our own efforts, whereas often, if we will just do nothing but listen quietly to what God has to say to us, we shall find that He sets us thinking and mending our faults by a quiet way which looks as though it had nothing to do with it; and then, when we come to about where our fault used to be, we find it gone, imperceptibly as it were, by our having been strengthened in another direction which lay, though we did not know it, at the real root of the matter.

HENRIETTA KERR

I have heard the murmurings of the children of Israel. EXODUS xvi. 12

SAVE our blessings, Master, save
 From the blight of thankless eye,
Teach us for all joys to crave
 Benediction pure and high,
Own them given, endure them gone,
Shrink from their hardening touch, yet prize them won,
Prize them as rich odors meet
For love to lavish at His sacred feet.

JOHN KEBLE

NOTHING so hinders us in what we are doing as to be longing after something else; in so doing, we leave off tilling our own field, to drive the plough through our neighbor's land, where we must not look to reap a harvest; and this is mere waste of time. If our thoughts and hopes are elsewhere, it is impossible for us to set our faces steadily towards the work required of us. ST. FRANCIS DE SALES

One thing is indisputable: the chronic mood of looking longingly at what we have not, or thankfully at what we have, realizes two very different types of character. And we certainly can encourage the one or the other. LUCY C. SMITH

Seek to cultivate a buoyant, joyous sense of the crowded kindnesses of God in your daily life. ALEXANDER MACLAREN

The mountains shall depart, and the hills be removed; but my kindness shall not depart from thee, neither shall the covenant of my peace be removed, saith the Lord that hath mercy on thee.

ISAIAH liv. 10

There hath not failed one word of all His good promise.

1 KINGS viii. 56

THERE is a persuasion in the soul of man that he is here for cause, that he was put down in this place by the Creator to do the work for which He inspires him, that thus he is an overmatch for all antagonists that could combine against him.

RALPH WALDO EMERSON

It is impossible for that man to despair who remembers that his Helper is omnipotent; and can do whatsoever He please. Let us rest there awhile,—He can, if He please: and He is infinitely loving, willing enough; and He is infinitely wise, choosing better for us than we can do for ourselves. God invites and cherishes the hopes of men by all the variety of His providence. He that believes does not make haste, but waits patiently, till the times of refreshment come, and dares trust God for the morrow, and is no more solicitous for the next year than he is for that which is past.

JEREMY TAYLOR

Blessed be God, even the Father of our Lord Jesus Christ, the Father of mercies and the God of all comfort; who comforteth us in all our tribulation, that we may be able to comfort them which are in any trouble, by the comfort wherewith we ourselves are comforted of God.

2 CORINTHIANS i. 3, 4

THE spirit of gracious and *expressed* affection. Ah, let no one shrink from expressing it! The heart has strange abysses of gloom, and often yearns for just one word of love to help. And it is just when the manner may be drier and less genial than usual that the need may be greatest.

LUCY C. SMITH

God puts within our reach the power of helpfulness, the ministry of pity: He is ever ready to increase His grace in our hearts, that as we live and act among all the sorrows of the world we may learn by slow degrees the skill and mystery of consolation. "If ye know these things, happy are ye if ye do them." There is no surer way of steadfast peace in this world than the active exercise of pity; no happier temper of mind and work than the lowly watching to see if we can lessen any misery that is about us: nor is there any better way of growth in faith and love.

FRANCIS PAGET

239

*Lay up for yourselves treasures in heaven, . . .
for where your treasure is, there will your heart
be also.*

MATTHEW vi. 20, 21

> SINCE I am coming to that holy room
> Where with the choir of saints forevermore
> I shall be made Thy music, as I come
> I tune the instrument here at the door,
> And, what I must do then, think here before.
>
> JOHN DONNE

To lay up treasure in heaven is to do arts which
promote, or belong to, the kingdom of God; and what
our Lord assures us of is that any act of our hands,
any thought of our heart, any word of our lips, which
promotes the divine kingdom by the ordering whether
of our own life or of the world outside—all such activity, though it may seem for the moment to be lost,
is really stored up in the divine treasure-house; and
when the heavenly city, the New Jerusalem, shall at
last appear, that honest effort of ours, which seemed
so ineffectual, shall be found to be a brick built into
that eternal and celestial fabric.

CHARLES GORE

We cannot remove the conditions under which our
work is to be done, but we can transform them. They
are the elements out of which we must build the
temples wherein we serve.

BROOKE FOSS WESTCOTT

If ye keep my commandments, ye shall abide in my love.

JOHN xv. 10

THIS did not once so trouble me,
That better I could not love Thee;
But now I feel and know
That only when we love, we find
How far our hearts remain behind
The love they should bestow.
RICHARD CHENEVIX TRENCH

OUR Lord gives the answer to a difficulty continually perplexing honest Christians—"How am I to learn to *love* God? I want to do my duty, but I do not feel as if I loved God." Our Lord gives the answer, "Where your treasure is, there will your heart be also." Act for God, do and say the things that He wills; direct your thoughts and intentions God-ward; and, depend upon it, in the slow process of nature, all that belongs to you—your instincts, your intelligence, your affections, your feelings—will gradually follow along the line of your action. Act for God; you are already *showing* love to Him and you will learn to *feel* it.

CHARLES GORE

They who, continuing faithful to divine grace, however partially communicated, serve God with their whole lives, will never fail of that one reward, the greatest which even He has to bestow, the being made able to love Him with their whole hearts.

DORA GREENWELL

AUGUST 29

The troubles of my heart are enlarged: Oh, bring Thou me out of my distresses.

PSALMS XXV. 17

Low at His feet lay thy burden of carefulness,
  High on His heart He will bear it for thee,
Comfort thy sorrows, and answer thy prayerfulness,
  Guiding thy steps as may best for thee be.
                              J. S. B. MONSELL

THE greatest burden we have to carry in life is self. The most difficult thing we have to manage is self. Our own daily living, our frames and feelings, our especial weaknesses and temptations, and our peculiar temperaments,—our inward affairs of every kind,— these are the things that perplex and worry us more than anything else, and that bring us oftenest into bondage and darkness. In laying off your burdens, therefore, the first one you must get rid of is yourself. You must hand yourself and all your inward experiences, your temptations, your temperament, your frames and feelings, all over into the care and keeping of your God, and leave them there. He made you and therefore He understands you, and knows how to manage you, and you must trust Him to do it.

                              HANNAH WHITALL SMITH

I am the Lord thy God which teacheth thee to profit, which leadeth thee by the way that thou shouldest go.

ISAIAH xlviii. 17

JUST as God leads me I would go;
  I would not ask to choose my way;
Content with what He will bestow,
  Assured He will not let me stray.
So as He leads, my path I make,
And step by step I gladly take,
  A child in Him confiding.

LAMPERTUS GEDICKE

HE has not made us for nought; He has brought us thus far, in order to bring us further, in order to bring us on to the end. He will never leave us nor forsake us; so that we may boldly say, "The Lord is my Helper; I will not fear what flesh can do unto me." We "may cast all our care upon Him who careth for us." What is it to us how our future path lies, if it be but His path? What is it to us whither it leads us, so that in the end it leads to Him? What is it to us what He puts upon us, so that He enables us to undergo it with a pure conscience, a true heart, not desiring anything of this world in comparison of Him? What is it to us what terror befalls us, if He be but a hand to protect and strengthen us?

JOHN HENRY NEWMAN

Behold, the Lord's hand is not shortened, that it cannot save; neither His ear heavy, that it cannot hear: but your iniquities have separated between you and your God, and your sins have hid His face from you.

ISAIAH lix. 1, 2

ONE thing alone, dear Lord! I dread;—
    To have a secret spot
That separates my soul from Thee,
    And yet to know it not.

FREDERICK W. FABER

IT is a condition of enjoying continued insight into the laws which govern spiritual truth, that we should conform our moral being to that measure of truth which we already see. A deliberate rejection of duty prescribed by already recognized truth cannot but destroy, or at least impair most seriously, the clearness of our mental vision. A single act may thus involve grave inward deterioration; it may land the soul upon a lower level of moral life, where passion is more imperious, and principle is weaker; where a man is less his own master, and more readily enslaved to the circumstances and beings around him.

H. P. LIDDON

It is a strange but inflexible spiritual law, that those who aim at anything short of the best according to their conception, as God has given them light, will sooner or later come to grief. It is merely a matter of time.

CHARLES H. BRENT

Fret not thyself, it tendeth only to evil-doing.
PSALMS XXXVII. 8 (R. V.)

> To anxious, prying thought,
> And weary, fretting care,
> The Highest yieldeth nought;
> He giveth all to prayer.
> PAUL GERHARDT

DO not be disquieted about your faults. Love without ceasing, and much will be forgiven you, because you have loved much. Faults perceived in peace, in the spirit of love, are immediately consumed by love itself; but faults perceived in a pettish fit of self-love disturb peace, interrupt the presence of God, and the exercise of perfect love. Vexation at a fault is generally more of a fault than the fault itself.

FRANCOIS DE LA MOTHE FÉNELON

Fight like a good soldier; and if thou sometimes fall through frailty, take again greater strength than before, trusting in my more abundant grace.

THOMAS À. KEMPIS

This alone is thy concern, to fight manfully, and never, however manifold thy wounds, to lay down thine arms, or to take to flight.

LORENZO SCUPOLI

SEPTEMBER 2

Thus saith the Lord, Let not the wise man glory in his wisdom, neither let the mighty man glory in his might, let not the rich man glory in his riches: but let him that glorieth glory in this, that he understandeth and knoweth me, that I am the Lord which exercise lovingkindness, judgment, and righteousness, in the earth; for in these things I delight, saith the Lord.

JEREMIAH ix. 23, 24

WHAT dost thou fear? His wisdom reigns
    Supreme confessed;
His power is infinite; His love
Thy deepest, fondest dreams above;—
    So trust and rest.

ADELAIDE A. PROCTER

THE firm belief of, and resting on, His power and wisdom, and love, gives a clear, satisfying answer to all doubts and fears. It suffers us not to stand to jangle with each trifling, grumbling objection, but carries all before it, makes day in the soul, and so chases away those fears that vex us only in the dark.

ROBERT LEIGHTON

I feel that goodness, and truth, and righteousness are realities, eternal realities, and that they cannot be abstractions, or vapors floating in a spiritual atmosphere, but that they necessarily imply a living, personal Will, a good, loving, righteous God, in whose hands we are perfectly safe, and who is guiding us by unfailing wisdom.

THOMAS ERSKINE

As a shepherd seeketh out his flock in the day that he is among his sheep that are scattered; so will I seek out my sheep, and will deliver them out of all places where they have been scattered in the cloudy and dark day.

EZEKIEL xxxiv. 12

The life which I now live in the flesh I live by the faith of the Son of God, who loved me, and gave Himself for me.

GALATIANS ii. 20

PERVERSE and foolish, oft I strayed,
But yet in love He sought me,
And on His shoulder gently laid,
And home rejoicing brought me.
SIR HENRY W. BAKER

TRY to feel, by imagining what the lonely Syrian shepherd must feel towards the helpless things which are the companions of his daily life, for whose safety he stands in jeopardy every hour, and whose value is measured to him not by price, but by his own jeopardy, and then we have reached some notion of the love which Jesus meant to represent; that Eternal tenderness which bends over us, and knows the name of each and the trials of each, and thinks for each with a separate solicitude, and gave itself for each with a sacrifice as special, and a love as personal, as if in the whole world's wilderness there were none other but that one.

FREDERICK WM. ROBERTSON

SEPTEMBER 4

Fulfil ye my joy, that ye be likeminded, having the same love, being of one accord, of one mind. . . . Let this mind be in you, which was also in Christ Jesus.

PHILIPPIANS ii. 2, 5

JESUS, Thy all-victorious love
    Shed in my heart abroad;
Then shall my feet no longer rove,
    Rooted and fixed in God.
My steadfast soul, from falling free,
    Shall then no longer move,
While Christ is all the world to me,
    And all my heart is love.

CHARLES WESLEY

LET our temper be under the rule of the love of Jesus: He can not alone curb it,—*He can* make us gentle and patient. Let the vow, that not an unkind word of others shall ever be heard from our lips, be laid trustingly at His feet. Let the gentleness that refuses to take offence, that is always ready to excuse, to think and hope the best, mark our intercourse with all. Let our life be one of self-sacrifice, always studying the welfare of others, finding our highest joy in blessing others. And let us, in studying the Divine art of doing good, yield ourselves as obedient learners to the guidance of the Holy Spirit. By His grace, the most common-place life can be transfigured with the brightness of a heavenly beauty, as the infinite love of the Divine nature shines out through our frail humanity.

ANDREW MURRAY

Ye yourselves are taught of God to love one another.

1 THESSALONIANS iv. 9

If we love one another, God dwelleth in us, and His love is perfected in us.

1 JOHN iv. 12

THIS is the great business and meaning of our life on earth: that we should more and more yield up our hearts to God's great grace of love; that we should let it enter ever more fully and more freely into us, so that it may even fill our whole heart and life. We must day after day be driving back, in His strength, the sin that doth so easily beset us, and the selfishness that sin has fastened in our hearts; and then His love will day by day increase in us. Prayer will win and keep it; work will strengthen and exercise it; the Bible will teach us how to know and prize it, how to praise God for it; the Holy Eucharist will ever renew and quicken its power in our hearts. And so (blessed be God!), love and joy and peace will grow in us, beyond all that we can ask or think; and He will forgive us, for love's sake, all the failures, all the faults in whatever work He has given us to do; and will bring us at last into the fulness of that life which even here He has suffered us to know; into that one Eternal Home, where Love is perfect, and unwearied, and unending; and where nothing ever can part us from one another or from Him.

FRANCIS PAGET

Bringing into captivity every thought to the obedience of Christ.

2 CORINTHIANS X. 5

"I WILL lift up mine eyes unto the hills." The vision of God unseals the lips of man. Herein lies strength for conflict with the common enemy of the praying world known as wandering thoughts. If the eye is fixed on God, thought may roam where it will without irreverence, for every thought is then converted into a prayer. Some have found it a useful thing when their minds have wandered off from devotion and been snared by some good but irrelevant consideration, not to cast away the offending thought as the eyes are again lifted to the Divine Face, but to take it captive, carry it into the presence of God and weave it into a prayer before putting it aside and resuming the original topic. This is to lead captivity captive.

CHARLES H. BRENT

Each wish to pray is a breath from heaven, to strengthen and refresh us; each act of faith, done to amend our prayers, is wrought in us by Him, and draws us to Him, and His gracious look on us. Neglect nothing which can produce reverence.

EDWARD B. PUSEY

I will abide in Thy tabernacle for ever; I will trust in the covert of Thy wings.

PSALMS lxi. 4

I will bless the Lord, who hath given me counsel.

PSALMS xvi. 7

Would it not be possible for every man to double his intellectual force by keeping much in the company of Infinite Wisdom?

E. P. TENNEY

I cannot help the thought which grows steadily upon me, that the better part of prayer is not the asking, but the kneeling where we can ask, the resting there, the staying there, drawing out the willing moments in heavenly communion with God, within the closet, with the night changed into the brightness of the day by the light of Him who all the night was in prayer to God. Just to be there, at leisure from ourselves, at leisure from the world, with our souls at liberty, with our spirit feeling its kinship to the Divine Spirit, with our life finding itself in the life of Gold,—this is prayer. Would it be possible that one could be thus with God, listening to Him, speaking to Him, reposing upon His love, and not come out with a shining face, a gladdened heart, an intent more constant and more strong to give to the waiting world which so sadly needs it what has been taken from the heart of God?

ALEXANDER MCKENZIE

SEPTEMBER 8

Sing unto the Lord, O ye saints of His, and give thanks at the remembrance of His holiness.

PSALMS XXX. 4

> GLAD with Thy light, and glowing with Thy love,
> So let me ever speak and think and move
>   As fits a soul new-touched with life from heaven;
> That seeks but so to order all her course
> As most to show the glory of that Source
>   By whom alone her strength, her life are given.
>
> C. J. P. SPITTA

OUR Christianity is apt to be of a very "dutiful" kind. We mean to do our duty, we attend church and go to our communions. But our hearts are full of the difficulties, the hardships, the obstacles which the situation presents, and we go on our way sadly, downhearted and despondent. We need to learn that true Christianity is inseparable from deep joy; and the secret of that joy lies in a continual looking away from all else—away from sin and its ways, and from the manifold hindrances to the good we would do—up to God, His love, His purpose, His will. In proportion as we do look up to Him we shall rejoice, and in proportion as we rejoice in the Lord will our religion have tone and power and attractiveness.

CHARLES GORE

Even as the Father hath loved me, I also have loved you; abide ye in my love.

JOHN xv. 9 (R. V.)

*A*BIDE IN ME: These words are the command of love, which is ever only a promise in a different shape. Think of this until all feeling of burden and fear and despair pass away, and the first thought that comes as you hear of abiding in Jesus be one of bright and joyous hope.

ANDREW MURRAY

When love is heard inviting more trust, more love, the encouragement to trust, to love, goes beyond the rebuke that our love is so little, and we take heart to confide in the love that is saying, "Give me thine heart," expecting that it will impart itself to us, and enable us to give the response of love which it desires. For indeed it must be with the blessed purpose to enable us to love Him that our God bids us love Him; for He knows that no love but what He Himself quickens in us can love Him.

Therefore always feel the *call* to love a gracious *promise* of strength to love, and marvel not at your own deadness, but trust in Him who quickeneth the dead.

JOHN MCLEOD CAMPBELL

*And above all these things put on love, which is
the bond of perfectness.*

COLOSSIANS iii. 14 (R. V.)

> THOU hatest hatred's withering reign;
> In souls that discord maketh dark
> Dost Thou rekindle love's bright spark,
> And make them one again.

PAUL GERHARDT

WE have cause to suspect our religion if it does
not make us gentle, and forbearing, and forgiving; if
the love of our Lord does not so flood our hearts as to
cleanse them of all bitterness, and spite, and wrath.
If a man is nursing anger, if he is letting his mind
become a nest of foul passions, malice, and hatred,
and evil wishing, how dwelleth the love of God in
him?

HUGH BLACK

Love me always, boy, whatever I do or leave undone. And—God help me—whatever you do or leave
undone, I'll love you. There shall never be a cloud
between us for a day; no, sir, not for an hour. We're
imperfect enough, all of us, we needn't be so bitter;
and life is uncertain enough at its safest, we needn't
waste its opportunities.

JULIANA HORATIA EWING

Love worketh no ill to his neighbor; therefore love is the fulfilling of the law.

ROMANS xiii. 10

In her tongue is the law of kindness.

PROVERBS xxxi. 26

THE worst kinds of unhappiness, as well as the greatest amount of it, come from our conduct to each other. If our conduct, therefore, were under the control of kindness, it would be nearly the opposite of what it is, and so the state of the world would be almost reversed. We are for the most part unhappy, because the world is an unkind world. But the world is only unkind for the lack of kindness in us units who compose it.

FREDERICK WM. FABER

You feel in some families as if you were living between the glasses of a microscope. Manner, accent, expression, all that goes to make up your "personality," all that you do or leave undone, is commented upon and found fault with.

H. BOWMAN

If you would be loved as a companion, avoid unnecessary criticism upon those with whom you live.

ARTHUR HELPS

SEPTEMBER 12

*If ye fulfil the royal law according to the scrip-
ture, Thou shalt love thy neighbor as thyself, ye
do well.*

JAMES ii. 8

Do you feel yourself alone and empty-hearted?
Then you have necessity indeed for fortitude and
brave endurance, but above all and before all you
must get out of your solitude. You cannot command
for yourself the love you would gladly receive; it
is not in our power to do that; but that noble love
which is not asking but giving,—that you can always
have. Wherever your life touches another life, there
you have opportunity. To mix with men and women
in the ordinary forms of social intercourse becomes
a sacred function when one carries into it the true
spirit. To give a close, sympathetic attention to every
human being we touch; to try to get some sense of
how he feels, what he is, what he needs; to make in
some degree his interest our own,—that disposition
and habit would deliver any one of us from isolation
or emptiness.

GEORGE S. MERRIAM

She [Annie Keary] did not try to set others right;
she only listened to and loved and understood her
fellow-creatures.

ELIZA KEARY

The peace of God, which passeth all understanding, shall keep your hearts and minds through Christ Jesus.

PHILIPPIANS iv. 7

> I TAKE Thee for my Peace, O Lord,
>   My heart to keep and fill;
> Thine own great calm, amid earth's storms,
>   Shall keep me always still,
> And as Thy Kingdom doth increase,
> So shall Thine ever-deepening peace.

ANNIE W. MARSTON

REMEMBER this, busy and burdened disciple; man or woman tried by uncertain health; immersed in secular duties; forced to a life of almost ceaseless publicity. Here is written an assurance, a guarantee, that not at holy times and welcome intervals only, not only in the dust of death, but in the dust of life, there is prepared for you the peace of God, able to keep your hearts and thoughts in Christ Jesus. It is found in Him, it is cultivated by intercourse with him. It is "the secret of His presence." Amidst the circumstances of your life, which are the expression of His will, He can maintain it, He can keep you in it. Nay, it is not passive; it "shall keep" you, alive, and loving, and practical, and ready at His call.

HANDLEY C. G. MOULE

I will walk within my house with a perfect heart.

PSALMS ci. 2

TEACH me, O God, Thy holy way,
And give me an obedient mind;
That in Thy service I may find
My soul's delight from day to day.

WILLIAM TIDD MATSON

As far as human frailty will permit, each little trifling piece of duty which presents itself to us in daily life, if it be only a compliance with some form of social courtesy, should receive a consecration, by setting God—His will, word, and Providence—before us in it, and by lifting up our hearts to Him in ejaculatory prayer, while we are engaged in it. The idea must be thoroughly worked into the mind, and woven into the texture of our spiritual life, that the minutest duties which God prescribes to us in the order of His Providence—a casual visit, a letter of sympathy, an obligation of courtesy, are not by any means too humble to be made means of spiritual advancement, if only the thing be done "as to the Lord, and not to men."

EDWARD MEYRICK GOULBURN

Learn to commend thy daily acts to God, so shall the dry every-day duties of common life be steps to heaven, and lift thy heart thither.

EDWARD B. PUSEY

If thou forbear to deliver them that are drawn unto death, and those that are ready to be slain; if thou sayest, Behold, we knew it not; doth not He that pondereth the hearth consider it, and He that keepeth thy soul, doth not He know it? and shall not He render unto every man according to his works.

PROVERBS xxiv. 11, 12

WHAT we value for ourselves we must seek to spread to others; and what we shrink from ourselves —lowering surroundings, a tainted atmosphere—what we shrink to think of those nearest and dearest to us being exposed to—let us do all we can to remove from others. "Lead *us* not into temptation. Deliver *us* from evil." Do what you can to sweeten the mental and moral atmosphere that surrounds you.

ARTHUR C. A. HALL

We have a more or less true ideal of what our own human life ought to be—of what opportunities we ought to have for the development of our faculties— of what home and school and college, youth and married life and old age, work and rest, ought to mean for ourselves and our families. We are to be as truly zealous and active for other classes or other individuals as we are for our own class or our own family or ourselves.

CHARLES GORE

SEPTEMBER 16

I will mention the lovingkindness of the Lord, and the praises of the Lord, according to all that the Lord hath bestowed on us.

ISAIAH lxiii. 7

Be content with such things as ye have.

HEBREWS xiii. 5

My God shall supply all your need according to His riches in glory by Christ Jesus.

PHILIPPIANS iv. 19

BEGIN with thanking Him for some little thing, and then go on, day by day, adding to your subjects of praise; thus you will find their numbers grow wonderfully; and, in the same proportion, will your subjects of murmuring and complaining diminish, until you see in everything some cause for thanksgiving. If you cannot begin with anything positive, begin with something negative. If your whole lot seems only filled with causes for discontent, at any rate there is some trial that has *not* been appointed you; and you may thank God for its being withheld from you. It is certain that the more you try to praise, the more you will see how your path and your lying down are beset with mercies, and that the God of love is ever watching to do you good.

PRISCILLA MAURICE

The meek shall inherit the earth, and shall delight themselves in the abundance of peace.

PSALMS xxxvii. 11

> Joy is Thy gift, O Father!
> Thou wouldst not have us pine;
> In darkest hours Thy comfort
> Doth aye most brightly shine;
> Ah, then how oft Thy voice
> Hath shed its sweetness o'er me,
> And opened heaven before me,
> And bid my heart rejoice!

PAUL GERHARDT

To be with God, in whatever stage of being, under whatever conditions of existence, is to be in heaven.

DORA GREENWELL

I perceive we postpone all our joys of Christ, till He and we be in our own house above, thinking that there is nothing of it here to be sought or found, but only hope and fair promises; and that Christ will give us nothing here but tears, sadness, crosses; and that we shall never feel the smell of the flowers of that high garden of paradise above, till we come there. Nay, but I find it possible to find young glory, and a young green paradise of joy even here. We dream of hunger in Christ's house, while we are here, although He alloweth feasts to all the bairns within God's household.

SAMUEL RUTHERFORD

261

Now unto Him that is able to do exceeding abun-
dantly above all that we ask or think, according
to the power that worketh in us, unto Him be
glory in the church by Christ Jesus throughout
all ages, world without end. Amen.

EPHESIANS iii. 20, 21

ALL the simplest, most living, and most genuine
Christians of our own time are such as rest their
souls, day by day, on this confidence and promise of
accruing power, and make themselves responsible, not
for what they have in some inherent ability, but for
what they can have in their times of stress and peril,
and in the continual raising of their own personal
quantity and power. Instead of gathering in their
souls timorously beforehand upon the little sufficiency
they find in possession, they look upon the great
world of the Saviour's Kingdom in it, as being
friendly and tributary, ready to pour in help, minister light, and strengthen them to victory, just according to their faith. And so they grow in courage,
confidence, personal volume, efficiency of every kind,
and instead of slinking into their graves out of impotent lives, they lie down in the honors of heroes.

HORACE BUSHNELL

Expect great things from God, attempt great things
for God.

WILLIAM CAREY

He that dwelleth in the secret place of the Most High shall abide under the shadow of the Almighty.

PSALMS xci. 1

AS soon as I woke in the morning I threw myself into the arms of Divine Love as a child does into its father's arms. I rose to serve Him, and to perform my daily labor simply that I might please Him. If I had time for prayer, I fell on my knees in His divine presence, consecrated myself to Him, and begged Him that He would accomplish His holy will perfectly in me and through me, and that He would not permit me to offend Him in the least thing all through the day. I occupied myself with Him and His praise as long as my duties permitted. Very often, I had not leisure to say even so much as the Lord's Prayer during the day; but that did not trouble me. I thought it as much my duty to work for Him as to pray to Him, for He Himself had taught me, that all that I should do for love of Him would be a true prayer. I loved Him and rejoiced in Him. If my occupations required all my attention, I had nevertheless my heart turned towards Him; and, as soon as they were finished, I ran to Him again, as to my dearest Friend. When evening came, and every one went to rest, I found mine only in the Divine Love, and fell asleep, still loving and adoring Him.

ARMELLE NICOLAS

*Great peace have they which love Thy law; and
they have none occasion of stumbling.*

PSALMS cxix. 165 (R. V.)

IN Thy might all things I bear,
In Thy love find bitter sweet,
And with all my grief and care,
Sit in patience at Thy feet.

A. H. FRANCKE

WHAT you need to do, is to put your will over
completely into the hands of your Lord, surrendering
to Him the entire control of it. Say, "Yes, Lord, YES!"
to everything, and trust Him so to work in you to
will, as to bring your whole wishes and affections into
conformity with His own sweet, and lovable, and
most lovely will. It is wonderful what miracles God
works in wills that are utterly surrendered to Him.
He turns hard things into easy, and bitter things into
sweet. It is not that He puts easy things in the place of
the hard, but He actually changes the hard thing
into an easy one.

HANNAH WHITALL SMITH

It has been well remarked, It is not said that *after*
keeping God's commandments, but *in* keeping them
there is great reward. God has linked these two things
together, and no man can separate them—obedience
and peace.

F. W. ROBERTSON

Choose life, . . . that thou mayest love the Lord thy God, and that thou mayest obey His voice, and that thou mayest cleave unto Him; for He is thy life, and the length of thy days.

DEUTERONOMY xxx. 19, 20

God gently calls us every day:
Why should we then our bliss delay?
He calls to heaven and endless light;
Why should we love the dreary night?

Praise, Lord, to Thee for Matthew's call,
At which he rose and left his all;
Thou, Lord, e'en now art calling me;
I will leave all, and follow Thee.

WILLIAM WALSHAM HOW

OBEY His blessed call now, and, having obeyed it once, never again disobey any call within you, to do His will. While we mourn our neglect of past calls, our sorrow, which is still His gift and call within us, will draw down His gladdening look, which will anew call us unto Him. Pass we by no call which, however indistinctly, we may have, and He will cheer us with clearer and gladlier calls. Our very sorrow and fear will be our joy and hope; our very stumblings our strength, and dimness our light, while stumbling or in darkness we feel after Him who is our Stay, our Light, our Joy.

EDWARD B. PUSEY

Beloved, think it not strange concerning the fiery trial which is to try you, as though some strange thing happened unto you: but rejoice, inasmuch as ye are partakers of Christ's sufferings.

1 PETER iv. 12, 13

> NOT more than I can bear I know
> Thou, dearest Lord, wilt on me lay,
> And I can learn of Thee to go
> Unfearing on my way.
>
> HARRIET MCEWEN KIMBALL

IT is a tremendous moment when first one is called upon to join the great army of those who suffer. That vast world of love and pain opens suddenly to admit us one by one within its fortress. We are afraid to enter into the land, yet you will, I know, feel how high is the call. It is as a trumpet speaking to us, that cries aloud, "It is your turn—endure." Play your part. As they endured before you, so now, close up the ranks—be patient and strong as they were. Since Christ, this world of pain is no accident untoward or sinister, but a lawful department of life, with experiences, interests, adventures, hopes, delights, secrets of its own. These are all thrown open to us as we pass within the gates—things that we could never learn or know or see, so long as we were well. God help you to walk through this world now opened to you, as through a kingdom, royal, and wide and glorious.

HENRY SCOTT HOLLAND

Take heed, and be quiet; fear not, neither be faint-hearted.

ISAIAH vii. 4

THOUGH everything without fall into confusion, and though thy body be in pain and suffering, and thy soul in desolation and distress, yet let thy spirit be unmoved by it all, placid and serene, delighted in and with its God inwardly, and with His good pleasure outwardly.

GERHARD TERSTEEGEN

To say each morning, "I must have things weariful, painful, to bear to-day, and they shall all be offered up beforehand as my heart's sacrifice; they shall be, not fought against, but received calmly and as welcome, for His sake who suffers them to come," gives a dignity, a purpose, nay, a very joy to what otherwise is all cheerless annoyance.

H. L. SIDNEY LEAR

As soon as anything presents itself to your mind as a suffering, and you feel a repugnance to it, resign yourself immediately to God with respect to it; give yourself up to Him in sacrifice, and you will find that, when the cross arrives, it will not be so very burdensome, because you had disposed yourself to a willing reception of it.

MADAME GUYON

Wait on the Lord; be of good courage, and He shall strengthen thine heart; wait, I say, on the Lord.

PSALMS xxvii. 14

I ASK not that my course be calm and still;
No, here too, Lord, be done Thy holy will:
    I ask but for a quiet childlike heart;
Though thronging cares and restless toil be mine,
Yet may my heart remain forever Thine;
    Draw it from earth, and fix it where Thou art.

C. J. P. SPITTA

TRUE union with God is to do His will without ceasing, in spite of all our natural disinclination, in all the wearisome and painful duties of our condition.

FRANÇOIS DE LA MOTHE FÉNELON

When persons have learnt to look upon the daily course of their ordinary life, with its duties and troubles, however common-place, as their offering to God, and as the safest school for themselves of perfection, they will have made a very important step in the spiritual life. Another step, so simple that it is often despised, is to do everything, however ordinary, as well as it can possibly be done, for God's sake. A third is to be always pressing forward; when a mistake is made, or a fault committed, to face and admit it freely; but having asked God to supply the deficiency caused by our own infirmity, to go on steadfastly and hopefully.

H. L. SIDNEY LEAR

He that in these things serveth Christ is acceptable to God, and approved of men.

ROMANS xiv. 18

Then shall I not be ashamed, when I have respect unto all Thy commandments.

PSALMS cxix. 6

TRUE fidelity consists in obeying God in all things, and in following the light that points out our duty, and the grace which guides us; taking as our rule of life the intention to please God in all things, and to do always not only what is acceptable to Him, but, if possible, what is *most* acceptable; not trifling with petty distinctions between sins great and small, imperfections and faults, for, though there may be such distinctions, they should have no weight with the soul that is determined to do *all* His will. To this sincere desire to do the will of God, we must add a cheerful spirit, that is not overcome when it has failed, but begins again and again to do better; hoping always to the very end to be able to do it; bearing with its own involuntary weakness, as God bears with it; waiting with patience for the moment when it shall be delivered from it; going straight on in singleness of heart, according to the strength that it can command; losing no time by looking back, nor making useless reflections upon its falls, which can only embarrass and retard its progress.

FRANÇOIS DE LA MOTHE FÉNELON

Commit thy way unto the Lord; trust also in Him, and He shall bring it to pass.

PSALMS xxxvii. 5

> PLAN not, nor scheme,—but calmly wait;
>   His choice is best.
> While blind and erring is thy sight,
> His wisdom sees and judges right,
>   So trust and rest.
>
> ADELAIDE A. PROCTER

"GREAT peace have they which love My law." They see that from Me, the sovereign Ruler of the world, who governth all things with infinite wisdom, order, and love, nothing but good can spring; and that I can take care of them and their affairs far better and more successfully than they could of themselves. Thus, considering that all that happens to them comes from Me, they are strong with an invincible patience, and bear all things, not only with resignation, but with cheerfulness and joy, tasting in all things that befall them externally or internally the sweetness of My ineffable love. And this is to believe, and meditate with a cheerful and grateful spirit, even in the midst of tribulations and difficulties, that it is I who sweetly dispose all things, and that whatever happens springs from the inexhaustible fountain of My goodness.

ST. CATHARINE OF SIENA

There is therefore now no condemnation to them which are in Christ Jesus, who walk not after the flesh, but after the Spirit.

ROMANS viii. 1

IT may be that recollections of the past hinder you, but you must reject them; anxious thoughts may arise, put them away; your fauls seem to raise up a barrier, but no past faults can separate a loving heart from God.

H. L. SIDNEY LEAR

Do not scrutinize so closely whether you are doing much or little, ill or well, so long as what you do is not sinful, and that you are heartily seeking to do everything for God. Try as far as you can to do everything well, but when it is done do not think about it; try rather to think of what is to be done next. Go on simply in the Lord's way, and do not torment yourself. We ought to hate our faults, but with a quiet, calm hatred, not pettishly and anxiously. We must learn to look patiently at them, and win through them the grace of self-abnegation and humility. Be constant and courageous, and rejoice that He has given you the will to be wholly His.

ST. FRANCIS DE SALES

Even to your old age, I am He; and even to hoar hairs will I carry you; I have made, and I will bear; even I will carry, and will deliver you.

ISAIAH xlvi. 4

The chariots of God are twenty thousand, even thousands of angels; the Lord is among them, as in Sinai, in the holy place.

PSALMS lxviii. 17

I HAVE not a shadow of doubt that if all our eyes could be opened to-day, we should see our homes, and our places of business, and the streets we traverse, filled with the "chariots of God." There is no need for any one of us to walk for lack of chariots. That cross inmate of your household, who has hitherto made life a burden to you, and who has been the Juggernaut car to crush your soul into the dust, may henceforth be a glorious chariot to carry you to the heights of heavenly patience and long-suffering. That misunderstanding, that mortification, that unkindness, that disappointment, that loss, that defeat, —all these are chariots waiting to carry you to the very heights of victory you have so longed to reach. Mount into them, then, with thankful hearts, and lose sight of all second causes in the shining of His love who will carry you in His arms safely and triumphantly over it all.

HANNAH WHITALL SMITH

Are they not all ministering spirits, sent forth to minister for them who shall be heirs of salvation?

HEBREWS i. 14

NEAR you in sympathy the angels stand,
Their unseen hosts encompass you around;
Strong and unconquerable the glorious band,
And loud their songs and hymns of victory sound.
And near you, though invisible, are those,
The good and just of every age and clime,
Who while on earth have fought the self-same foes,
And won the fight through faith and love sublime;
Let not the hosts of sin inspire a fear,
For lo! far mightier hosts are ever near!

JONES VERY

WITH every evil overcome, and every new likeness of Christ inwardly put on, you are brought more completely within the circle of the great cloud of witnesses, the myriads of angels in full assembly, and the spirits of good men made perfect; their strength passes mightily into your soul and their peace is laid brightly within the heart. This is one of the essential elements of our strength when we are supported and buoyed up in doing the Divine will. You are not marching alone. You feel it; you know it. Visible or invisible, a mighty host is with you; you are marching with them in countless and serried numbers; one spirit moves the whole and lifts their feet, and they keep step to the same music.

EDMUND H. SEARS

SEPTEMBER 30

Ye shall not fear them; for the Lord your God He shall fight for you.

DEUTERONOMY iii. 22

And behold God Himself is with us for our captain.

2 CHRONICLES xiii. 12

> OH, for trust that brings the triumph
> When defeat seems strangely near!
> Oh, for faith that changes fighting
> Into victory's ringing cheer—
> Faith triumphant, knowing not defeat or fear!
>
> HERBERT BOOTH

HOPEFULNESS of final victory is ours, if we only remember that we are fighting God's battles. And can He know defeat? He who is the God of the great world around us is the God of the little world within. It is He who is contending in thee; thou art but His soldier, guided by His wisdom, strengthened by His might, shielded by His love. Keep thy will united to the Will of God, and final defeat is impossible; for He is invincible.

GEORGE BODY

Our only victory over temptations is through persisting courage, and an indomitable cheerfulness.

FREDERICK W. FABER

Courage, it shall be well: we follow a conquering general; yea, who hath conquered already; and He that hath conquered for us shall ever conquer in us.

ROBERT LEIGHTON

Nevertheless, I am continually with Thee: Thou hast holden me by my right hand.

PSALMS lxxiii. 23

FAITH is a grasping of Almighty power;
The hand of man laid on the arm of God;
   The grand and blessed hour
In which the things, impossible to me,
Become the possible, O Lord, through Thee.
ANNA E. HAMILTON

NOTHING is necessary for you in maintaining a triumphant Christian life, but just to stay by the helm, and put yourself in where the power is. Come unto God, unite yourself to God, and the doing power you have is infinite!—and is none the less yours because it is His. Trim your ship steadily to the course, and God's own gales will waft it.

HORACE BUSHNELL

Gaze intently with the eye of faith at the infinite wisdom and omnipotence of God, to whom nothing is impossible or difficult, and consider that His goodness is unbounded, and unspeakable His willingness to give, hour by hour, and moment by moment, all things needful for the spiritual life, and for complete victory over self, if we will throw ourselves with confidence into His arms.

LORENZO SCUPOLI

Whatever God tells us to do, He also helps us to do.
DORA GREENWELL

OCTOBER 2

*And in every work that he began in the service
of the house of God, and in the law, and in the
commandments, to seek his God, he did it with all
his heart, and prospered.*

2 CHRONICLES xxxi. 21

HELP me in Christ to learn to do Thy will,
That I may have from Him eternal life;
And here on earth Thy perfect love fulfil,
Then home return victorious from the strife.

JONES VERY

THERE is no other way in which one's life will be
so surely, so quickly transfigured, as in the faithful,
happy, cheerful doing of every-day tasks. We need to
remember that this world is not so much a place for
doing things as for making character. Right in the
midst of what some people call drudgery is the very
best place to get the transformed, transfigured life.
The doing of common tasks patiently, promptly,
faithfully, cheerfully, makes the character beautiful
and bright. But we must take heed always that we
do our tasks, whatever they are, with love in our
heart. Doing any kind of work unwillingly, with complaint and murmuring, hurts the life.

J. R. MILLER

God weigheth more with how much love a man
worketh, than how much he doeth. He doeth much
that loveth much. He doeth much that doeth a thing
well.

THOMAS À KEMPIS

These things I have spoken unto you, that in me ye might have peace. In the world ye shall have tribulation: but be of good cheer; I have overcome the world.

JOHN xvi. 33

THEE will I love, my Crown of gladness,
  Thee will I love, my God and Lord,
Amid the darkest depths of sadness;
  Not for the hope of high reward,—
For Thine own sake, O Light Divine,
  So long as life is mine.

JOHANN SCHEFFLER

WHAT is the secret of serenity? We all want to know it. Indeed, we do know it already. There is no secret about it. St. Paul speaks it out plainly enough. Everybody can see what it is. All things work together for good to them that love God. We must love God; that is the heart of it. Happiness, content, and right satisfaction, all doubts answered, all dark places lighted up, heaven begun here—this is the reward of loving God. In this world, tribulation; yes, but good cheer in spite of that, for the Son of God, whom we love, has overcome the world.

GEORGE HODGES

Man's happiness consists in present peace, even in the midst of the greatest trials, and in more than hope of a glorious future.

CHARLES G. GORDON

OCTOBER 4

Bless the Lord, all His works in all places of His dominion · bless the Lord, O my soul.

PSALMS cii. 22

O MOST high, almighty, good Lord God, to Thee belong praise, glory, honor, and all blessing.

Praised be my Lord God with all His creatures, and specially our brother the sun, who brings us the day; fair is he and shines with a very great splendor; O Lord, he signifies to us Thee. Praised be my Lord for our sister the moon, and for the stars, the which He has set clear and lovely in heaven.

Praised be my Lord for our sister water, who is very serviceable unto us, and humble and precious and clean. Praised be Thou, my Lord, for our brother fire; he is bright and pleasant and very mighty and strong. Praised be my Lord for our mother the earth, who doth sustain us and keep us, and bringeth forth divers fruits and flowers of many colors, and grass.

Praised be my Lord for all those who pardon one another for His love's sake, and who endure weakness and tribulation. Praised be Thou, my Lord, for our sister, the death of the body, from which no man escapeth.

Praise ye and bless ye the Lord, and give thanks unto Him and serve Him with great humility.

ST. FRANCIS OF ASSISI

OCTOBER 5

It is a good thing to give thanks unto the Lord,
and to sing praises unto Thy name, O most High:
to show forth Thy lovingkindness in the morning,
and Thy faithfulness every night.

PSALMS xcii. 1, 2

PRAISE to the Holiest in the height,
  And in the depth be praise;
In all His words most wonderful,
  Most sure in all His ways.
JOHN HENRY NEWMAN

IF our hearts were tuned to praise, we should see causes unnumbered, which we had never seen before, for thanking God. Thanksgiving is spoken of as a "sacrifice well pleasing unto God." It is a far higher offering than prayer. When we pray we ask for things which we want; or we tell out our sorrows. We pray, in order to bring down blessings upon ourselves; we praise, because our hearts overflow with love to God, and we must speak it out to Him. It flows out of pure love, and then the love goes back to our hearts, and warms them anew, and revives and quickens them.
PRISCILLA MAURICE

Learn the lesson of thanksgiving. It is due to God, it is due to ourselves. Thanksgiving for the past makes us trustful in the present and hopeful for the future. What He has done is the pledge of what He will do.
A. C. A. HALL

OCTOBER 6

Rest in the Lord, and wait patiently for Him.

PSALMS XXXVII. 7

> Is it the Lord that shuts me in?
>   Then I can bear to wait!
> No place so dark, no place so poor,
> So strong and fast no prisoning door,
>   Though walled by grievous fate,
> But out of it goes fair and broad
> An unseen pathway, straight to God,
>   By which I mount to Thee.

SUSAN COOLIDGE

WE cannot be useless while we are doing and suffering God's will, whatever it may be found to be. And we can always do that. If we are bringing forth the fruits of the Spirit, we are not useless. And we can always do that. If we are increasing in the knowledge of God's will in all wisdom and spiritual understanding, we are not useless. And we can always do that. While we pray we cannot be useless. And we can always do that. God will always find us a work to do, a niche to fill, a place to serve, nay, even a soul to save, when it is His will, and not ours, that we desire to do; and if it should please Him that we should sit still for the rest of our lives, doing nothing else but waiting on Him, and waiting for Him, why should we complain? *Here is the patience of the saints.*

ANTHONY W. THOROLD

*As his share is that goeth down to the battle, so
shall his share be that tarrieth by the stuff: they
shall share alike.*

1 SAMUEL XXX. 24 (R. V.)

WORSHIP or service,—which? Ah, that is best
To which He calls us, be it toil or rest,—
To labor for Him in life's busy stir,
Or seek His feet, a silent worshipper.

CAROLINE A. MASON

LET us no more yearn for present employment
when God's providence bids us "be still," than we
would think it good to yearn after cessation while
God bids work. Shall we not miss a blessing if we
call rest a weariness and a discontent, no less than if
we called God's work a thankless labor? If we would
be holy in body and spirit, shall we not keep smooth
brow, light heart, whether He bids us serve His table,
or wait our summons?

EDWARD WHITE BENSON

He who acts with a view to please God alone,
wishes to have that only which it pleases God that he
should have, and at the time and in the way which
may be most agreeable to Him; and, whether he have
it or not, he is equally tranquil and contented, because in either case he obtains his wish, and fulfils his
intention, which was no other than purely to please
God.

LORENZO SCUPOLI

281

Fear none of those things which thou shalt suffer.
REVELATION ii. 10

Let Thy tender mercies come unto me, that I may live: for Thy law is my delight.
PSALMS cxix. 77

> O BLESSED life! the heart at rest
> When all without tumultuous seems;
> That trusts a higher Will, and deems
> That higher Will, not mine, the best.
> WILLIAM TIDD MATSON

NOTHING is so trying to nature as suspense between a faint hope and a mighty fear; but we must have faith as to the extent of our trials, as in all else. Our sensitiveness makes us often disposed to fancy that we are tried beyond our strength; but we really know neither our strength to endure nor the nature of God's trials. Only He who knows both these, and every turn of the hearts which He has made, knows how to deal out a due proportion. Let us leave it all to Him, and be content to bear in silence.

FRANÇOIS DE LA MOTHE FÉNELON

It is not the sunny side of Christ that we must look to, and we must not forsake Him for want of that. Oh, how sweet a thing were it for us to learn to make our burdens light, by framing our hearts to the burden, and making our Lord's will a law!

SAMUEL RUTHERFORD

*So is he that layeth up treasure for himself, and
is not rich toward God.*

LUKE xii. 21

IT seems as if God gathered into His storehouse,
from each of our lives, fruit in which He delights.
And the daily cross-bearings and self-denials, the
bright word spoken when head and heart are weary,
the meek endurance of misunderstanding, the steady
going on in one unbroken round, with a patient
cheerfulness that knows nothing of "moods,"—all
these are garnered there, and add to our riches towards Him.

H. BOWMAN

It is a great matter to learn to look upon troubles
and trials not as simply evils. How can that be evil
which God sends? And those who can repress complaints, murmurs, and peevish bemoaning—better
still, the vexed feelings which beset us when those
around inflict petty annoyances and slights on us—
will really find that their little daily worries are turning into blessings.

H. L. SIDNEY LEAR

> JUST to leave in His dear hand
>   *Little* things;
> All we cannot understand,
>   All that stings.
> Just to let Him take the care
>   Sorely pressing,
> Finding all we let Him bear
>   Changed to blessing.

FRANCES R. HAVERGAL

Our heart shall rejoice in Him, because we have trusted in His holy name.

PSALMS xxxiii. 21

TAKE anxious care for nought,
  To God your wants make known;
And soar on wings of heavenly thought
  Toward His eternal throne;
So, though our path is steep,
  And many a tempest lowers,
Shall His own peace our spirits keep,
  And Christ's dear love be ours.

JOHN MOULTRIE

CHERISH thankfulness with prayer. St. Paul gives us in two words this secret of peace. "In everything," (he excepts nothing, so do not you) "by prayer and supplication with *thanksgiving* let your requests be made known unto God. And the peace of God which passeth all understanding *shall* keep your hearts and minds through Christ Jesus." He does not say it as a benediction only: he tells us, it *"shall* keep your hearts and minds." Do the one and God will do the other. Ask what you will, be thankful; and not peace only, but peace which passeth all which our poor minds can think, shall keep these poor breaking, restless hearts—these ever wearying, worrying minds of ours—in Christ Jesus.

E. B. PUSEY

The cup which my Father hath given me, shall I not drink?

JOHN xviii. 11

Be ye transformed by the renewing of your mind, that ye may prove what is that good, and acceptable, and perfect will of God.

ROMANS xii. 2

W E are often greatly hindered in the fulfilment of our duties by an unconscious clinging to self, which holds us back from God, and which leads us to seek our rest in something other than the simple fulfilment of His most holy will. If we honestly sought nothing save His will, we should always be in a state of perfect peace, let what may happen. But, very often, even when we ask that God's will may be done, we still wish it to be done after our fashion.

PÈRE HYACINTHE BESSON

When we are fully delivered from the influence of selfish considerations, and have become conformed to the desires and purposes of the Infinite Mind, we shall drink the cup, and drink it cheerfully, whatever it may be. In a word, we shall necessarily be submissive and happy in all trials, and in every change and diversity of situation. Not because we are seeking happiness, or thinking of happiness, as a distinct object, but because the glorious will of Him whom our soul loves supremely, is accomplished in us.

THOMAS C. UPHAM

Ye said also, Behold, what a weariness is it.

MALACHI i. 13

My soul cleaveth unto the dust; quicken Thou me according to Thy word.

PSALMS cxix. 25

Awake, thou that sleepest, and arise from the dead, and Christ shall give thee light.

EPHESIANS v. 14

THERE are some who give up their prayers because they have so little feeling in their prayers—so little warmth of feeling. But who told us that feeling was to be a test of prayer? The work of prayer is a far too noble and necessary work to be laid aside for any lack of feeling. Press on, you who are dry and cold in your prayers, press on as a work and as a duty, and the Holy Spirit will, in His good time, refresh your prayers Himself.

ARTHUR F. WINNINGTON INGRAM

You do not feel in the spirit of prayer; you have no spiritual uplift; you are simply indifferent. Give that unhappy mood no heed. You know very well what you ought to do. You ought to present yourself before God; you ought to say your prayers. Do that, and the devout attitude, the bended knees, the folded hands, the quiet and the silence, the lips busied with holy words, will induce the consciousness of the divine presence, and help you to pray in spirit and in truth.

GEORGE HODGES

We have known and believed the love that God hath to us.

1 JOHN iv. 16

> NOT what I am, O Lord, but what Thou art!
> That, that alone can be my soul's true rest;
> Thy love, not mine, bids fear and doubt depart,
> And stills the tempest of my tossing breast.
>
> HORATIUS BONAR

WHEN you go to prayer, your first thought must be: The Father is in secret, the Father waits me there. Just because your heart is cold and prayerless, get you into the presence of the loving Father. As a father pitieth his children, so the Lord pitieth you. Do not be thinking of how little you have to bring God, but of how much He wants to give you. Just place yourself before Him, and look up into His face; think of His love, His wonderful, tender, pitying love. Tell Him how sinful and cold and dark all is; it is the Father's loving heart will give light and warmth to yours.

ANDREW MURRAY

God is not found in multiplicity, but in simplicity of thoughts and words. If one word suffice for your prayer, keep to that word, and to whatever short sentence will unite your heart with God.

MARGARET MARY HALLAHAN

My soul melteth for heaviness: strengthen Thou me according unto Thy word.

PSALMS cxix. 28

That their hearts might be comforted, being knit together in love.

COLOSSIANS ii. 2

WHEN I am with Thee as Thou art with me,
  Life will be self-forgetting power;
Love, ever conscious, buoyant, clear, and free
  Will flame in darkest hour.

GEORGE MACDONALD

EVERYTHING becomes possible to those who love. The commands of the Lord are no longer grievous, for the soul that loves is gifted by that love with fresh energies; it discovers in itself unsuspected possibilities, and is supplied with ever-flowing currents of new vigor. We shall be enabled to do so much if only we love. We live by loving, and the more we love the more we live; and therefore, when life feels dull and the spirits are low, turn and love God, love your neighbor, and you will be healed of your wound. Love Christ, the dear Master; look at His face, listen to His words, and love will waken, and you will do all things through Christ who strengtheneth you.

HENRY SCOTT HOLLAND

The noble love of Jesus impels a man to do great things, and stirs him up to be always longing for what is more perfect.

THOMAS À KEMPIS

This commandment have we from Him, That he who loveth God love his brother also.

1 JOHN iv. 21

He who loves God all else above,
　His own shall also clasp
In circles ampler far of love
　Than weaker arms can grasp;
And farther down through space and time
His sympathies descend and climb.

SIR AUBREY DE VERE

THE true proficiency of the soul consists not so much in deep thinking, or eloquent speaking, or beautiful writing; as in much and warm loving. Now, if you ask me in what way this much and warm love may be acquired, I answer,—By resolving to do the will of God, and by watching to do His will as often as occasion offers. Those who truly love God love all good wherever they find it. They seek all good to all men. They commend all good, they always acknowledge and defend all good. They have no quarrels. They bear no envy. O Lord, give me more and more of this blessed love! It will be a magnificent comfort in the hour of death to know that we are on our way to be judged by Him whom we have loved above all things. We are not going to a strange country, since it is His country whom we love and who loves us.

ST. TERESA

OCTOBER 16

Let all bitterness, and wrath, and anger, and clamor, and evil-speaking, be put away from you, with all malice.

EPHESIANS iv. 31

THE wider vision of the mind;
  The spirit bright with sun;
The temper like a fragrant wind,
  Chilling and grieving none;
The quickened heart to know God's will,
  And on His errands run.

SUSAN COOLIDGE

IT is of the very greatest moment to know the occasions of our sin, and the way in which it shows itself. To know the occasions, puts us on our guard; to know how our sin shows itself, gives us the means of stopping it. Thus, as to these occasions; one is made angry, if he is found fault with roughly, or even at all, or slighted, or spoken slightly of, or laughed at, or kept waiting, or treated rudely, or hurt even unintentionally, or if his will is crossed, or he is contradicted, or interrupted, or not attended to, or another be preferred to him, or if he cannot succeed in what he has to do. These sound little things when we speak of them in the presence of God, and in the sight of eternity. But these and such like little things make up our daily trials, our habits of mind, our life; our likeness or unlikeness to God, who made us in His own image; our eternity.

E. B. PUSEY

Behold, I give unto you power to tread on serpents and scorpions, and over all the power of the enemy: and nothing shall by any means hurt you.

LUKE X. 19

SHED down on me Thy mighty power,
  To strengthen for each coming hour;
And then, through flood, through fire and sword,
  I'll follow Thee, my Lord, my Lord!

JOHANN RAMBACH

WHY do we grow so little in grace? It is because we do not use our intellect to meditate upon the forces of the unseen world amidst which we live, or our will to draw upon them. We know that we are weak, and sin and Satan are strong, and we know the truth. But there is a third power stronger than either our weakness or the forces of evil, which we commonly forget, and which will never disclose itself except in our using of it. We must stir up the gift within us. Within us we have the Spirit of power, the Spirit of Jesus, the life of Jesus. It remains to us to appeal to it; in constant acts of faith to draw upon it and to use it. Thus it will become to each of us as much a truth of experience as it was to St. Paul, and no vague language of metaphor, that "it is no longer merely I that live, but Christ that liveth in me."

CHARLES GORE

*Our light affliction, which is but for a moment,
worketh for us a far more exceeding and eternal
weight of glory.*

2 CORINTHIANS iv. 17

ONLY be still, and wait His leisure
  In cheerful hope, with heart content
To take whate'er thy Father's pleasure,
  And all-discerning love hath sent;
Nor doubt our inmost wants are known
To Him who chose us for His own.

GEORG NEUMARK, 1657

OH, how is the face of life altered, as soon as a man has in earnest made his first object to do his Father's will! Oh, how do, what before seemed grievous burdens, bodily sickness, domestic trial, privations, losses, bereavement, the world's scorn, man's unthankfulness, or whatever grief his Father may put upon him, how do these things change! To those, whose hope is in heaven, everything becomes a means of discipline, an instrument of strengthening their cheerful acceptance of their Father's will. Their irksome tasks, privations, sickness, heaviness of heart, unkindness of others, and all the sorrows which their Father allots them in this world, are so many means of conforming them to their Saviour's image. Then doth everything which God doeth with them seem to them "very good," even because He doth it.

EDWARD B. PUSEY

*O my Father, if this cup may not pass away
from me except I drink it, Thy will be done.*

MATTHEW xxvi. 42

> To do or not to do,—to have,
>   Or not to have I leave to Thee;
> To be or not to be, I leave,—
>   Thy only will be done to me:
> All my requests are lost in one,
> Father, Thy only will be done!
>
> C. WESLEY

> DEAR Lord, in all our loneliest pains
> Thou hast the largest share,
> And that which is unbearable,
> 'Tis Thine, not ours, to bear.
>
> FREDERICK W. FABER

OFFER thyself as a sacrifice to God in peace and quietness of spirit. And the better to proceed in this journey, and support thyself without weariness and disquiet, dispose thy soul at every step, by widening out thy will to meet the Will of God. The more thou dost widen it, the more wilt thou receive. Thy will must be disposed as follows: to will everything and to will nothing, if God wills it or wills it not.

LORENZO SCUPOLI

You must make, at least once every week, a special act of love to God's will above all else, and that not only in things supportable, but also in things insupportable.

ST. FRANCIS DE SALES

My soul waiteth for the Lord more than they that watch for the morning: I say, more than they that watch for the morning.

PSALMS CXXX. 6

The Lord my God will enlighten my darkness.

PSALMS xviii. 28

A SOUL that is patient waits with calm endurance for light before acting, and in virtue of this calm and patient endurance suffers no pain or anxiety, because the soul possesses herself and waits for light; and when the mind waits patiently for light, sooner or later it is sure to come. Trials of mind affect us more deeply than pains of body, and if we give way to anxiety such trials become troubles, and are immensely increased. But this cannot happen to those patient souls, who feel that they are in the hands of God, and are encircled with His fatherly providence, and that all things are in His disposal. When we see not our way through some trial or difficulty, we have only to look to God, and to wait in patience, and in due time His light will come and guide us. This very attitude of waiting, this very patience of expecting, will dispose the mind to receive, and the will to rightly use, the needful light. Whenever you are perplexed as to what course you should take, if you go blindly into action you will be sure to repent it. Wait for light, wait with patience, and light will not fail you.

WILLIAM BERNARD ULLATHORNE

Thou shalt speak all these words unto them; but they will not hearken to thee.

JEREMIAH vii. 27

HIS eyes were bright with intelligence and trained powers of observation; and they were beautiful with kindliness, and with the well-bred habit of giving complete attention to other people and their affairs when he talked with them.

JULIANA H. EWING

There is a grace of kind listening, as well as a grace of kind speaking. Some men listen with an abstracted air, which shows that their thoughts are elsewhere. Or they seem to listen, but by wide answers and irrelevant questions show that they have been occupied with their own thoughts, as being more interesting, at least in their own estimation, than what you have been saying. Some interrupt, and will not hear you to the end. Some hear you to the end, and then forthwith begin to talk to you about a similar experience which has befallen themselves, making your case only an illustration of their own. Some, meaning to be kind, listen with such a determined, lively, violent attention, that you are at once made uncomfortable, and the charm of conversation is at an end. Many persons, whose manners will stand the test of speaking, break down under the trial of listening. But all these things should be brought under the sweet influences of religion.

FREDERICK WM. FABER

OCTOBER 22

Ye have not chosen me, but I have chosen you.

JOHN xv. 16

Ye are my friends, if ye do whatsoever I command you.

JOHN xv. 14

> We have not chosen Thee,
> But us Thou deign'st to choose,—
> Not servants, but Thy friends to be,
> Whom Thou wilt never lose:
> For never wilt Thou change—
> Who art all change above:
> Nor life nor death shall us estrange
> From Thy most perfect love.
>
> GEORGE B. BUBIER

We offer Christ the submission of our hearts, and the obedience of our lives; and He offers us His abiding Presence. We take Him as our Master, and He takes us as His friends. Our Lord takes us up into a relationship of love with Himself, and we go out into life inspired with His spirit to work His work. It begins with the self-surrender of love; and love, not fear or favor, becomes the motive. To feel thus the touch of God on our lives changes the world. Its fruits are joy and peace, and confidence that the events of life are suffused, not only with meaning, but with a meaning of love. The soul that is bound by this personal attachment to Jesus has a life in the eternal, which transfigures the life in time with a great joy.

HUGH BLACK

Now thanks be unto God, which always causeth us to triumph in Christ.

2 CORINTHIANS ii. 14

FIGHT the good fight
With all thy might;
Christ is thy Strength, and Christ thy Right;
Lay hold on life,
And it shall be
Thy joy and crown eternally.

J. B. S. MONSELL

LET the first act on waking be to place yourself, your heart, mind, faculties, your whole being, in God's hands. Ask Him to take entire possession of you, to be the Guide of your soul, your Life, your Wisdom, your Strength. He wills that we seek Him in all our needs, that we may both know Him truly, and draw closer and closer to Him; and in prayer we gain an invisible force which will triumph over seemingly hopeless difficulties.

H. L. SIDNEY LEAR

However matters go, it is our happiness to win new ground daily in Christ's love, and to purchase a new piece of it daily, and to add conquest to conquest.

SAMUEL RUTHERFORD

This ought to be our endeavor,—to conquer ourselves, and daily to wax stronger, and to make a further growth in holiness.

THOMAS À KEMPIS

Your life is hid with Christ in God.

COLOSSIANS iii. 3

Put on therefore a heart of compassion, kindness, humility, longsuffering; forbearing one another, and forgiving each other; even as the Lord forgave you so also do ye.

COLOSSIANS iii. 12-13 (R. V.)

> IT is not the deed we do,
>   Though the deed be never so fair,
> But the love that the dear Lord looketh for,
>   Hidden with holy care
>   In the heart of the deed so fair.
>
> HARRIET MCEWEN KIMBALL

THESE are duties which belong to us alike, whatever our outward lot be, whether rich or poor, honored or despised, amid outward joys or sorrows. For as our life is hidden in Christ, so have we all an outward and an inward, a hidden life. Outwardly, we seem busied for the most part about common things, with trivial duties, worthless tasks. Inwardly we are, or ought to be, studying how, in all, to please God, walking in His sight, doing them in His Presence, seeking to know how He would have them done. So amid trivial things we may be, nay men are, in every station of life, pleasing God, that is, leading angels' lives, in that they are doing His will on earth, as the angels in heaven. They are "servants of His, doing His pleasure."

EDWARD B. PUSEY

*My meat is to do the will of Him that sent me,
and to finish His work.*

JOHN iv. 34

THEY who tread the path of labor follow where My feet have
  trod;
They who work without complaining do the holy will of God.

HENRY VAN DYKE

WHENCE comes it that we have so many complaints, each saying that his occupation is a hindrance to him, while notwithstanding his work is of God, who hindereth no man? Whence comes this inward reproof and sense of guilt which torment and disquiet you? Dear children, know that it is not your work which gives you this disquiet. No; it is your want of order in fulfilling your work. If you performed your work in the right method, with a sole aim to God, and not to yourselves, your own likes and dislikes, nor sought your own gain or pleasure, but only God's glory, in your work, it would be impossible that it should grieve your conscience. It is a shame for a man if he have not done his work properly, but so imperfectly that he has to be rebuked for it. For this is a sure sign that his works are not done in God, with a view to His glory and the good of his neighbor.

JOHN TAULER

I will give thee the treasures of darkness, and hidden riches of secret places, that thou mayest know that I, the Lord, which call thee by thy name, am the God of Israel.

ISAIAH xlv. 3

GOD! Thou art Love! I build my faith on that!
I know Thee, Thou hast kept my path and made
Light for me in the darkness—tempering sorrow,
So that it reached me like a solemn joy:
It were too strange that I should doubt Thy love.

ROBERT BROWNING

IF I believe in God, in a Being who made me, and fashioned me, and knows my wants and capacities and necessities, because He gave them to me, and who is perfectly good and loving, righteous, and perfectly wise and powerful,—whatever my circumstances inward or outward may be, however thick the darkness which encompasses me, I yet can trust, yea, be assured, that all will be well, that He can draw light out of darkness, and make crooked things straight.

THOMAS ERSKINE

Though sorrows, heaviness, and faintings of heart ever so much increase; yet, if thy faith increase also, it will bear thee up in the midst of them. I would fain have it go well with thee, and that thou mightest not want the holy Counsellor and Adviser, in any strait or difficulty which the wise and tender God orders to befall thee.

ISAAC PENINGTON

Strengthened with all might, according to His glorious power, unto all patience and longsuffering with joyfulness.

COLOSSIANS i. 11

REJOICE in Christ alway!
  When earth looks heavenly bright,
When joy makes glad the livelong day,
  And peace shuts in the night.
Rejoice, when care and woe
  The fainting soul oppress,
When tears at wakeful midnight flow,
  And morn brings heaviness.

JOHN MOULTRIE

A GREAT point is gained when we have learned not to struggle against the circumstances God has appointed for us.

H. L. SIDNEY LEAR

All mental discomfort comes from our minds being in divergence from God's; when the two are agreed no warfare occurs, for they work together, and man's mind accepts God's rule, but reason tells us that disagreement must bring conflicts. He will have His way, and would have us accept all events with the knowledge that He is love, whatever and however contradictory those events may be to our comprehension of Him.

CHARLES GEORGE GORDON

Something is wrong, when the Christian cannot rejoice in all the dear dispensations of his Father's providence.

ISABELLA CAMPBELL, 1825

301

OCTOBER 28

*Who then is willing to consecrate his service this
day unto the Lord?*

1 CHRONICLES xxix. 5

MY blessed task from day to day
Is humbly, gladly, to obey.

HARRIET MCEWEN KIMBALL

THE only way to restore a weakened will is by
exercising itself in details of duty, it may be in smallest acts of obedience, regularly done, "here a little,
and there a little," content to grow by slow degrees
into the use of lost powers through repeated acts of
observance however trivial or unobserved. Faithfulness to every smallest call of obedience, as it comes,
is the means of gaining gradual accessions of strength,
and thus tending more and more to higher degrees
of conformity to the Will of God. Only by such simple
practical dutifulness can habits be formed.

T. T. CARTER

Break off some one evil, seek to uproot some one
sin, cut off some one self-indulgence, deny thyself some
one vanity; do it as an offering to God, for the love
of God, in hope once to see God; and some gleam of
faith, and life, and love will stream down upon thy
soul from the everlasting Fount of love. Follow on,
and thou shalt never lose that track of light.

EDWARD B. PUSEY

I will walk at liberty: for I seek Thy precepts.

PSALMS cxix. 45

To be made with Thee one spirit,
  Is the boon that I lingering ask,
To have no bar 'twixt my soul and Thine;
My thoughts to echo Thy will divine,
  Myself Thy servant for any task.

LUCY LARCOM

THERE is more effort, more steadfastness, involved in a diligent attention to little duties than appears at first sight, and that because of their continual recurrence. Such heed to little things implies a ceaseless listening to the whispers of grace, a strict watchfulness against every thought, wish, word or act which can offend God ever so little, a constant effort to do everything as perfectly as possible. All this, however, must be done with a free, childlike spirit, without restlessness and anxiety. He does not ask a fretted, shrinking service. Give yourself to Him, trust Him, fix your eye upon Him, listen to His voice, and then go on bravely and cheerfully, never doubting for an instant that His grace will lead you in small things as well as great, and will keep you from offending His law of love.

JEAN NICOLAS GROU

OCTOBER 30

In quietness and in confidence shall be your strength.

ISAIAH XXX. 15

BE still, my soul—for just as thou art still,
Can God reveal Himself to thee; until
   Through thee His love, and light, and life can freely
   flow.
In stillness God can work through thee and reach
The souls around thee. He then through thee can teach
   His lessons—and His power in weakness show.

BESSIE PORTER

WE are always wanting to be doing, to be giving, to be planning for the future, to be mapping out all our life; instead of resting and receiving day by day, leaving the morrow to our God, and rejoicing in Jesus Christ amidst all our falls and failures. Instead of going on rejoicing in Jesus, we are tempted to despond, and to go on desponding, after every failure, negligence, and sin.

GEORGE H. WILKINSON

We seek God afar off, in projects perhaps altogether unattainable, and we do not consider that we possess Him now in the midst of confusion, by the exercise of simple faith, provided we bear humbly and bravely the annoyances which come from others, and our own imperfections.

FRANÇOIS DE LA MOTHE FÉNELON

Thou shalt remember all the way which the Lord thy God led thee.

DEUTERONOMY viii. 2

> NOT mindless of the growing years
> Of care and loss and pain,
> My eyes are wet with thankful tears
> For blessings that remain.
>
> J. G. WHITTIER

THE years of available and happy life which have been already enjoyed ought to be the cause of thankfulness, even if "the days of darkness" were many. "The sorrow's crown of sorrow is remembering happier things," says Tennyson. Surely, in the sphere of Faith, at least, there is some mistake here. "For what we *have* received the Lord make us truly thankful."

JAMES SMETHAM

A bright, happy soul, rejoicing in all God's gifts, seeing cause for thankfulness and gladness in everything, counting up mercies rather than trials, looking at the bright side, even of sickness, bereavement, and death—what a very fountain of goodness and love of Christ such an one is! I remember one who, worn with sickness and sleepless nights, answered to the question if the nights did not seem interminable: "Oh no, I lie still, and count up my blessings!"

H. L. SIDNEY LEAR

NOVEMBER 1

That He might gather together in one all things in Christ, both which are in heaven, and which are on earth.

EPHESIANS i. 10

> FOR all the saints who from their labors rest,
> Who Thee by faith before the world confessed,
> Thy name, O Jesu, be for ever blessed.
>> Alleluia!
>
> Oh, blest communion! fellowship divine!
> We feebly struggle, they in glory shine;
> Yet all are one in Thee, for all are Thine.
>> Alleluia!
>>> WILLIAM W. HOW

IN the glorious company of the apostles, the goodly fellowship of the prophets, the noble army of martyrs, the holy Church throughout all the world is one. Therefore year by year let us reverently commemorate their names, remembering what they were, but steadfastly gazing at what they are. Their very words are still ringing in our ears: of some the beloved image too is full before us. Let us live as they would bid us, could they still speak: let us fulfil their known behests, following in their steps, filling up the works that they began, carrying on their hallowed offices, now bequeathed to our care; let us be like them in deadness to sin, and unceasing homage to our unseen Lord. As we grow holier, we grow nearer to them; to be like them is to be with them; even now they are not far from us, we know not how nigh.

HENRY EDWARD MANNING

Giving thanks unto the Father, which hath made us meet to be partakers of the inheritance of the saints in light.

COLOSSIANS i. 12

NOT their own, ah! not from earth was flowing
  That high strain to which their souls were tuned;
Year by year we saw them inly growing
  Liker Him with whom their hearts communed.
Then to Him they passed; but still unbroken,
  Age to age, lasts on that goodly line,
Whose pure lives are, more than all words spoken,
  Earth's best witness to the life divine.

JOHN CAMPBELL SHAIRP

ONLY to remember that such have been, that we walked for a season with them, is a chastening, a purifying, yea, and however much we may miss and mourn them, a gladdening thought.

RICHARD CHENEVIX TRENCH

The beatitude of the Saints is the matured result of the long course of patient strivings, which may have passed wholly unobserved because of their minuteness. One step has followed another in the mysterious progress of daily, hourly acts, each seeming to pass away, as footprints on the sand are obliterated by the advancing tide; but the end is the Vision of God, and the recompense is the perfection of a nature made one with the Mind of God.

T. T. CARTER

Though He slay me, yet will I trust in Him.

JOB xiii. 15

Behold, I have refined thee, but not with silver;
I have chosen thee in the furnace of affliction.

ISAIAH xlviii. 10

I WILL not let Thee go; Thou Help in time of need!
    Heap ill on ill,
    I trust Thee still,
E'en when it seems that Thou wouldst slay indeed!
    Do as Thou wilt with me,
    I yet will cling to Thee;
Hide Thou Thy face, yet, Help in time of need,
    I will not let Thee go.

WOLFGANG C. DESSLER

YOUR afflictions are not eternal, time will end them, and so shall ye at length see the Lord's salvation; His love sleepeth not, is still in working for you; His salvation will not tarry nor linger; and suffering for Him is the noblest cross out of heaven. Your Lord hath the choice of ten thousand other crosses, beside this, to exercise you withal; but His wisdom and His love choosed out this for you, beside them all; and take it as a choice one, and make use of it. Let the Lord absolutely have the ordering of your evils and troubles, and put them off you, by recommending your cross and your furnace to Him, who hath skill to melt His own metal, and knoweth well what to do with His furnace.

SAMUEL RUTHERFORD

As bond-servants [margin] of Christ, doing the will of God from the heart.

EPHESIANS vi. 6 (R. V.)

LORD Jesus, turn us from the noise
Of endless strivings and empty joys,
To find forever Thy one true peace,
Rest from sorrow, from sin release!

HARRIET MCEWEN KIMBALL

CAN He not enable you to do that will from your heart, in your surroundings? Are you sorely tried by those surroundings? Are they, in themselves, humiliating to you, or exasperating to you? Are they full of acute heart-pangs, or heavy with a chronic heartache? Not one of these things is forgotten before your Lord. Your slightest pain finds response in His sympathy. But let that thought be but the stepping-stone to this, that for you as for the slave-saint of Ephesus there lies open in that same Lord the blessed secret of a life which shall move amidst these same unwelcome surroundings as a life free, and at leisure, and at peace, full of love and rest, blessed and blessing; a life hid with Christ in God; a life in which *everything*, from your rising up to your lying down, the smallest cross and the largest, is seen in the light of the holy, the beloved, will of God, and so is met not with a sigh, or a murmur, but "from the soul."

HANDLEY C. G. MOULE

NOVEMBER 5

Love never faileth.

1 CORINTHIANS xiii. 8 (R. V.)

Your heart shall live for ever.

PSALMS xxii. 26

> DEATH has no bidding to divide
> The souls that dwell in Thee;
> Yes, all who in the Lord abide
> Are of one family.
>
> THOMAS H. GILL

WILL not our own lamented and beloved be there, in the array of happy spirits? Will they not hail our coming with delight? Do they not remember us now, even in the sight of God? For to see His face does not extinguish but perfect all holy loves. God's love gathers up and perfects all pure love like His own, all love that is for His sake. When we meet our beloved in Him, we shall both know and love them so as we have neither loved or known before.

HENRY EDWARD MANNING

She is not sent away, but only sent before; like unto a star, which, going out of our sight, doth not die and vanish, but shineth in another hemisphere: ye see her not, yet she doth shine in another country.

SAMUEL RUTHERFORD

Cast thy burden upon the Lord, and He shall sustain thee: He shall never suffer the righteous to be moved.

PSALMS lv. 22

> To Thee I bring my care,
>   The care I cannot flee;
> Thou wilt not only share,
>   But bear it all for me.
> O loving Saviour, now to Thee
> I bring the load that wearies me.
>
> FRANCES R. HAVERGAL

"CAST thy burden upon the Lord, and He will sustain thee"—burden and all. "Thee" is the greatest burden that thou hast! All other burdens are but slight, but this is a crushing burden. But when we come to the Lord with our burden, He just lifts up His child, burden and all, and bears him all the way home.

CHARLES A. FOX

He lays his affairs and himself on God, and so hath no pressing care; no care but the care of love, how to please, how to honor his Lord. And in this, too, he depends on Him, both for skill and strength; and, touching the success of things, he leaves that as none of his to be burdened with, casts it on God, and since He careth for it, they need not both care, His care is sufficient. Hence springs peace, inconceivable peace.

ROBERT LEIGHTON

NOVEMBER 7

*As we have therefore opportunity, let us do good
unto all men.*

She hath done what she could.

VERY consoling words, if we can be sure they apply
to us. Very pungent condemnation if they apply not,
and we suffer opportunities to go by. The rule demands no impossibilities; but it does demand that
every sphere, however humble, shall be filled with
divine endeavors. You have not done what you could
if you have not made it the problem of every day; how
many burdens can I make lighter? how much heart
sunshine can I shed about me? how much can I increase the sum of human blessing in the circle where
my lines have fallen? How easily we slide into the
delusion that we should do a great deal more good
if we had the means, overlooking the means that lie
close about us!

EDMUND H. SEARS

There is no act too trifling to be made by God the
first link in a chain of blessing; whether some trifling
incident is allowed on our part to drop unobserved,
or is taken up and placed in its intended position,
often depends on the entertainment we have given to
some previously-suggested idea of duty.

SARAH W. STEPHEN

Whosoever therefore shall break one of these least commandments, and shall teach men so, he shall be called the least in the Kingdom of heaven.
MATTHEW v. 19

THE great sterling duties, the exact truth of word, the resolute refusal to countenance wrong, the command of temper, the mastery of indolence, the unstained purity,—these, and such as these, form the character, and fashion our souls into instruments in God's hands for high and heavenly purposes in His Providence. But the carefulness over details, the watchfulness against faults which we know to be faults, but which, notwithstanding, seem venial, the devout regularity and attention in our private prayers, the invariable good-humor of our manners, the seeking for occasions of kindness and unselfishness, the avoidance of little temptations, the care not to cause little annoyances and little troubles,—to attend to all this for the sake of Christ our Master is the natural and fitting expression of a loving heart.
FREDERICK TEMPLE

The sins by which God's Spirit is ordinarily grieved are the sins of small things—laxities in keeping the temper, slight neglects of duty, sharpness of dealing.
HORACE BUSHNELL

Continuing steadfastly in prayer.

ROMANS xii. 12 (R. V.)

PRAYER is a preparation for danger, it is the armor for battle. Go not into the dangerous world without it. You kneel down at night to pray and drowsiness weighs down your eyelids. A hard day's work is a kind of excuse, and you shorten your prayer, and resign yourself softly to repose. The morning breaks, and it may be you rise late, and so your early devotions are not done, or done with irregular haste. It is no marvel if that day in which you suffer drowsiness to interfere with prayer be a day on which you betray Him by cowardice and soft shrinking from duty.

FREDERICK WM. ROBERTSON

Prayer to God regular and earnest, never intermittent for any reason, never hurried over for any weariness or for any coldness; this is one chief means of keeping our spiritual growth healthy and alive. If we would live in any degree by that ideal which our better selves sometimes set before us, we must steadily maintain the habit of regular prayer. For whether or not we are conscious of it at the time, there is a calm and unceasing strength which can be thus engrafted on our souls, and thus only.

FREDERICK TEMPLE

Therefore wait ye upon me, saith the Lord.

ZEPHANIAH iii. 8

That ye might be filled with all the fulness of God.

EPHESIANS iii. 19

WHAT is our work when God a blessing would impart?
To bring the empty vessel of a needy heart.

RICHARD CHENEVIX TRENCH

IN praying, we are often occupied with ourselves, with our own needs, and our own efforts in the presentation of them. In waiting upon God, the first thought is of *the God upon whom we wait.* God longs to reveal Himself, to fill us with Himself. Waiting on God gives Him time in His own way and divine power to come to us. Before you pray, bow quietly before God, to remember and realize who He is, how near He is, how certainly He can and will help. Be still before Him, and allow His Holy Spirit to waken and stir up in your soul the child-like disposition of absolute dependence and confident expectation. Wait on God till you know you have met Him; prayer will then become so different. And when you are praying, let there be intervals of silence, reverent stillness of soul, in which you yield yourself to God, in case He may have aught He wishes to teach you or to work in you.

ANDREW MURRAY

I have learned, in whatsoever state I am, therein to be content.

PHILIPPIANS iv. 11 (R. V.)

FORGIVE us, Lord, our little faith;
And help us all, from morn till e'en,
Still to believe that lot the best
Which is,—not that which might have been.

GEORGE ZABRISKIE GRAY

THOU givest within and without precisely what the soul needs for its advancement in a life of faith and self-renunciation. I have then only to receive this bread, and to accept, in the spirit of self-sacrifice, whatever Thou shalt ordain, of bitterness in my external circumstances, or within my heart. For whatever happens to me each day is my daily bread, provided I do not refuse to take it from Thy hand, and to feed upon it.

FRANÇOIS DE LA MOTHE FÉNELON

Judge that only necessary which God, in His eternal wisdom and love, proportions out unto us. And when thou comest hither, thou wilt come to thy rest; and as thou abidest here, thou wilt abide in thy soul's true rest, and know the preciousness of that lesson, and of whom thou art to learn it, even, *in every state to be content.*

ISAAC PENINGTON

Rejoice in the Lord alway; and again I say, Rejoice.

PHILIPPIANS iv. 4

REJOICE in hope and fear;
  Rejoice in life and death;
Rejoice when threatening storms are near,
  And comfort languisheth:
When should not they rejoice
  Whom Christ His brethren calls,—
Who hear and know His guiding voice
  When on their hearts it falls?

JOHN MOULTRIE

To "give thanks to Him for all things," is, indeed, a very difficult duty; for it includes giving thanks for trials of all kinds; for suffering and pain; for languor and weariness; for the crossing of our wills; for contradiction; for reproaches; for loneliness; for privations. Yet they who have learned submission will not find it a hard duty; for they will so entirely love all that God wills and appoints, that they will see it is the very best thing for them. Hereafter they will see all the links of the chain, and how wonderfully even those have fitted, which at the time seemed to have no adaptation or agreement. This belief enables them to praise Him, and give thanks *now* for each thing, assured that as it has been, so it will be—that the God of love will do all things well.

PRISCILLA MAURICE

Not as though I had already attained, either were already perfect; but I follow after, if that I may apprehend that for which also I am apprehended of Jesus Christ.

PHILIPPIANS iii. 12

LET no man think that sudden in a minute
  All is accomplished and the work is done;—
Though with thine earliest dawn thou shouldst begin it,
  Scarce were it ended in thy setting sun.

FREDERIC W. H. MYERS

NOTHING so purifies the thoughts, heightens the acts, shuts out self, admits God, as, in all things, little or great, to look to Jesus. Look to Him, when ye can, as ye begin to act, to converse, or labor; and then desire to speak or be silent, as He would have you; to say this word, or leave that unsaid; to do this, or leave that undone; to shape your words, as if He were present, and He *will* be present, not in body, but in spirit, not by your side, but in your soul. Faint not, any who would love Jesus, if ye find yourselves yet far short of what He Himself who is Love saith of the love of Him. Perfect love is heaven. When ye are perfected in love, your work on earth is done. There is no short road to heaven or to love. Do what in thee lies by the grace of God, and He will lead thee from strength to strength, and grace to grace, and love to love.

EDWARD B. PUSEY

I pray not that Thou shouldest take them out of the world, but that Thou shouldest keep them from the evil.

JOHN xvii. 15

IN the hour of trial,
  Jesu, plead for me;
Lest by base denial
  I depart from Thee.
      JAMES MONTGOMERY

OUR Lord would have His people to be in the world, and yet to be separate from it. He would have them be separated, not by isolation from it, but by living loyally under Him as their King, where His claims are denied and His rule is rejected; by courageously living in obedience to righteousness where desire is too generally the impelling and formative power. To live in the world as Christ's soldiers and servants; to witness for Him by word and deed as we live in obedience to His will—this is the separation which Christ teaches, this is the separation that gives glory to God. Woe be to us if we fail in expressing by loyal obedience here our loyalty to Christ as our King! To fail here is to bear stamped on us the brand of a traitor's moral cowardice, and a brand of greater shame than it no mortal brow can bear.

GEORGE BODY

Trouble and anguish have taken hold on me; yet Thy commandments are my delights.

PSALMS cxix. 143

WHEN black despair beats down my wings,
  And heavenly visions fade away—
Lord, let me bend to common things,
  The tasks of every day;

As, when th' aurora is denied,
  And blinding blizzards round him beat,
The Samoyed bends, and takes for guide
  The moss beneath his feet.

WILLIAM CANTON

WHATEVER bad times may come, or whatever perplexity, there is almost always close at hand, waiting for one, some plain thing to be done. It may be a mere matter of routine, an item in the day's regular business; it may be the exercise of some consideration for another; it may be only silent patience; but it is always *something*. And always one has the choice to do it or decline it. One can go through his work well or shirk it. One can consider his neighbor or neglect him. One can repress the fever-fit of impatience or give it wild way. And the perpetual presence of such a choice leaves no hour without guidance.

GEORGE S. MERRIAM

The will of the Lord be done.

ACTS xxi. 14

> BUT if in parallel to Thine
>   My will doth meekly run,
> All things in heaven and earth are mine,
>   My will is crossed by none;
>   Thou art in me,
>   And I in Thee,—
> Thy will—and mine—are done!

W. M. L. JAY

SUFFERINGS arising from anxiety, in which the soul adds, to the cross imposed by the hand of God, an agitated resistance, and a sort of unwillingness to suffer,—such troubles arise only because we live to ourselves. A cross wholly inflicted by God, and fully accepted without any uneasy hesitation, is full of peace as well as of pain. On the contrary, a cross not fully and simply accepted, but resisted by the love of self, even slightly, is a double cross; it is even more a cross, owing to this useless resistance, than through the pain it necessarily entails.

FRANÇOIS DE LA MOTHE FÉNELON

The basis of all peace of mind, and what must be obtained before we get that peace, is a cessation of the conflict of two wills—His and ours.

CHARLES G. GORDON

Whatsoever is born of God overcometh the world; and this is the victory that overcometh the world, even our faith.

1 JOHN v. 4

WHAT is victory over the world? It is to cut off as far as we may, every hold which everything out of God has over us; to study wherein we are weak, and there seek in His strength to be made strong. Be your temptation the love of pleasure, it is to forego it; if of food, to restrain it; if of praise, to put forward others rather than yourself; if of being right in the sight of men, be content to be misjudged, and to keep silence; if of self-indulgence, use hardness; if of display, cut off the occasions and give to the poor; if of having thine own will, practice the submission of it to the wills of others.

EDWARD B. PUSEY

If we aspire to walk in the power of the new life, we must cast away all hindrances, and it must cost something we really value.

CHARLES G. GORDON

The Faith presses upon man his noblest desires as obligations, and makes their attainment possible by the gift of the Spirit.

BROOKE FOSS WESTCOTT

Ye shall observe to do therefore as the Lord your God hath commanded you: ye shall not turn aside to the right hand or to the left.

DEUTERONOMY v. 32

No duty, however hard and perilous, should be feared one-half so much as failure in the duty. People sometimes shrink from responsibility, saying they dare not accept it because it is so great. But in shrinking from duty they are really encountering a far more serious condition than that which they evade. It is a great deal easier to do that which God gives us to do, no matter how hard it is, than to face the responsibility of not doing it. We have abundant assurance that we shall receive all the strength we need to perform any duty God allots to us; but if we fall out of the line of obedience, and refuse to do anything which we ought to do, we find ourselves at once out of harmony with God's law and God's providence, and cannot escape the consequences of our failure.

J. R. MILLER

Knowledge is a call to action; an insight into the way of perfection is a call to perfection.

J. H. NEWMAN

He knoweth what is in the darkness, and the light dwelleth with Him.

DANIEL ii. 22

TAKE it on trust a little while;
Soon shalt thou read the mystery right
In the full sunshine of His smile.

JOHN KEBLE

GOD is too wise not to know all about us, and what is really best for us to be, and to have. And He is too good, not to desire our highest good; and too powerful, desiring, not to effect it. If, then, what He has appointed for us does not seem to us the best, or even to be good, our true course is to remember that He sees further than we do, and that we shall understand Him in time, when His plans have unfolded themselves; meanwhile casting all our care upon Him, since He careth for us.

HENRY PARRY LIDDON

To be out of harmony with the things, acts, and events, which God in His providence has seen fit to array around us—that is to say, not to meet them in a humble, believing, and thankful spirit—is to turn from God. And, on the other hand, to see in them the developments of God's presence, and of the divine will, and to accept that will, is to turn in the opposite direction, and to be in union with Him.

THOMAS C. UPHAM

The Lord will lighten my darkness.

2 SAMUEL xxii. 29

Upon whom doth not His light arise?

JOB xxv. 3

HOPE, then, though woes be doubled,
 Hope, and be undismayed;
Let not thy heart be troubled,
 Nor let it be afraid.
This prison where thou art,
 Thy God will break it soon,
And flood with light thy heart
 In His own blessed noon.

PAUL GERHARDT

A CHRISTIAN may for many days together see neither sun nor star, neither light in God's countenance, nor light in his own heart, though even at that time God darts some beams through those clouds upon the soul; the soul again by a spirit of faith sees some light through those thickest clouds, enough to keep it from utter despair, though not to settle it in peace. In this dark condition, if they do as St. Paul and his company did, cast an anchor even in the dark night of temptation, and pray still for day, God will appear, and all shall clear up, we shall see light without and light within; the day-star will arise in their hearts.

RICHARD SIBBES

NOVEMBER 21

Lord, what wilt Thou have me to do?

ACTS X. 6

EVERY task, however simple, sets the soul that does it free;
Every deed of love and mercy, done to man is done to Me.
HENRY VAN DYKE

FOR each one of us, whether on a bed of pain, in feebleness and uncertainty of purpose such as comes with ill-health or overstrained nerves, or whatever else may be our immediate condition, nothing is more urgent, nothing more behooves us than to ask, "What wouldst Thou have me to do?" For, whatever our state, however helpless and incapable, however little service to God or to our neighbor seems within our power, there is no doubt at all as to His willing us to do *something*. Not necessarily any great thing; it may be only some little message of sympathy and comfort to carry to one even more lonely than we are; it may be some tiny pleasure to a little child, or a kindly word or glance to one whose own fault has cut him off from general kindness and pity; it may be even only in humble patience to stand and wait till He makes His will plain, abstaining the while from murmur and fretfulness; but, in some shape or other, be certain that your Master and Lord hears and will answer your question, "What wouldst Thou have me to do?"

H. L. SIDNEY LEAR

*Therefore, brethren, we were comforted over you
in all our affliction and distress by your faith.*

1 THESSALONIANS iii. 7

JUST as God leads I am content:
I rest me calmly in His hands;
That which He has decreed and sent—
That which His will for me commands—
I would that He should all fulfil;
That I should do His gracious will
In living or in dying.

LAMPERTUS GEDICKE

DIVINE Providence means the arrangement of
all our life, not only of its bright side, but also of its
dark. It may mean sickness as well as health; death
as well as life; loss as well as gain; peril as well as
safety; shipwreck by sea and accident by land; mur-
rain to our flocks; sickness in our homes.

ANTHONY W. THOROLD

Howbeit your faith seeth but the black side of
Providence, yet it hath a better side, and God shall
let you see it. We know that all things work together
for good to them that love God; hence I infer that
losses, disappointments, ill tongues, loss of friends,
houses or country, are God's workmen, set on work
to work out good to you, out of everything that be-
falleth you. When the Lord's blessed will bloweth
cross your desires, it is best, in humility, to strike sail
to Him, and to be willing to be led any way our Lord
pleaseth.

SAMUEL RUTHERFORD

*That the Lord thy God may bless thee in all the
work of thine hand which thou doest.*

DEUTERONOMY xiv. 29

FIRM against every doubt of Thee
    For all my future way,—
To walk in heaven's eternal light
    Throughout the changing day.
Ah! such a day as Thou shalt own
    When suns have ceased to shine!
A day of burdens borne by Thee,
    And work that all was Thine.

ANNA L. WARING

LET us give ourselves to God without any reserve,
and let us fear nothing. He will love us, and we shall
love Him. His love, increasing every day, will take the
place of everything else to us. He will fill our whole
hearts; He will deprive us only of those things that
make us unhappy. He will cause us to do in general,
what we have been doing already, but which we have
done in an unsatisfactory manner; whereas, hereafter,
we shall do them well, because they will be done for
His sake. Even the smallest actions of a simple and
common life will be turned to consolation and recompense. We shall meet the approach of death in peace;
it will be changed for us into the beginning of the
immortal life.

FRANÇOIS DE LA MOTHE FÉNELON

*We command and exhort by our Lord Jesus Christ
that with quietness they work.*

2 THESSALONIANS iii. 12

THERE is an order in our daily life,
Like that the holy angels constant keep;
And though its outward show seems but a strife,
There dwells within a peace like oceans deep.

JONES VERY

THE enemy of that grand central habit of interior
patience is *haste*: haste of thought, haste of judgment,
haste of manner, haste of speech. Even natural powers
of every kind become true strength, when they work
submissively and harmoniously under the direction of
Divine light and the movement of Divine grace; and
this disciplined subjection at every point under the
dominion of Christ our Lord, ruling us by His grace,
makes the soul the serene organ of the Holy Spirit,
for the animating, controlling, and guiding of our
souls.

WILLIAM BERNARD ULLATHORNE

We are conformed to Him in proportion as our
lives grow in quietness, His peace spreading within
our souls. Even amid all that outwardly disturbs us
we have, if we have Him, the same peace, because
He is our peace, sustaining our whole being.

T. T. CARTER

NOVEMBER 25

*Joy and gladness shall be found therein, thanks-
giving, and the voice of melody.*

ISAIAH li. 3

IF thou art living a righteous and a useful life, doing
thy duty orderly and cheerfully where God has put
thee, then thou art making sweeter melody in the
ears of the Lord Jesus Christ, than if thou hadst the
throat of a nightingale; for then thou in thy humble
place art copying the everlasting harmony and melody which is in heaven.

CHARLES KINGSLEY

In proportion as the perfect obedience of the life
of Christ comes, through humility and prayer and
thought, to be the constant aim of all our efforts; in
proportion as we try, God helping us, to think and
speak and act as He did, and through all the means of
grace to sanctify Him in our hearts; we shall, with
growing hope and with a wonder that is ever lost in
gratitude, know that even our lives are not without
the earnest of their rest in an eternal harmony; that
through them there is sounding more and more the
echo of a faultless music: and that He who loves that
concord, He who alone can ever make us what He
bids us be, will silence in us every harsh and jarring
note; that our service too may blend with the con-
senting praise of all His Saints and Angels.

FRANCIS PAGET

He that contemneth small things shall fall by little and little.

ECCLESIASTICUS xix. 1

Watch ye, stand fast in the faith, quit you like men, be strong.

1 CORINTHIANS xvi. 13

STAND then in His great might,
With all His strength endued;
But take, to arm you for the fight,
The panoply of God.
Leave no unguarded place,
No weakness of the soul;
Take every virtue, every grace,
And fortify the whole.

CHARLES WESLEY

LET every one consider what his weak point is; in that is his trial. His trial is not in those things which are easy to him, but in that one thing, in those several things, whatever they are, in which to do his duty is against his nature. Never think yourself safe because you do your duty in ninety-nine points; it is the hundredth which is to be the ground of your self-denial. It is with reference to this you must watch and pray; pray continually for God's grace to help you, and watch with fear and trembling lest you fall. Oh that you may (as it were) sweep the house diligently to discover what you lack of the full measure of obedience! for, be quite sure, that this apparently small defect will influence your whole spirit and judgment in all things.

JOHN HENRY NEWMAN

*God is faithful, by whom ye were called unto
the fellowship of His Son Jesus Christ our Lord.*
1 CORINTHIANS 1, 9

> GIVE me a new, a perfect heart,
> From doubt, and fear, and sorrow free;
> The mind which was in Christ impart,
> And let my spirit cleave to Thee.
>
> CHARLES WESLEY

SINCE I attained to a clear consciousness, by inward experience, that there is no way of satisfying the needs of the soul, or tranquillizing the heart's longings, but by the inner life in Christ, I am aware of an increase of power for the work of my calling, whatever it be, and of joy and spirit in performing it.

CHRISTIAN K. J. BUNSEN

In my daily life I am to ask "How would *Christ* have acted in my circumstances? How would He have me act? How would *Christ* fulfil my duties, do my work, fill my place, meet my difficulties, turn to account all my capacities and opportunities?" This is to be the law and inspiration of my whole life; not only of my outward acts, but of all my inward thoughts and desires. There is to be a manifestation of the Divine Nature in *me*.

A. C. A. HALL

Whoso keepeth His word, in him verily is the love of God perfected; hereby know we that we are in Him.

1 JOHN ii. 5

I have called you friends.

JOHN xv. 15

THE hands that tend the sick tend Christ; the willing feet that go on errands of love, work for Christ; the words of comfort to the sorrowful, and of sympathy to the mourner, are spoken in the name of Christ—Christ comforts the world through His friends. How much have you done for Him? What sort of a friend have you been to Him? God is working through His people; Christ is succoring through His friends—it is the vacancies in the ranks of His friends wherein the mischief lies: come and fill one gap.

ARTHUR F. WINNINGTON INGRAM

It is true that love cannot be forced, that it cannot be made to order, that we cannot love because we ought, or even because we want. But we can bring ourselves into the presence of the lovable. We can enter into Friendship through the door of Discipleship; we can learn love through service; and the day will come to us also, when the Master's word will be true, "I call you no longer servant, but friend."

HUGH BLACK

Through His will, loved and done, lies the path to His love.

ANDREW MURRAY

Thanks be to God, which giveth us the victory through our Lord Jesus Christ.

1 CORINTHIANS xv. 57

KEEP close to Christ, if conflict sore betide;
Stand fast, remembering He is at your side
  To give you strength
In battle, and the victor's palm at length.
German, tr. by FRANCES E. COX

IF we would endeavor, like men of courage, to stand in the battle, surely we should feel the favorable assistance of God from heaven. For He who giveth us occasion to fight, to the end we may get the victory, is ready to succor those that fight manfully, and do trust in His grace.

THOMAS À. KEMPIS

He will give the victory into thy hands, if only thou wilt fight manfully by His side, trusting not in thyself, but in His power and goodness. And if the Lord delay awhile to give thee the victory, be not disheartened, but believe assuredly (and this will also help thee to fight resolutely) that He will turn all things which may befall thee, those even which to thee may seem farthest removed from, yea, most adverse to thy success, all will He turn to thy good and profit, if thou wilt but bear thyself as a faithful and generous warrior.

LORENZO SCUPOLI

*He saith unto them, Follow me . . . and they
straightway left their nets, and followed Him.*

MATTHEW iv. 19, 20

> JESUS calls us; o'er the tumult
>   Of our life's wild, restless sea,
> Day by day His sweet voice soundeth,
>   Saying, "Christian, follow me."
> As of old St. Andrew heard it
>   By the Galilean lake,
> Turned from home, and toil, and kindred,
>   Leaving all for His dear sake.

CECIL F. ALEXANDER

THE will of God will be done; but, oh, the unspeakable loss for us if we have missed our opportunity of doing it!

BROOKE FOSS WESTCOTT

God, who calleth us, Himself gives us the strength to obey His call. He who is with us now to call us, will be ever present with us, in all whereto He calleth us. All in His purpose and love, every degree of grace and glory, lies wrapped up in His next call. All eternity of bliss and the love of God will, through His grace, forecoming, accompanying, following, lie in one strong, earnest, undivided, giving of thy whole self to God, to do in thee, through thee, with thee, His gracious, loving will.

EDWARD B. PUSEY

DECEMBER 1

Be strong and courageous, be not afraid nor dismayed; with us is the Lord our God, to help us, and to fight our battles.

2 CHRONICLES xxxii. 7, 8

WE fling aside the weight and sin,
Resolved the victory to win;
No shrinking from the desperate fight,
No thought of yielding or of flight;
With the brave heart and steady eye,
We onward march to victory.

HORATIUS BONAR

IF you, your heart, your will, are enlisted on the good side, if you are wishing and trying that the good in you should conquer the bad, then you are on the side of God Himself, and God is on your side; and "if God be for us, who shall be against us?" Take courage, then. If thou dislikest thy sins, so does God. If thou art fighting against thy worst feelings, so is God. On thy side is God who made all, and Christ who died for all, and the Holy Spirit who alone gives wisdom purity, nobleness. How canst thou fail when He is on thy side? On thy side are all spirits of just men made perfect, all wise and good souls in earth and heaven, all good and wholesome influences, whether of nature or of grace, of matter or of mind. How canst thou fail if they are on thy side?

CHARLES KINGSLEY

These things have I spoken unto you, that my joy might remain in you, and that your joy might be full.

JOHN xv. 11

THOU bringest all again; with Thee
Is light, is space, is breadth and room
For each thing fair, beloved, and free,
To have its hour of life and bloom.
Each heart's deep instinct unconfessed;
Each lowly wish, each daring claim;
All, all that life hath long repressed,
Unfolds, undreading blight or blame.

DORA GREENWELL

LET us offer up to Him each day, and all its occupations, yes, and all its relaxations—as it begins, —and beg Him to let us somehow "see" Him throughout it. Let us trust Him with the hallowing of our ordinary "secular" interests, let us try to shape each day's life so as best to please Him. "Would our Lord like me to say this or to read that? Would He sanction this train of thought or of fancy? When I go with that companion, can I imagine His drawing near and walking beside us?" This habitual "looking up to Jesus," this repeated reference to His will and pleasure—does it seem to us likely to be oppressive, restrictive, burdensome? Let us only try it, and judge for ourselves: it will turn out to be a source of peace and comfort indescribable.

WILLIAM BRIGHT

DECEMBER 3

Because Thou hast been my help, therefore in the shadow of Thy wings will I rejoice.

PSALMS lxiii. 7

ON our way rejoicing gladly let us go;
Conquered hath our Leader, vanquished is our foe!
Christ without, our safety! Christ within, our joy!
Who, if we be faithful, can our hope destroy?
On our way rejoicing as we homeward move,
Hearken to our praises, O Thou God of love!

J. B. S. MONSELL

I CANNOT understand why those who have given themselves up to God and His goodness are not always cheerful, for what possible happiness can be equal to that? No accidents or imperfections which may happen ought to have power to trouble them, or to hinder their looking upward.

ST. FRANCIS DE SALES

Why should we go to heaven weeping, as if we were like to fall down through the earth for sorrow? If God were dead (if I may speak so, with reverence of Him who liveth for ever and ever,) we might have cause to look like dead folks; but "the Lord liveth, and blessed be the Rock of our salvation." None have right to joy but we; for joy is sown for us, and an ill summer or harvest will not spill the crop.

SAMUEL RUTHERFORD

338

That ye may know what is the hope of His call-
ing, and what the riches of the glory of His in-
heritance in the saints, and what is the exceeding
greatness of His power to us-ward who believe.
EPHESIANS i. 18, 19

THOU dost well,
And my heaven is here and now,
Day-star of my soul, if Thou
Wilt but deign in me to dwell.
WOLFGANG C. DESSLER

THROW open all the windows of your soul to the influence of Jesus. By prayer, thought, and action, let His divine power move in and through your life; and be sure that a mighty work is within His power and your possibility. Not that of lifting you into ordinary spiritual vitality, but of transforming you through and through with His Spirit.

WILLIAM LAWRENCE

The life which we are meant to lead under the dispensation of the Spirit who has been given for our guidance into Truth, is one which does not take us out of the world, but keeps us from its evil, enabling us to live a heavenly existence on earth, and so to span over the chasm which divides us from heaven.

EDWARD THRING

That I may know Him, and the power of His resurrection, and the fellowship of His sufferings, being made conformable unto His death.

PHILIPPIANS iii. 10

WHAT within me and without
　　Hourly on my spirit weighs,
Burdening heart and soul with doubt,
　　Darkening all my weary days;
In it I behold Thy will,
　　God, who givest rest and peace;
And my heart is calm and still,
　　Waiting till Thou send release.

A. H. FRANCKE

WHATEVER thy grief or trouble be, take every drop in thy cup from the hand of Almighty God. He with whom "the hairs of thy head are all numbered," knoweth every throb of thy brow, each hardly drawn breath, each shoot of pain, each beating of the fevered pulse, each sinking of the aching heart. Receive, then, what are trials to *thee*, not in the main only, but one by one, from His all-loving hands; thank His love for each; unite each with the sufferings of thy Redeemer; pray that He will thereby hallow them to thee. Thou wilt not know now what He thereby will work in thee; yet, day by day, shalt thou receive the impress of the likeness of the ever-blessed Son, and in thee, too, while thou knowest it not, God shall be glorified.

E. B. PUSEY

Casting all your care upon Him; for He careth for you.

1 PETER v. 7

HOW gentle God's commands!
How kind His precepts are!
Come, cast your burdens on the Lord,
And trust His constant care.
His goodness stands approved
Down to the present day;
I'll drop my burden at His feet,
And bear a song away.

PHILIP DODDRIDGE

SHE was not accustomed in these days to meet troubles, small or great, with the small stock of strength her mind or body could afford. She had acquired, by long habit, the power of putting them from her until she could take them into the presence of her Lord, and there, in secret, commune with Him of all that was in her heart.

SARAH W. STEPHEN

The Lord calls for our burdens, would not have us wrestle with them ourselves, but roll them over on Him. Now, the desires that are breathed forth in prayer are, as it were, the very unloading of the heart; each request that goes forth, carries out somewhat of the burden with it, and lays it on God. Tell Him what are your desires, and leave them there with Him, and so you are sure to be rid of all further disquieting care of them.

ROBERT LEIGHTON

DECEMBER 7

*As ye have therefore received Christ Jesus the
Lord, so walk ye in Him.*

COLOSSIANS ii. 6

We have the mind of Christ.

1 CORINTHIANS ii. 16

NEVER further than Thy cross;
Never higher than Thy feet;
Here earth's precious things seem dross;
Here earth's bitter things grow sweet.

Here we learn to serve and give,
And, rejoicing, self deny;
Here we gather love to live,
Here we gather faith to die.

ELIZABETH R. CHARLES

ARE we assimilating His mind, His way of looking at things, His judgments, His spirit? Is the Christ-conscience being developed in us? Have we an increasing interest in the things which interest Him, an increasing love of the things that He loves, an increasing desire to serve the purposes He has at heart? "Ye are my friends, if ye do whatsoever I command you," is the test by which we can try ourselves.

HUGH BLACK

This I saw, that when a soul loves God with a supreme love, God's interests and his are become one. It is no matter when nor where nor how Christ should send me, nor what trials He should exercise me with, if I may be prepared for His work and will.

DAVID BRAINERD

Lord, Thou wilt ordain peace for us: for Thou hast also wrought all our works for us.

ISAIAH xxvi. 12 (R. V.)

> WITH that deep hush subduing all
>   Our words and works that drown
> The tender whisper of Thy call,
> As noiseless let Thy blessing fall
>   As fell the manna down.
>
> JOHN G. WHITTIER

PRAY to be calm and quiet and hushed, and that He will vouchsafe you the sense of His blessed presence; that you may do all things beneath His eye; to sit with Mary calmly at His feet and hear His voice, and then calmly rise and minister to Him.

EDWARD BOUVERIE PUSEY

Try so to live in the light of God's love that it becomes a second nature to you, tolerate nothing adverse to it, be continually striving to please Him in all things, take all that He sends patiently; resolve firmly never to commit the smallest deliberate fault, and if, unhappily you are overtaken by any sin, humble yourself, and rise up speedily. You will not be always thinking of God consciously, but all your thoughts will be ruled by Him, His Presence will check useless or evil thoughts, and your heart will be perpetually fixed on Him, ready to do His holy will.

JEAN NICOLAS GROU

Beloved, if God so loved us, we ought to love one another.

1 JOHN iv.11

By this shall all men know that ye are my disciples, if ye have love one to another.

JOHN xiii. 35

Do I find love so full in my nature, God's ultimate gift,
That I doubt His own love can compete with it? Here, the parts shift?
Here, the creature surpass the Creator, —the end, what Began?
Would I fain in my impotent yearning do all for this man,
And dare doubt He alone shall not help him, who yet alone can?

ROBERT BROWNING

"COME unto me," says the holy Jesus, "all ye that labor and are heavy laden, and I will refresh you." Beg of Him to be the light and life of your soul; love the sound of His name; for Jesus is the *love*, the *sweetness*, the *compassionate goodness* of the Deity itself; which became man, that so men might have the power to become the sons of God. Love, and pity, and wish well to every soul in the world; dwell in love and then you dwell in God.

WILLIAM LAW

The Lord's love is the love of communicating all that He has to all His creatures; for He desires the happiness *of* all; and a similar love prevails in those who love Him, because the Lord is in them.

EMANUEL SWEDENBORG

That we . . . may grow up in all things into Him, which is the head, even Christ; from whom all the body fitly framed and knit together through that which every joint supplieth, according to the working in due measure of each several part, maketh the increase of the body unto the building up of itself in love.

EPHESIANS iv. 14-16 (R. V.)

W E become the living means to a great end; and all our inner salvation—our finding of Jesus—is seen, not to centre in ourselves, in our own gain, our own rescue, our own peace; but to lead out beyond itself; to have been our qualification for use and office, without which we could not be taken up, as workers with God, into that eternal husbandry whereby He sets Himself to win over the stubborn and thorny field of the world. Our eyes are taken off ourselves; we are not absorbed in rehearsing our own experiences, however blessed. We are caught up into the counsels; we serve to widen the frontiers of the Kingdom; through us, correlated as we are, by joints and bands, into the articulated body, the Spirit of Christ can get abroad, can take a fresh step forward. We are become its vantage-ground from which it can again advance. Oh, that we were more quick to His touch, more ready for His needs, more serviceable in His ministry!

HENRY SCOTT HOLLAND

DECEMBER 11

Light is sown for the righteous, and gladness for the upright in heart.

PSALMS xvii. 11

> SUN of the soul, Thou light divine,
> Around and in us brightly shine,
>   To strength and gladness wake us.
> Where Thou shinest, life from heaven
> There is given; we before Thee
> For that precious gift implore Thee.
>
> MICHAEL SCHIRMER

THAT is what our sacrifice of ourselves should be—
"full of life." Not desponding, morbid, morose; not gloomy, chilly, forbidding; not languid, indolent, inactive; but full of life, and warmth, and energy; cheerful, and making others cheerful; gay, and making others gay; happy, and making others happy; contented, and making others contented; doing good, and making others do good, by our lively vivid vitality,—filling every corner of our own souls and bodies, filling every corner of the circle in which we move, with the fresh life-blood of a warm, genial, kindly Christian heart. Doubtless this requires a sacrifice; it requires us to give up our own comfort, our own ease, our own firesides, our dear solitude, our own favorite absorbing pursuits, our shyness, our reserve, our pride, our selfishness.

ARTHUR P. STANLEY

346

*My soul shall be joyful in the Lord; it shall
rejoice in His salvation.*   PSALMS XXV. 9

*The living God, who giveth us richly all things
to enjoy.*

1 TIMOTHY vi. 17

Behold, My servants shall sing for joy of heart.
ISAIAH lxv. 14

GIVE me, O Lord, a heart of grace,
A voice of joy, a shining face,
That I may show where'er I turn
Thy love within my soul doth burn!

A tenderness for all that stray,
With strength to help them on the way
A cheerfulness, a heavenly mirth,
Brightening my steps along the earth!
LADY GILBERT

THOSE who love God are encompassed with gladness on every side, because in every passing moment
they see and feel a Father's love, and nothing of this
world can take it away or lessen it.

H. L. SIDNEY LEAR

To be happy is properly the beginning of all
schemes for *making* happy.

SARAH W. STEPHEN

My life is so strangely free from all trial and
trouble, that I cannot doubt my own happiness is one
of the talents entrusted to me to "occupy" with, till
the Master shall return, by doing something to make
other lives happy.

CHARLES L. DODGSON

When the enemy shall come in like a flood, the Spirit of the Lord shall lift up a standard against him.

ISAIAH lix. 19

STILL more and more do Thou my soul redeem,
From every bondage set me wholly free;
Though Evil oft the mightest power may seem,
Still make me more than conqueror, Lord, in Thee.

C. J. P. SPITTA

WAIT on the Lord in humility of heart, that thou mayest daily feel the change which is wrought in the heart and conscience by the holy, eternal, ever-living Power; and so thou mayest witness, "that which is born of the Spirit, is spirit." And then thou wilt feel that this birth of the Spirit cannot fulfil the lusts of the flesh, but will be warring and fighting the good fight against them; and thus, in faithfulness to the truth, and waiting upon the Lord, thou shalt witness an overcoming, in His due time. Oh, the conquering faith, the overcoming life and power of the Spirit! We cannot but speak of those things; and cry up the perfect gift, and the power of Him, who is not only able to perfect His work in the heart, but delights so to do; and even to tread down Satan under the feet of those that wait in patience for the perfect conquest.

ISAAC PENINGTON

Perplexed, but not in despair; cast down, but not destroyed.

2 CORINTHIANS iv. 8, 9

Faint, yet pursuing.

JUDGES viii. 4

I, even I, am He that blotteth out thy transgressions for mine own sake, and will not remember thy sins.

ISAIAH xliii. 25

I DON'T think it is possible to overrate the hardness of the first close struggle with any natural passion, but indeed the easiness of after-steps is often quite beyond one's expectations. The free gift of grace with which God perfects our efforts may come in many ways, but I am convinced that it is the common experience of Christians that it does come. There *may* be some souls, whose brave and bitter lot it is to conquer comfortless. Perhaps some terrible inheritance of strong sin from the father is visited upon the son, and, only able to keep his purpose pure, he falls as fast as he struggles up, and still struggling falls again. Soft moments of peace with God and man may never come to him. He may feel himself viler than a thousand trumpery souls who could not have borne his trials for a day. For you and me is reserved no such cross and no such crown as theirs who falling still fight, and fighting fall, with their faces Zionwards, into the arms of the everlasting Father. "As one whom his mother comforteth" shall be the healing of *their* wounds.

JULIANA HORATIA EWING

349

These things I command you, that ye love one another.

JOHN xv. 17

> YET habits linger in the soul;
>   More grace, O Lord! more grace!
> More sweetness from Thy loving heart,
>   More sunshine from Thy face!
>
> FREDERICK W. FABER

IF thy disturbance of mind proceeds from a person who is so disagreeable to thee, that every little action of his annoys or irritates thee, the remedy is to force thyself to love him, and to hold him dear; not only because he is a creature formed by the same sovereign hand as thou art, but also because he offers thee an opportunity (if thou wilt accept it) of becoming like unto thy Lord, who is kind and loving unto all men.

LORENZO SCUPOLI

The habit of letting every foolish or uncharitable thought, as it arises, find words, has a great deal to do with much evil in the world. Check the habit of uttering the words, and gradually you will find that you check the habit of thought too. A resolution always to turn to some distinctly good thought when a complaining or unkind one arises in the mind, is a great help—as it is to turn every thought condemnatory of our neighbor into a prayer for him. We never can long continue to dislike people for whom we pray.

H. L. SIDNEY LEAR

Moreover, as for me, God forbid that I should sin against the Lord, in ceasing to pray for you.

1 SAMUEL xii. 23

MORE things are wrought by prayer
Than this world dreams of. Wherefore, let thy voice
Rise like a fountain for me night and day.
For what are men better than sheep or goats
That nourish a blind life within the brain,
If, knowing God, they lift not hands of prayer
Both for themselves and those who call them friend?
For so the whole round earth is every way
Bound by gold chains about the feet of God.

ALFRED TENNYSON

PERHAPS we do not think enough what an effective service prayer is, especially intercessory prayer. We do not believe as we should how it might help those we so fain would serve, penetrating the hearts we cannot open, shielding those we cannot guard, teaching where we cannot speak, comforting where our words have no power to soothe; following the steps of our beloved through the toils and perplexities of the day, lifting off their burdens with an unseen hand at night. No ministry is so like that of an angel as this—silent, invisible, known but to God.

ELIZABETH RUNDLE CHARLES

Intercessory prayer might be defined as loving our neighbor on our knees.

CHARLES H. BRENT

The Master is come, and calleth for thee.

JOHN xi. 28

STIR in us the might of faith,
Light in us the fire of love!
Then will smile Thine angel Death,
Opener of the gate above;
Sweet Thy summons then will come;
Gladsome then shall we go home.

THOMAS H. GILL

BEYOND all secondary causes, deeper than disease or accident, lies the loving will of Him who is the Lord of life and death. Death is Christ's minister, "mighty and beauteous, though his face be dark," and he, too, stands amidst the ranks of the "ministering spirits sent forth to minister to them that shall be heirs of salvation."

ALEXANDER MACLAREN

Until our Master summons us, not a hair of our head can perish, not a moment of our life be snatched from us. When He sends for us, it should seem but the message that the child is wanted at home.

ANTHONY W. THOROLD

Death to a good man is but passing through a dark entry out of one little dusky room of his father's house into another that is fair and large, lightsome and glorious.

ANONYMOUS

Now therefore, our God, we thank Thee, and praise Thy glorious name.

1 CHRONICLES xxix. 13

Rejoice in the Lord, ye righteous; and give thanks at the remembrance of His holiness.

PSALMS xcvii. 12

AND now the wants are told, that brought
　　Thy children to Thy knee;
Here, lingering still, we ask for nought,
　　But simply worship Thee.

The hope of heaven's eternal days
　　Absorbs not all the heart
That gives Thee glory, love, and praise
　　For being what Thou art.

WILLIAM BRIGHT

LET praise—I say not merely thanksgiving, but praise—always form an ingredient of thy prayers. We thank God for what He is to us; for the benefits which He confers, and the blessings with which He visits us. But we praise Him for what He is in Himself,—for His glorious excellences and perfections, independently of their bearing on the welfare of the creature. And it shall often happen that when thy heart is numb and torpid, and yields not to the action of prayer, it shall begin to thaw, and at last burst, like streams under the breath of spring, from their icy prison, with the warm and genial exercise of praise.

EDWARD M. GOULBURN

DECEMBER 19

*And thine ears shall hear a word behind thee,
saying, This is the way, walk ye in it, when ye
turn to the right hand, and when ye turn to the
left.*

ISAIAH XXX. 21

*The ways of the Lord are right, and the just shall
walk in them.*

HOSEA xiv. 9

YET more and more this truth doth shine
From failure and from loss,
The will that runs transverse to Thine
Doth thereby make its cross:
Thine upright will
Cuts straight and still
Through pride and dream and dross.

W. M. L. JAY

LET us remember that it is not God who makes
many of the crosses that we find in our way, such as
we commonly call "crosses." Our Heavenly Father
makes "straight paths for our feet," and, if we would
go in His way, if we would straighten our wills to His
will, and lay them side by side, there would be no
crosses. But when the path that God points out goes
north and south, and our stubborn wills lead us east
and west, the consequence is *"a cross"*—a cross of our
own making, not that which our Master bids us "take
up and carry after Him," and of which it has been
well said, "He always carries the heaviest end Himself."

ANNIE WEBB-PEPLOE

I would have you to be free from cares.

1 CORINTHIANS vii. 32 (R. V.)

He that trusteth in the Lord, mercy shall compass him about.

PSALMS xxii. 10

> I HAVE no cares, O blessed Will!
> For all my cares are Thine;
> I live in triumph, Lord, for Thou
> Hast made Thy triumphs mine.
> FREDERICK W. FABER

LET my soul roll itself on Him, and adventure there all its weight. He bears greater matters, upholding the frame of heaven and earth, and is not troubled or burdened with it.

ROBERT LEIGHTON

What is needed for happy effectual service is simply to put your work into the Lord's hand, and leave it there. Do not take it to Him in prayer, saying, "Lord, guide me, Lord, give me wisdom, Lord, arrange for me," and then arise from your knees, and take the burden all back, and try to guide and arrange for yourself. *Leave* it with the Lord, and remember that what you trust to Him you must not worry over nor feel anxious about. Trust and worry cannot go together.

HANNAH WHITALL SMITH

I am the way, the truth, and the life: no man cometh unto the Father, but by me.

JOHN xiv. 6

Blessed are they that have not seen, and yet have believed.

JOHN xx. 29

THE Way, the Truth, the Life Thou art,
   This, this I know; to this I cleave;
The sweet new language of my heart,
   "Lord, I believe."
I have no doubts to bring to Thee;
My doubt has fled; my faith is free.

HARRIET MCEWEN KIMBALL

WE have been placed upon the Way. We have been taught the Truth. We have been made partakers of the Life. The Way must be traversed; the Truth must be pursued; the Life must be realized. Then cometh the end. Our pilgrimage, long as it may be or short, if we have walked in Christ, will leave us by the throne of God; our partial knowledge, if we have looked upon all things in Christ, will be lost in open sight; our little lives, perfected, purified, harmonized in Him whom we have trusted, will become, in due order, parts of the One Divine Life, when God is all in all.

BROOKE FOSS WESTCOTT

Love is the life of faith; obedience, the life of love. Yea, rather, Christ Himself is the life of the soul.

EDWARD B. PUSEY

He that dwelleth in the secret place of the most High shall abide under the shadow of the Almighty.

PSALMS xci. 1

The upright shall dwell in Thy presence.

PSALMS cxl. 13

MY soul and all its powers
  Thine, wholly Thine shall be;
All, all my happy hours
  I consecrate to Thee:
Me to Thine image now restore,
And I shall praise Thee evermore.

CHARLES WESLEY

IF the wish is wakened in our soul to be ever in His presence, let us go to Him this moment, and ask Him what to do, and how to feel, believing that He is more ready to hear than we to pray. He will give us realization of His love, and convictions of duty. Let us follow those convictions implicitly; let us ask Him every day to teach us more, and help us more; and we shall soon say, with Paul, "Thanks be unto God, for His unspeakable gift!"

WILLIAM R. HUNTINGTON

The all-important thing is not to live apart from God, but as far as possible to be consciously with Him. It must needs be that those who look much into His face will become like Him.

CHARLES H. BRENT

DECEMBER 23

Thus shall ye do in the fear of the Lord, faithfully, and with a perfect heart.

2 CHRONICLES xix. 9

IN little things of common life,
There lies the Christian's noblest strife,
  When he does conscience make
Of every thought and throb within;
And words and looks of self and sin
  Crushes for Jesus' sake.

J. B. S. MONSELL

WHERESOEVER we be, whatsoever we are doing, in all our work, in our busy daily life, in all schemes and undertakings, in public trusts, and in private retreats, He is with us, and all we do is spread before Him. Do it, then, as to the Lord. Let the thought of His eye unseen be the motive of your acts and words. Do nothing you would not have Him see. Say nothing which you would not have said before His visible presence. This is to do all in His name.

HENRY EDWARD MANNING

If one sign surer than any other be chosen to mark the progress of the Divine life, it is when sanctity prevails even in the minutest points of character, and in ordinary ways. The least look, the faintest expression, the casual act, may tell more of the secret power of Jesus in the soul, than world-famed acts of self-devotion.

T. T. CARTER

There was no room for them in the inn.

LUKE ii. 7

GOD often would enrich, but finds not where to place
His treasure,—nor in hand nor heart a vacant space.
RICHARD CHENEVIX TRENCH

THE soul, in its highest sense, is a vast capacity for God. It is like a curious chamber added on to being, and somehow involving being, a chamber with elastic and contractile walls, which can be expanded, with God as its guest, illimitably, but which without God shrinks and shrivels until every vestige of the Divine is gone.

HENRY DRUMMOND

All that God desires is to give you His great love, so that it may dwell in you, and be the principle of your life and service; and all that withstands God's desire and His gift is the want of room for it, and for its free movement, when that room is taken up with yourselves and your little personal interests.

WILLIAM BERNARD ULLATHORNE

By rooting out our selfish desires, even when they appear to touch no one but ourselves, we are preparing a chamber of the soul where the Divine Presence may dwell.

ELLEN WATSON

359

I live; yet not I, but Christ liveth in me.

GALATIANS ii. 20

Christ in you, the hope of glory.

COLOSSIANS i. 27

THOUGH Christ a thousand times in Bethlehem be born,
If He's not born in thee, thy soul is still forlorn.

JOHANN SCHEFFLER

THE great mystery of the Gospel does not lie in Christ without us only (though we must know also what He has done for us); but the very pith and kernel of it consists in Christ inwardly formed in our hearts.

RALPH CUDWORTH

When therefore the first spark of a desire after God arises in thy soul, cherish it with all thy care, give all thy heart into it; it is nothing less than a touch of the divine loadstone, that is to draw thee out of the vanity of time, into the riches of eternity. Get up therefore, and follow it as gladly as the wise men of the east followed the star from heaven that appeared to them. It will do for thee as the star did for them, it will lead thee to the birth of Jesus, not in a stable at Bethlehem in Judea, but to the birth of Jesus in the dark centre of thine own soul.

WILLIAM LAW

They loved not their lives unto the death.

REVELATION xii. 11

Our Lord Jesus Christ, who died for us, that, whether we wake or sleep, we should live together with Him.

1 THESSALONIANS v. 9, 10

> BE ours the faith that sees Thee stand
>   Beside the throne of God on high,
> To succor with Thy strong right hand
>   Thy soldiers when to Thee they cry.
>
> Be ours the love, divine and free,
>   Which asks forgiveness for our foes;
> Which draws, in life, its life from Thee,
>   And, dying, finds in Thee repose.
>
> J. F. THRUPP

"IF He has done so much for me, what can I do for Him?" is the question which a Christian life should answer. He may ask little or much. He may demand heroic sacrifices, or He may require only punctual attention to daily and prosaic duty. But He has a right to make any demands He will, and it should be a point of honor with every Christian to satisfy Him. It is this simple self-surrender, in a spirit of love for God and for the souls of men, which makes life strong and noble, as was the life of St. Stephen. It is this self-surrender which makes death, whenever or wherever it may come, a "falling asleep in Christ."

HENRY PARRY LIDDON

DECEMBER 27

They took knowledge of them, that they had been with Jesus.

ACTS iv. 13

> O HEARTS of love! O souls that turn
> Like sunflowers to the pure and best!
> To you the truth is manifest;
> For they the mind of Christ discern
> Who lean like John upon His breast.
>
> JOHN G. WHITTIER

WILT thou with St. John rest on the loving heart of our Lord Jesus Christ, thou must be transformed into the beauteous image of our Lord by a constant, earnest contemplation thereof, considering His holy meekness and humility, the deep, fiery love that He bore to His friends and His foes, and His mighty, obedient resignation which He manifested in all the paths wherein His Father called Him to tread. And now ye must gaze much more closely and deeply into the glorious image of our Lord Jesus Christ than I can show you with my outward teaching, and maintain a continual, earnest effort and aspiration after it. Then look attentively at thyself, how unlike thou art to this image, and behold thy own littleness. Here will thy Lord let thee rest on Him. In the glorious likeness of Christ thou wilt be made rich, and find all the solace and sweetness in the world.

JOHN TAULER

Verily I say unto you, Whosoever shall not re-
ceive the Kingdom of God as a little child shall
in no wise enter therein.

LUKE xviii. 17

DEAR Soul, couldst thou become a child
While yet on earth, meek, undefiled,
Then God Himself were ever near,
And Paradise around thee here.
GERHARD TERSTEEGEN

CHILDLIKENESS, in its Scripture sense, is a perfectness of trust, a resting in a Father's love, a being borne on in its power, living in it—it means a simplicity which resolves all into the one idea of lowly submissiveness to One in whom it lives; a buoyancy of spirit, which is a fountain of joy in itself, always ready to spring forth afresh brightly and happily to meet the claims of the present hour, not looking lingeringly back to the past, nor making plans independently, as of oneself, for the future; a resting contented in one's lot, whatever that lot may be; a singleness of intention; a pliancy, a yielding of the will, a forgetfulness of self in another's claims. To be thus childlike in the pure sense of such an ideal, is to be living in God, as one's Father, one's Preserver, one's Guide, felt to be a perpetual Presence and Providence.

T. T. CARTER

*With good will doing service, as to the Lord, and
not to men.*

EPHESIANS vi. 7

YET take the tiny stones which I have wrought,
  Just one by one, as they were given by Thee,
Not knowing what came next in Thy wise thought.
Set each stone by Thy Master-hand of grace;
  Form the mosaic as Thou wilt for me,
And in Thy temple pavement give it place.

FRANCES RIDLEY HAVERGAL

WHAT God may hereafter require of you, you
must not give yourself the least trouble about. Everything He gives you to do, you must do as well as ever
you can, and that is the best possible preparation for
what He may want you to do next. If people would
but do what they have to do, they would always find
themselves ready for what came next.

GEORGE MACDONALD

Nothing can excuse the neglect of the duties of the
position of life which God has conferred upon us. All
is delusive where these are not attended to, and made
much of.

FREDERICK W. FABER

If you would advance in true holiness, you must
aim steadily at perfection in little things.

ABBÉ GUILLORÉ

Whatsoever ye do in word or deed, do all in the name of the Lord Jesus, giving thanks to God and the Father by Him.

COLOSSIANS iii. 17

YEA, through life, death, through sorrow and through sinning,
He shall suffice me, for He hath sufficed:
Christ is the end, for Christ was the beginning;
    Christ the beginning for the end is Christ.

F. W. H. MYERS

LET this be thy whole endeavor, this thy prayer, this thy desire,—that thou mayest be stripped of all selfishness, and with entire simplicity follow Jesus only.

THOMAS À KEMPIS

Do what is pleasing to Jesus Christ, and neglect nothing which pleases Him.

LORENZO SCUPOLI

To "do all things in the name of Jesus" is the lesson of a life; do not be angry with yourselves, nor despair of ever learning it, because thou art slow to learn the first few syllables. When thou hast learned to do all things to Jesus, it will shed pleasure over all dull things, softness over all hard things, peace over all trial and woe and suspense. Then will life be glad, when thou livest to Jesus; and how sweet death, to die in Jesus; with Him, and to Him, and in Him, to live for evermore.

E. B. PUSEY

DECEMBER 31

We are laborers together with God.

1 CORINTHIANS iii. 9

> THEN bear a joy where joy is not,
>   Go, speak a kindly word in love,
> Less bitter make some loveless lot,
>   Now earth is linked to heaven above.
>   FREDERICK G. LEE

Do what you can—give what you have. Only stop not with feelings; carry your charity into deeds; do and give what costs you something.

J. H. THOM

"Up and be *doing*," is the word that comes from God for each of us. Leave some "good work" behind you that shall not be wholly lost when you have passed away. *Do* something worth living for, worth dying for. Is there no want, no suffering, no sorrow that you can relieve? Is there no act of tardy justice, no deed of cheerful kindness, no long-forgotten duty that you can perform? Is there no reconciliation of some ancient quarrel, no payment of some long-outstanding debt, no courtesy, or love, or honor to be rendered to those to whom it has long been due; no charitable, humble, kind, useful deed by which you can promote the glory of God, or good will among men, or peace upon earth? If there be any such deed, in God's name, in Christ's name, go and do it.

ARTHUR P. STANLEY

index of authors

PROSE SELECTIONS

INDEX OF AUTHORS

PROSE SELECTIONS

INDEX OF AUTHORS

POETICAL SELECTIONS

INDEX OF AUTHORS